Advanced Turbo Pascal®:

Programming & Techniques

Advanced Turbo Pascal®:

Programming & Techniques

Herbert Schildt

Osborne **McGraw-Hill**
Berkeley, California

Osborne **McGraw-Hill**
2600 Tenth Street
Berkeley, California 94710
U.S.A.

For information on translations and book distributors outside of the U.S.A., please write to Osborne **McGraw-Hill** at the above address.

Turbo Pascal is a registered trademark of Borland International.
MS-DOS is a registered trademark of Microsoft Corporation.
IBM is a registered trademark of International Business Machines, Inc.
CP/M is a registered trademark of Digital Research.
UNIX is a trademark of Bell Laboratories.

Advanced Turbo Pascal®: Programming & Techniques

1234567890 DODO 89876

ISBN 0-07-881220-8

Jon Erickson, Acquisitions Editor
Lorraine Aochi, Technical Editor
Albert Holt of Borland International, Technical Reviewer
Kevin Shafer, Senior Editor
Lynn Heimbucher, Editorial Assistant
Lyn Cordell, Project Editor
Kay Luthin, Copy Editor
Yashi Okita, Cover Design

To my parents

Contents

Introduction

I have been fortunate to be able to write the kind of programming book that I always wanted. Years ago, when I began to program, I tried to find a book that presented algorithms for such tasks as sorts, linked lists, simulations, and expression parsers in a straightforward way. I also wanted a book that would give insights into many of the common problems I might find in programming. I never found exactly the book I was looking for. Now, as an experienced programmer, I have written that book.

This book covers a wide range of subjects and contains many useful algorithms, procedures, functions, and approaches written in the Turbo Pascal language. Turbo Pascal is the de facto standard for Pascal programmers who use microcomputers. Turbo Pascal compilers are available for virtually all microcomputers. I used the IBM PC Turbo Pascal compiler for the examples in this book; with few exceptions, the examples will compile and run on any of the Turbo Pascal compilers.

Chapter 1 begins with a short overview of the language. Chapter 2 discusses sorting, including arrays and disk files. Chapter 3 deals with stacks, queues, linked lists, and binary trees. This may seem like a lot to cover in one chapter, but the subjects form a solid unit.

Chapter 4 discusses dynamic allocation methods, and Chapter 5 presents an overview of operating-system interfacing and assembly language linkage. Chapter 6's topic is statistics, and it includes a complete statistics program. Chapter 7 is about codes, ciphers, and data compression, and it includes a short history of cryptography. Chapter 8 describes several random number generators and then discusses how to use them in two simulations: a checkout line in a store and a random-walk portfolio management program.

Chapter 9, my personal favorite, contains the complete code to a recursive descent parser. (Years ago, I would have given just about anything to have had that code.) Chapter 9 is for those who need to evaluate expressions. Chapter 10's subject is converting programs from other languages into Turbo

Pascal. Chapter 11 finishes the book with a discussion of efficiency, porting, and debugging.

   If you would like to obtain an IBM PC-compatible diskette that contains all of the programs and algorithms presented in this book, please complete the order form and mail it with your payment enclosed. If you are in a hurry, call (217) 586-4021 and place your order by telephone.

H.S.

Please send me _____ copies, at $29.95 each, of the programs in *Advanced Turbo Pascal: Programming & Techniques*. For foreign orders, please add $5.00 for shipping and handling.

Name _____

Address _____

City _____ State _____ ZIP _____

Telephone _____

Method of payment: Check _____ Visa _____ MC _____

Credit card number: _____

Expiration date: _____

Signature: _____

Send to: Herbert Schildt
            RR 1, Box 130
            Mahomet, IL 61853

ONE

A Review of Pascal

This book uses a problem-solving approach to illustrate advanced concepts in the Pascal programming language, with special emphasis on Borland's Turbo Pascal. Each chapter presents a different area of programming and offers one or more solutions to programming tasks, focusing on style and structure. Through this approach, advanced Pascal topics are explored, as well as the general programming theory behind each algorithm. You should have a working knowledge of Pascal, know how to operate the Turbo Pascal system, and be able to enter and compile simple programs.

For easy identification, all variable names, Pascal keywords, function names, and procedure names will be boldface throughout this book.

The Origins of Pascal

Pascal was invented by Niklaus Wirth in the early 1970s. (It is named after Blaise Pascal, the 17th-century philosopher.) The Pascal programming language was intended originally to be an instructional language—it would help beginning programmers develop good habits by allowing them to write clear, concise, and structured programs. Prior to Pascal, most students were taught FORTRAN, a much older, unstructured computer language. Professor Wirth believed that many common programming errors could be avoided if a block-structured language that had strong type-checking were used.

Pascal is a *strongly typed language*. This means that variables and constants of one type may not be freely mixed with variables and constants of another. For example, both sides of the assignment statement must be of the same type, with the exception that the variable on the left side can be a **real**, while the expression on the right side can be **integer**. Strong type-checking helps prevent program errors by forcing the programmer to always have compatible expressions.

In Turbo Pascal, variable names consist of a letter or underscore followed by letters, digits, or underscores. The maximum allowable length is 127 characters, but you should use shorter names for practical purposes.

All strings in Turbo Pascal are enclosed between single quotation marks. This differs from such languages as C or BASIC, where double quotation marks are used.

Pascal has five scalar data types:

Keyword	Meaning
char	A character, 1 byte long
byte	An integer, 1 byte long, with a value between 0 and 255
integer	A whole number with a value between −32768 and 32767
real	A decimal number with 11 digits of precision
Boolean	TRUE or FALSE

Although **byte** and **char** appear to be the same, Pascal's strong type-checking prevents them from being used interchangeably. A **byte** variable is used primarily over an **integer** variable to achieve faster execution, because on some machines byte operations are faster than integer operations. In addition to the five scalar types, Pascal allows arrays of each scalar type.

Although Pascal was initially developed as an educational language, its ease of use and highly structured approach won many converts who had programmed in other languages. As Pascal began to be used increasingly for commercial software development, several extensions were needed. Prior to Turbo Pascal, each compiler developer supported a slightly different set of extensions, which made portability difficult. (Portability is the subject of Chapter 11.) However, because Turbo Pascal has emerged as the de facto standard, many of the extensions can be freely used.

Pascal as a Structured Language

Pascal is a structured language with some similarities to Algol and C. The distinguishing feature of a block-structured language is its ability to *compartmentalize code and data*. This means it can section off and hide from the rest of the program all information and instructions necessary to perform a specific task. Generally, compartmentalization is accomplished by subroutines, often called *subprograms*, with *local variables*, which are temporary. In this way, it is possible to write subroutines so that the events occurring within them will cause no side effects in other parts of the program. Excessive use of *global variables* (variables known throughout the entire program) may allow bugs to creep into a program by allowing unwanted side effects. In Pascal, all subprograms are either discrete functions or procedures.

Functions and procedures are the building blocks of Pascal. A specific task in a program can be defined and coded separately into a function or procedure. After debugging the function or procedure, a programmer can rely on it to work properly without creating side effects in other parts of the program. All variables declared in that function or procedure are known only to that subroutine.

In Pascal, using blocks of code creates program structures. A *block of code* is a logically connected group of program statements that can be treated as a unit. It is created by placing lines of code between the keywords **begin** and **end**, as shown here:

```
if x < 10  then
begin
      WriteLn('too low, try again');
      ResetCounter(-1);
end;
```

In this example the two statements located after **if** and between **begin** and **end** are both executed if **x** is less than 10. The first statement prints the line **too low, try again** on the screen, and the other line is a procedure call. These two statements can be thought of as one unit—a block of code. They are linked together: one statement cannot execute without the other also executing. In Pascal, every statement can be either a single statement or a block of statements. The use of code blocks creates readable programs with easy-to-follow logic. Code blocks also help you write better, bug-free programs, because the meaning of each statement is clear.

As Pascal grew in popularity, many programmers began to use Pascal to program any task they needed. Because there are Pascal compilers for virtually all computers, you can take code written for one machine and then compile and run it on another with few or no changes. This saves both time and money.

A Turbo Pascal programmer can create and maintain a personal library of functions tailored to the programmer's personality. Because Turbo Pascal allows separate source-code files to be included at compile time, large projects can easily be managed.

Turbo Pascal Enhancements

If you are already an experienced Turbo Pascal programmer, you may skip to Chapter 2. However, if you are an experienced standard Pascal programmer, you should read the remainder of this chapter, because it discusses the important enhancements added to Pascal by Borland and makes note of a few differences. Because this book uses many of these enhancements in the examples, it is important that you are familiar with them.

The decision to enhance a language must be based on a good reason. Each extension intrinsically reduces the portability of programs that use those enhancements, and enhancements therefore make the language nonstandard. Usually enhancements are added only because the standard form of the language lacks some necessary function. They are necessary to standard Pascal because it lacks a few things that a professional programmer needs and expects, such as strings, absolute addressing, and overlay facilities. Remember that Pascal was invented as a teaching language; Borland made it into a general-purpose language.

The enhancements Borland added fall into two categories: language statements (keywords) and built-in procedures. This section looks first at the statements, then at the built-in procedures, and finally at a few differences between standard Pascal and Turbo Pascal.

Absolute

One of the most important enhancements found in Turbo Pascal is the **absolute** modifier. Standard Pascal has no way of making a variable reside at a specific memory address. This ability was never needed in a teaching situation; however, in a real-world software development environment, it is essential.

For example, imagine that you want to write a program that puts information into a shared memory area, such as a video memory. To do this you must be able to specify that a variable resides at a certain location. In Turbo Pascal you simply add the **absolute** modifier to the variable declaration statement after the type declaration. For the IBM PC and related machines, the address must be in *segment:offset* form; for others, it is in standard address form. For the IBM PC, the following statement declares a variable of type **real** and locates it in segment 0, offset 9000.

```
count: real absolute 0:9000;
```

Remember, when declaring **absolute** variables you must be careful, or you will crash your program or operating system.

You can also use **absolute** to make two variables share the same address space. To do this, use the name of the variable that you want another variable to share space with as the target of the **absolute** modifier. The following example allows **test** and **count** to share the same space:

```
test: integer;
count: integer absolute test;
```

External

In standard Pascal a program cannot use functions or procedures that are not written in Pascal. However, there are many occasions on which this might be useful. For example, a device like a speech synthesizer may need to be controlled through a special assembly language module. For this situation, Turbo Pascal allows external subroutines to be linked with a Pascal program by using the **external** modifier.

The **external** modifier informs the Pascal program that an assembly language routine is going to be used and what disk file the routine resides in. You must declare an external subprogram without its body in your Pascal program; you only need a heading to specify both the parameters (if there are any) and the disk file the subroutine is in. For example, to declare a procedure called **Speech** with one **string** parameter as **external** in file **talk**, you would write

```
procedure Speech(word:string); external 'talk';
```

You can declare a function in the same way.

Before using **external** subprograms, you must know assembly language programming and understand the architecture of your computer. This book later examines interfacing to assembly language routines in greater detail.

Inline

Turbo Pascal allows you to insert assembly language instructions directly into your Pascal source code by using **inline**. This ability can be useful for both interfacing to special hardware devices and writing fast routines that use Turbo Pascal's support features. Although the use of **inline** is examined in detail in Chapter 5, here is the basic method.

The machine code that you wish to insert in your program follows the keyword **inline** in parentheses. Each byte or word is separated by a backslash (\ ). You can use plus and minus signs to add and subtract. An asterisk (*) specifies a location-counter reference. All code is entered as numbers; that is, you may not use mnemonics as you do with an assembler. Because **inline** is a statement, it ends with a semicolon. For example, the statement

```
inline ($C9\$E900);
```

inserts three bytes into your program: $C9, $E9, and 00.

Overlay

One of Turbo Pascal's most important enhancements is the **overlay** command. It allows you to create programs that are larger than will fit into memory. It does this by automatically loading subprograms, called *overlays*, which are stored on disk as needed while your program is executing.

Generally, to create an overlay, you put **overlay** in front of the function or procedure that you want to use. When Turbo Pascal encounters the **overlay** command, it automatically compiles that subprogram into a separate overlay file. Refer to the *Turbo Pascal User Manual*, which provides an excellent description of creating overlays.

shr and shl

shr stands for "shift right" and **shl** stands for "shift left." These are operations that can be used on variables of type **integer** only. Essentially, they cause the bits in the operand to be shifted either right or left by the specified number of places. This type of operation is used for writing system-specialized code or device drives. The general forms for these operations are

$$\textit{integer expression } \textbf{shr } \textit{number}$$
$$\textit{integer expression } \textbf{shl } \textit{number}$$

where *number* must be between 1 and 15.

To see how these operations work, look at the binary representation of an integer called **count** whose value is 8:

$$0\ 0\ 0\ 0 \quad 1\ 0\ 0\ 0$$

After Turbo Pascal executes the statement

```
count := count shr 1;
```

count has the value 4, and it looks like

$$0\ 0\ 0\ 0 \quad 0\ 1\ 0\ 0$$

because all of the bits have been shifted to the right by one position. If Turbo Pascal executes

```
count := count shl 3;
```

count has the value 32 and looks like this:

$$0\ 0\ 1\ 0\ \ \ \ 0\ 0\ 0\ 0$$

As you may have noticed, a shift right actually divides by two, and a shift left multiplies by two. Right or left shifts are often used as quick ways to halve or double a number.

String

In standard Pascal there is no easy way to manipulate character strings. However, Turbo Pascal has added a special character-array type called **string**, which allows you to manipulate strings easily. Strings must be between 1 and 255 characters in length, and they are declared much like character arrays. For example, to declare a string with a maximum length of 20, you would write

```
test_string : string[20];
```

Unlike a character array, which must have a fixed length, a variable of type **string** may have any length greater than zero and less than or equal to the specified maximum length.

XOR

The **XOR** exclusive-or operator can be applied to either **integer** or **Boolean** operands. For **integer** operands, it causes an XOR operation to be performed between each bit of the two integers. For **Boolean** operands, a TRUE/FALSE outcome is determined.

In the **integer XOR** operation, each bit in the result is set according to this truth table:

XOR	0	1
0	0	1
1	1	0

Each bit is set to 1 *if and only if* exactly one bit is 1 and the other is 0, as shown here:

```
        1   0   1   1   0   0   1   0
 XOR    0   1   1   0   1   0   0   1
      ─────────────────────────────────
        1   1   0   1   1   0   1   1
```

With **Boolean** operators, the result of an **XOR** operation is determined by this truth table:

XOR	F	T
F	F	T
T	T	F

The outcome of an **XOR** operation is TRUE if and only if exactly one operand is TRUE. For example, if **X** and **Y** are two **Boolean** variables, and if **X** is TRUE and **Y** is FALSE, then **X XOR Y** is TRUE.

Built-in Procedures

Turbo Pascal has a rich assortment of built-in procedures that make programming much easier. They generally fall into three areas: screen control, strings, and operating-system interfacing. Although these extra procedures are covered later in this book, here is a quick look at a few of them.

Screen and Graphics Procedures

Here is a list of Turbo Pascal's basic screen procedures and their effects:

Procedure	Effect
CrtEol	Clears to the end of a line
CrtExit	Sends a terminal reset string
CrtInit	Sends a terminal initialization string
ClrScr	Clears the screen
DelLine	Deletes to the end of the line
GotoXY	Positions the cursor at the specified X,Y screen coordinates
InsLine	Inserts a blank line at the current cursor position
LowVideo	Produces low-intensity display
NormVideo	Produces normal-intensity display

These screen functions are used in many of the programs in this book.

In addition to these common screen functions, Turbo Pascal for the IBM PC includes a complete set of color graphics, turtle graphics, and window routines that can be used to make your programs look very professional.

String Functions

As previously stated, one of Turbo Pascal's most important enhancements is that it allows you to create variables of type **string**. In order to support this new data type, Turbo Pascal includes the following special string procedures, which are not found in standard Pascal:

Procedure	Effect
Delete	Removes a substring, given its starting position and length
Insert	Inserts one string into another, given the starting position of the second string
Str	Converts an **integer** or **real** into a string
Val	Converts a string into an **integer** or **real**

The following functions also support the **string** data type:

Function	Effect
Copy	Returns a substring copy of a string
Concat	Returns a concatenation of two strings listed as its parameters
Length	Returns the integer length of a string
Pos	Returns the starting position of a substring within a second string

Operating-System Interfacing Procedures

Turbo Pascal has a special procedure that allows Pascal programs to access operating-system routines. For CP/M-80 and CP/M-86, there are two procedures, called **Bdos** and **Bios**, that allow CP/M operating-system calls. For the IBM PC and MS-DOS in general, there is a procedure called **MsDOS**. Essentially, all three procedures work the same way: a function number and parameters are passed via these functions into the operating system. The use of these functions is the subject of Chapter 5.

Differences Between Turbo Pascal And Standard Pascal

In addition to the extensions and enhancements to standard Pascal already discussed, Turbo Pascal differs from standard Pascal in a few other ways. If you are an experienced Pascal programmer but are new to Turbo Pascal, it is important to keep in mind the following differences:

- The **new** procedure, which allocates a dynamic variable for use with pointers, does not accept variant record specifications. If necessary, you can work around this by using the **getmem** procedure.

- A **goto** must not branch outside of the block it is in. This means that both the label and the **goto** must be in the same block.

- For CP/M-80 users only: recursive subprograms must not use **var** type parameters.

- The **get** and **put** are not implemented; rather, **read** and **write** have been extended to accommodate disk I/O.

- The keyword **packed** may be used but has no effect. Also, the procedures **pack** and **unpack** are not implemented.

- The **page** procedure is not implemented.

TWO

Sorting and Searching

In the world of computer science, perhaps no other tasks are more fundamental or as extensively analyzed as those of sorting and searching. Sorting and searching routines are used in virtually all database programs, as well as in compilers, interpreters, and operating systems. This chapter introduces you to the basics of sorting and searching. Since sorting data generally makes searching that data easier and faster, sorting is discussed first.

Sorting

Sorting is the process of arranging a set of similar pieces of information into an increasing or decreasing order; specifically, given an increasing sorted list i of n elements,

$$i_1 <= i_2 <= ... <= i_n$$

There are two categories of sorting algorithms: the sorting of arrays, both in memory and in random-access disk files; and the sorting of sequential disk or tape files. This chapter focuses on the first category because it is of most interest to the microcomputer user. However, the general method of sorting sequential files is introduced later.

The main difference between sorting arrays and sorting sequential files is that each element of the array is available all of the time. This means that any element may be compared or exchanged with any other element at any time. In contrast, only one element is available at any one time in a sequential file. Because of this difference, the sorting techniques differ greatly between the two.

Generally, when information is sorted, only a portion of that information is used as the *sort key* on which comparisons are based. When an exchange must be made, the entire data structure is transferred. In a mailing list, for example, the ZIP code field might be used as the key, but the entire name and address accompanies the ZIP code when the exchange is made. For the sake of simplicity, examples of the various sorting methods presented here focus on sorting character arrays. Later you will learn how to adapt any of these methods to any type of data structure.

Classes of Sorting Algorithms

There are three ways to sort arrays:

- By exchange
- By selection
- By insertion.

Imagine a deck of cards. To sort the cards by *exchange*, you would spread the cards, face up, on a table and then proceed to exchange out-of-order cards until the deck was ordered.

To sort by *selection*, you would spread the cards on the table, select the lowest-value card, and hold it in your hand. Then, from the remaining cards on the table, you would select the next lowest card and place it behind the one already in your hand. This process would continue until all of the cards were in your hand. Because you always selected the lowest card from those remaining on the table, when the process was complete, the cards in your hand would be sorted.

To sort by *insertion*, you would hold the cards in your hand, taking one at a time from the deck. As you took each card, you would place it into a new deck on the table, always inserting it in the correct position. The deck would be sorted when you had no cards in your hand.

Judging Sorting Algorithms

There are many algorithms for each sorting method. Each algorithm has its merits, but the general criteria for judging a sorting algorithm are based on the answers to the following questions.

- How fast can the algorithm sort information in an average case?
- How fast are its best and worst cases?
- Does the algorithm exhibit *natural* or *unnatural* behavior?
- Does it rearrange elements with equal keys?

How fast a particular algorithm sorts is of great concern. The speed with which an array can be sorted is directly related to the number of comparisons and the number of exchanges required, with exchanges taking more time. Later in this chapter, you will see that some sorts require an exponential amount of time per element to sort, and some require logarithmic time.

Best- and worst-case run times are important if you expect to encounter best- and worst-case situations frequently. A sort will often have a good average case but a terrible worst case, or vice versa.

A sort is said to exhibit *natural behavior* if it works least when the list is already in order, works harder as the list becomes less ordered, and works hardest when a list is in inverse order. How hard a sort works is based on the number of comparisons and moves that are executed.

To understand the importance of rearranging elements with equal keys, imagine a database that is sorted on a main key and a subkey—for example, a mailing list with the ZIP code as the main key and the last name within the same ZIP code as the subkey. When a new address is added to the list and the list is sorted again, you do not want the subkeys to be rearranged. To guarantee this, a sort must not exchange main keys of equal value.

In the following sections, representative sorts from each class of sorting algorithms are analyzed to judge their efficiency. Each sort will use the two user-defined types shown here:

```
type
   DataItem = char;
   DataArray = array [1..80] of char;
```

Therefore, to change the type of data each sort uses requires changing only these two type definitions. The array dimension is arbitrary, and you may change it as necessary.

THE BUBBLE SORT The best-known (and most infamous) sort is the *Bubble sort*. Its popularity is derived from its catchy name and its simplicity. However, it is one of the worst sorts ever made.

The Bubble sort uses the exchange method of sorting. It uses repeated comparisons and, if necessary, exchanges of adjacent elements. Its name comes from the method's similarity to bubbles in a tank of water, where each bubble seeks its own level. The simplest form of the Bubble sort is shown here:

```
procedure  Bubble(var item: DataArray; count:integer);
var
   i,j: integer;
   x: DataItem;
begin
```

```
   for i:=2 to count do
   begin for j:=count downto i do
      if item[j-1]>item[j] then
      begin     { now swap the elements  }
         x:=item[j-1];
         item[j-1]:=item[j];
         item[j]:=x;
      end;
   end;
end; { Bubble sort }
```

In this form, **item** is the array of **DataItem**s to be sorted, and **count** is the number of elements in the array.

A Bubble sort is driven by two loops. Since there are **count** elements in the array, the outer loop causes the array to be scanned **count**−1 times. This ensures that, in the worst case, every element is in its proper position when the procedure terminates. The inner loop actually performs the comparisons and exchanges.

This version of the Bubble sort can sort a character array into ascending order. For example, the following short program sorts a string that is read from a disk file called **test.dat**. The same program can be used with the other sort routines in this chapter by changing the sort procedure.

```
program SortDriver;

{ this program will read in 80 or less characters from a
disk file called 'test.dat', sort them, and display
the results on the screen. }

type
    DataItem = char;
    DataArray = array [1..80] of char;
var
    test: DataArray;
    t,t2: integer;
    testfile: file of char;

procedure  bubble(var item: DataArray; count:integer);
var
    i,j: integer;
    x: DataItem;
begin
    for i:=2 to count do
    begin for j:=count downto i do
       if item[j-1]>item[j] then
       begin
          x:=item[j-1];
          item[j-1]:=item[j];
          item[j]:=x;
       end;
    end;
end; { bubble sort }

begin
```

```
      Assign(testfile, 'test.dat');
      Reset(testfile);
      t:=1;

      while not Eof(testfile) do begin
         read(testfile,test[t]);
         t:=t+1;
      end;

      t:=t-2;   { get rid of control-z at end of file}

      Bubble(test,t);   { sort the array }

      for t2:=1 to t do write(test[t2]);
      WriteLn;
end.
```

To illustrate how the Bubble sort works, here are the passes used to sort the array **dcab**:

```
            initial   d c a b
            pass 1    a d c b
            pass 2    a b d c
            pass 3    a b c d
```

When analyzing any sort, you must determine how many comparisons and exchanges will be performed for the best, average, and worst cases. With the Bubble sort, the number of comparisons is always the same because the two **for** loops still repeat the specified number of times, whether the list is initially ordered or not. This means that the Bubble sort always performs $1/2(n^2-n)$ comparisons, where n is the number of elements to be sorted. This formula is derived from the fact that the outer loop of the Bubble sort executes $n-1$ times and the inner loop sorts $n/2$ times. Multiplying these together produces the formula just given.

The number of exchanges is 0 for the best case—an already sorted list. The number of exchanges is $3/4(n^2-n)$ for the average case and $3/2(n^2-n)$ for the worst cases. It is beyond the scope of this book to explain the derivation of these numbers, but you can see that as the list becomes less ordered, the number of elements that are out of order approaches the number of comparisons. (There are three exchanges in a Bubble sort for every element out of order.) The Bubble sort is called an *n-squared algorithm* because its execution time is a multiple of the square of the number of elements. A Bubble sort is very bad for a large number of elements, because execution time is directly related to the number of comparisons and exchanges.

For example, if you ignore the time it takes to exchange any out-of-position element, you can see that if each comparison takes 0.001 seconds, then sorting 10 elements will take about 0.05 seconds, sorting 100 elements will take about

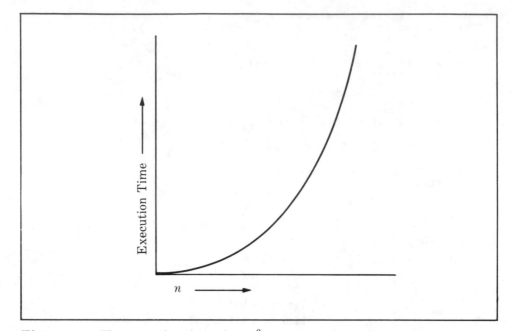

Figure 2-1.   The execution time of an n^2 sort in relation to array size

5 seconds, and sorting 1000 elements will take about 500 seconds. A 100,000-element sort—the size of a small phone book—would take about 5,000,000 seconds, or about 1400 hours (about two months of continuous sorting)! The graph in Figure 2-1 shows how execution time increases in relation to the size of the array.

You can make some improvements to the Bubble sort in order to speed it up—and help its image a bit. For example, the Bubble sort has one peculiarity: an out-of-order element at the large end, such as the **a** in the **dcab** example, will go to its proper position in one pass, but a misplaced element in the small end, such as the **d**, will rise very slowly to its proper place. Instead of always reading the array in the same direction, subsequent passes could reverse direction. Greatly out-of-place elements will travel more quickly to their correct position. Shown here, this version of the Bubble sort is called the *Shaker sort* because of its "shaking" motion over the array:

```
procedure  Shaker(var item: DataArray; count:integer);

{ this is an improved version of the Bubble sort }

var
   j,k,l,r: integer;
```

```
      x: DataItem;
begin
   l:=2; r:=count; k:=count;
   repeat
      for j:= r downto l do
         if item[j-1]>item[j] then
         begin     { swap  }
            x:=item[j-1];
            item[j-1]:=item[j];
            item[j]:=x;
            k:=j;
         end;

         l:=k+1;

         for j:=l to r do
            if item[j-1]>item[j] then
            begin     { swap  }
               x:=item[j-1];
               item[j-1]:=item[j];
               item[j]:=x;
               k:=j;
            end;

         r:=k-1;

   until l>r
end; { Shaker sort }
```

Although the Shaker sort is an improvement over the Bubble sort, it cannot be recommended because it still executes on the order of n^2. The number of comparisons is unchanged and the number of exchanges has only been reduced by a relatively small constant.

SORTING BY SELECTION   A *Selection sort* selects the element with the lowest value and exchanges it with the first element. From the remaining $n-1$ elements, the element with the next-lowest value is found and exchanged with the second element, and so on up to the last two elements. For example, if the Selection sort were used on the array **bdac**, each pass would look like this:

initial   b d a c

pass 1   a d b c

pass 2   a b d c

pass 3   a b c d

A simple form of the Selection sort is shown here:

```
procedure  Select(var item: DataArray; count:integer);
var
   i,j,k: integer;
   x: DataItem;
```

```
begin
   for i:=1 to count-1 do
   begin
      k:=i;
      x:=item[i];
      for j:=i+1 to count do      { find smallest element }
         if item[j]<x then
         begin
            k:=j;
            x:=item[j];
         end;
         item[k]:=item[i];     { swap }
         item[i]:=x;
   end;
end; { Selection sort }
```

Unfortunately, as in the Bubble sort, the outer loop executes $n-1$ times and the inner loop $n/2$ times. This means that the Selection sort requires $1/2(n^2-n)$ comparisons, which makes it too slow for a large number of items. The number of exchanges for the best case is $3(n-1)$ and for the worst case is $n^2/4+3(n-1)$. For the best case—if the list is ordered—only $n-1$ elements need to be moved, and each move requires 3 exchanges. The worst case approximates the number of comparisons.

Although determining the average case is beyond the scope of this book to develop, it is $n(\ln n+y)$, where y is Euler's constant, about 0.577216. This means that although the numbers of comparisons for both the Bubble sort and the Selection sort are the same, the number of exchanges in the average case is far less for the Selection sort.

THE INSERTION SORT   The Insertion sort is the last of the simple sorting algorithms. The Insertion sort initially sorts the first two members of the array. The algorithm then inserts the third member into its sorted position in relation to the first two members. The fourth element is then inserted into the list of three elements. The process continues until all elements have been sorted. For example, in the array **dcab**, the Insertion sort would look like this:

initial d c a b

pass 1 c d a b

pass 3 a c d b

pass 4 a b c d

A version of the Insertion sort is shown here:

```
procedure  Insert(var item: DataArray; count:integer);
var
   i,j: integer;
   x: DataItem;
```

```
begin
   for i:=2 to count do
   begin
      x:=item[i];
      j:=i-1;
      while (x<item[j]) and (j>0) do
      begin
         item[j+1]:=item[j];
         j:=j-1;
      end;
      item[j+1]:=x;
   end
end; { Insertion sort }
```

Unlike the Bubble sort and the Selection sort, the number of comparisons that occur when the Insertion sort is used depends upon how the list is initially ordered. If the list is in order, then the number of comparisons is $n-1$. If the list is out of order, then the number of comparisons is $1/2(n^2+n)-1$, while the average is $1/4(n^2+n-2)$.

The number of exchanges for each case is as follows:

Best	$2(n-1)$
Average	$1/4(n^2+9n-10)$
Worst	$1/2(n^2+3n-4)$

Therefore, the number for the worst case is as bad as those for the Bubble and Selection sorts, and the number for the average case is only slightly better. However, the Insertion sort does have two advantages. First, it behaves naturally: it works the least when the array is already sorted and the hardest when the array is sorted in inverse order. This makes the Insertion sort useful for lists that are almost in order. Second, it leaves the order of equal keys unchanged: if a list is sorted using two keys, after an Insertion sort it remains sorted for both keys.

Even though the number of comparisons may be fairly good for certain sets of data, the fact that the array must constantly be shifted means that the number of moves can be significant. However, the Insertion sort still behaves naturally, with the least exchanges occurring for an almost-sorted list and the most exchanges for an inversely ordered array.

Improved Sorts

Each algorithm shown so far has the fatal flaw of executing in n^2 time. For large amounts of data, these sorts would be slow — at some point, too slow to use. Every computer programmer has heard or told the horror story of the "sort that took three days." Unfortunately, these stories are often true.

When a sort takes too long, it may be the fault of the underlying algorithm. However, a sad commentary is that the first response is often, "Let's write it in assembly code." Although assembler will almost always speed up a routine by a constant factor, if the underlying algorithm is bad, the sort will still be slow, no matter how optimal the coding. Remember, when the time of a routine is n^2, increasing the speed of the coding or of the computer will only cause a slight improvement, because the rate at which the run time increases will change exponentially. (The graph in Figure 2-1 is shifted to the right slightly, but the curve is unchanged.) Keep in mind that if something is not fast enough written in Turbo Pascal, it won't be fast enough written in assembler. The solution is to use a better sorting algorithm.

In this section, two excellent sorts are developed. The first is the Shell sort and the second is the QuickSort, which is generally considered the best sorting routine. These sorts run so fast that if you blink, you will miss them.

THE SHELL SORT   The Shell sort is named after its inventor, D. L. Shell. However, the name seems to have stuck because its method of operation resembles sea shells piled upon one another.

The general method, derived from the Insertion sort, is based on diminishing increments. Figure 2-2 gives a diagram of a Shell sort on the array **fdacbe**. First, all elements that are three positions apart are sorted. Next, all elements that are two positions apart are sorted. Finally, all elements adjacent to each other are sorted.

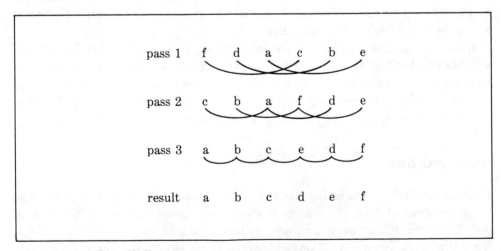

Figure 2-2.   The Shell sort

```
procedure shell(var item: data_array; count:integer);
const
    t = 5;
var
    i,j,k,s,m: integer;
    h: array[1..t] of integer;
    x: data_item;
begin
    h[1]:=9; h[2]:=5; h[3]:=3; h[4]:=3;  h[5]:=1;
    for m:=1 to t do
    begin
        k:=h[m];
        s:=-k;
        for i:=k+1 to count do
        begin
            x:=item[i];
            j:=i-k;
            if s=0 then
            begin
                s:=-k;
                s:=s+1;
                item[s]:=x;
            end;
            while (x<item[j]) and (j>0) and (j<=count) do
            begin
                item[j+k]:=item[j];
                j:=j-k;
            end;
            item[j+k]:=x;
        end;
    end;
end ; { shell sort }
```

It may not be obvious that this method yields good results, or even that it will sort the array, but it does both. This algorithm is efficient because each sorting pass involves either relatively few elements or elements that are already in reasonable order, so that each pass increases the order of the data.

The exact sequence for the increments can be changed. The only rule is that the last increment must be 1. For example, the sequence 9, 5, 3, 1 works well and is used in the Shell sort shown here. Avoid sequences that are powers of 2 because, for complex mathematical reasons, they reduce the efficiency of the sorting algorithm. (However, even if you use them, the sort will still work.)

The inner **while** loop has two test conditions. The **x<item[j]** is a comparison necessary for the sorting process. The tests **j>0** and **j<=count** keep the sort from overrunning the boundary of the array **item**. This extra check degrades the performance of the Shell sort somewhat. Slightly different versions of the Shell sort employ special array elements called *sentinels*, which are not actually part of the information to be sorted. Sentinels hold special termination values that indicate the least and greatest possible elements. This makes boundary checking unnecessary. However, using sentinels requires a specific knowledge of the data, which limits the generality of the sort procedure.

The analysis of the Shell sort presents some difficult mathematical problems that are beyond the scope of this discussion. However, execution time is proportional to $n^{1.2}$ for sorting n elements. This is a significant improvement over the n^2 sorts of the previous section, as shown in Figure 2-3, which graphs an n^2 curve and an $n^{1.2}$ curve together. However, before you decide to use the Shell sort, you should know that the QuickSort is even better.

THE QUICKSORT   The QuickSort, invented and named by C. A. R. Hoare, is generally considered the best sorting algorithm currently available. It is based on the exchange method of sorting. This is surprising if you consider the terrible performance of the Bubble sort—the simplest version of an exchange sort.

The QuickSort is built on the idea of partitions. The general procedure selects a value called the *comparand*, and then partitions the array into two parts, with all elements greater than or equal to the partition value on one side and those less than the partition value on the other. This process is repeated for each remaining part, until the array is sorted. For example, given the array **fedacb** and using the partition value **d**, the first pass of the QuickSort would rearrange the array like this.

initial	f e d a c b
pass 1	b c a d e f
pass 2	a b c d e f

This process is repeated for each part, **bca** and **def**. The process is essentially recursive in nature; indeed, the cleanest implementations of QuickSort are recursive algorithms.

The selection of the middle comparand value can be accomplished in two ways. The value can be chosen either at random or by averaging a small set of values taken from the array. For optimal sorting it is best to select a value that is precisely in the middle of the range of values. However, this is not easy to do for most sets of data. Even in the worst case—in which the value chosen is at one extremity—QuickSort still performs reasonably well.

The version of QuickSort shown here selects the middle element of the array. Although this may not always result in a good choice, it is a simple, quick technique, and the sort will still perform correctly.

```
procedure quickSort(var item: DataArray; count:integer);
   procedure qs(l,r:integer; var it:DataArray);
      var
      i,j: integer;
      x,y: DataItem;
      begin
         i:=l; j:=r;
```

```
        x:=it[(l+r) div 2];
        repeat
            while it[i] < x do i:= i+1;
            while x < it[j] do j:=j-1;
            if i<=j then
            begin
                y:=it[i];
                it[i]:=it[j];
                it[j]:=y;
                i:=i+1; j:=j-1;
            end;
        until i>j;
        if l<j then qs(l,j,it);
        if l<r then qs(i,r,it)
    end;
begin
    qs(1,count,item);
end; { QuickSort }
```

Here, the procedure **QuickSort** sets up a call to the main sorting procedure, called **qs**. This allows the common interface of **item** and **count** to be maintained.

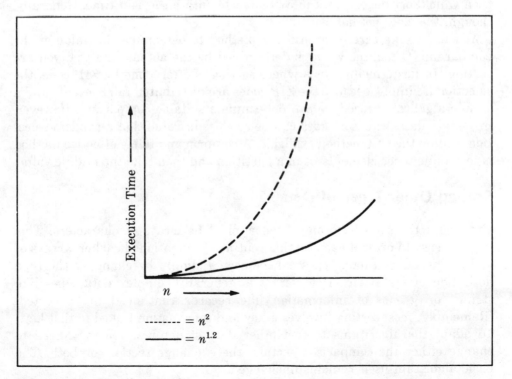

Figure 2-3. The n^2 and $n^{1.2}$ curves

The derivation of the number of comparisons and the number of exchanges that QuickSort performs requires mathematics beyond the scope of this book. However, you can assume that the number of comparisons is $n \log n$ and that the number of exchanges is about $n/6 \log n$. These are significantly better than any of the sorts shown so far.

The equation

$$N = a^x$$

can be rewritten as

$$x = \log_a N$$

This means, for example, that if 100 elements were to be sorted, QuickSort would require an average of 100 * 2, or 200, comparisons because log 100 is 2. Compared with the Bubble sort's average of 990 comparisons, this number is quite good.

However, there is one nasty aspect of QuickSort that you should be aware of. If the comparand value for each partition happens to be the largest value, then QuickSort degenerates into "slowsort" with an n^2 run time. Generally, though, this does not happen.

You must take care in choosing a method to determine the value of the comparand. Often, the value is determined by the actual data that you are sorting. In large mailing lists where sorting is often done by ZIP code, the selection is simple, because the ZIP codes are distributed fairly evenly and a simple algebraic procedure can determine a suitable comparand. However, in certain databases, sort keys can be so close in value that a random selection is often the best method available. A common and fairly effective method is to sample three elements from a partition and then take the middle value.

Sorting Other Types of Data

Until now, the sorts have only been applied to arrays of characters. This made it easy to present each sorting routine. As mentioned earlier, arrays of any of the built-in data types can be sorted simply by changing the type definition of **DataItem**. However, it is generally complex data types like strings or groups of information like records that need to be sorted. (Remember, most sorting involves a key and information linked to that key.) To adapt the algorithms to sort other data structures, you may need to change either the comparison section, the exchange section, or both. The basic algorithm itself remains unchanged.

Because QuickSort is one of the best general-purpose routines available at this time, it will be used in the examples. The same techniques, however, apply to any of the sorts previously described.

SORTING STRINGS   The easiest way to sort strings is to create an array of strings by using Turbo Pascal's **string** data type. This allows you to maintain easy indexing and exchanging, while keeping the basic QuickSort algorithm unchanged. The version shown here sorts the strings into alphabetical order:

```
type
   DataItem = string[80];
   DataArray = array [1..80] of DataItem;

Procedure  QsString(var item: DataArray; count:integer);
   procedure QS(l,r:integer; var it:DataArray);
      var
      i,j: integer;
      x,y: DataItem;
      begin
         i:=l; j:=r;
         x:=it[(l+r) div 2];
         repeat
            while it[i] < x do i:= i+1;
            while x < it[j] do j:=j-1;
            if i<=j then
            begin
               y:=it[i];
               it[i]:=it[j];
               it[j]:=y;
               i:=i+1; j:=j-1;
            end;
         until i>j;
         if l<j then qs(l,j,it);
         if l<r then qs(i,r,it)
      end;
begin
   QS(1,count,item);
end; { QsString }
```

Notice that only the type definition of **DataItem** had to be changed to enable QuickSort to sort strings instead of characters. This is due to Borland's excellent job of integrating **string** types into Pascal. In standard Pascal, sorting strings would have required much more code.

Keep in mind that string comparisons take longer than character comparisons, because several elements must be tested in each case.

SORTING RECORDS   Most application programs that require a sort will probably need to have a group of data sorted. A mailing list is an excellent example because a name, street, city, state, and ZIP code are all linked together. When this conglomerate unit of data is sorted, a sort key is used, but the entire record is also exchanged. To understand this process, you first need to create a *record* to hold the information. If you use the mailing address as an example, a convenient record to hold the information would be as follows:

```
type
    address = record
            name : string[30];
            street: string[40];
            city: string[20];
            state: string[2];
            zip: string[9];
    end;
```

After **address** has been defined, you must change the type definition of **DataItem** to the following:

```
DataItem = address;
```

When these changes have been made, you must change the comparison sections of QuickSort based on the field you are sorting. In the version of Quick-Sort shown here, the **name** field is used. This means that the mailing list is sorted in alphabetical order based on the name.

```
procedure  QsRecord(var item: DataArray; count:integer);
    procedure qs(l,r:integer; var it:DataArray);
        var
        i,j: integer;
        x,y: DataItem;
        begin
            i:=l; j:=r;
            x:=it[(l+r) div 2];
            repeat
                while it[i].name < x.name do i:= i+1;
                while x.name < it[j].name do j:=j-1;
                if i<=j then
                begin
                    y:=it[i];
                    it[i]:=it[j];
                    it[j]:=y;
                    i:=i+1; j:=j-1;
                end;
            until i>j;
            if l<j then qs(l,j,it);
            if l<r then qs(i,r,it)
        end;
begin
    qs(1,count,item);
end; { QsRecord }
```

Sorting Disk Files

There are two types of disk files: *sequential* and *random-access*. If a disk file is small enough, it may be read into memory so that the array-sorting routines presented earlier can sort it most efficiently. However, many disk files are too large to be sorted easily in memory and require special techniques.

SORTING RANDOM-ACCESS DISK FILES   Used by most microcomputer database applications, random-access disk files have two major advantages over sequential disk files. First, they are easy to maintain: you can update information without having to copy the entire list over. Second, they can be treated as a large array on disk, which greatly simplifies sorting.

Applying this method allows you to use the basic QuickSort with modifications to seek different records on the disk, in the same way as indexing an array. Unlike sorting a sequential disk file, sorting a random file in place also means that a full disk does not need to have room for both the sorted and unsorted files.

Each sorting situation differs according to the exact data structure that is sorted and the key that is used. However, the general concept of sorting random-access disk files can be understood by studying a sort program that sorts the mailing-list record called **address** that was defined earlier. This sample program assumes that the number of elements is fixed at 80; but in real applications, a record count would have to be dynamically maintained.

```
program MlistSort;

type
    address = record
            name : string[30];
            street: string[40];
            city: string[20];
            state: string[2];
            zip: string[9];
    end;
    str80 = string[80];
    DataItem = address;
    DataArray = array [1..80] of DataItem; { arbitrary number }
    recfil = file of address;

var
    test: DataItem;
    t,t2: integer;
    testfile: file of address;

function Find(var fp:recfil; i:integer): str80;
var
    t:address;
begin
    i:=i-1;
    Seek(fp,i);
    Read(fp,t);
    Find:=t.name;
end;{ Find}

procedure   QsRand(var fp:recfil; count:integer);
    procedure QS(l,r:integer);
        var
        i,j,s: integer;
```

```
      x,y,z: DataItem;
      begin
         i:=l; j:=r;
         s:=(l+r) div 2;
         Seek(fp,s-1);  { get a record }
         Read(fp,x);
         repeat
            while Find(fp,i) < x.name do i:= i+1;
            while x.name < Find(fp,j) do j:=j-1;
            if i<=j then
            begin   { swap records on disk  }
               Seek(fp,i-1); Read(fp,y);
               Seek(fp,j-1); Read(fp,z);
               Seek(fp,j-1); Write(fp,y);
               Seek(fp,i-1); Write(fp,z);
               i:=i+1; j:=j-1;
            end;
         until i>j;

         if l<j then QS(l,j);
         if l<r then QS(i,r)
      end;
begin
    QS(1,count);
end; { QsRand }

begin

    Assign(testfile, 'rectest.dat');
    Reset(testfile);
    t:=1;
    while not Eof(testfile) do begin
       Read(testfile,test);  { count the file }
       t:=t+1;
    end;
    t:=t-1;

    QS_Rand(testfile,t);

end.
```

The function **Find** was written in order to keep the QuickSort code essentially unchanged. **Find** returns the **name** string from a record on disk. The reason you must constantly subtract 1 from the arguments to **Seek** and **Find** is that disk-file records are numbered starting with 0.

SORTING SEQUENTIAL FILES   Unlike random-access files, sequential files generally do not use fixed record lengths, and they may be organized on storage devices that do not allow easy random access. Therefore, sequential disk files are common because a specific application is best suited to variable record lengths or because the storage device is sequential in nature. For example, most text files are sequential.

Although sorting a disk file as if it were an array has several advantages, this method cannot be used with sequential files — there is no way to achieve quick access to any arbitrary element. For example, no quick way exists to reach arbitrary records of a sequential file that is located on tape. For this reason, it would be difficult to apply any of the previously presented array-sorting algorithms to sequential files.

There are two approaches to sorting sequential files. The first approach reads the information into memory and sorts by using one of the standard array-sorting algorithms. Although this approach is fast, memory constraints limit the size of the file that can be sorted.

The second approach, called a *Merge sort*, divides the file to be sorted into two files of equal length. Using these files, the sort reads an element from each file, orders that pair, and writes the elements to a third disk file. The new file is then divided, and the ordered doubles are merged into ordered quadruples. The new file is split again, and the same procedure is followed until the list is sorted. This Merge sort is called a *three-tape merge* because it requires three files (tape drives) to be active at one time.

To understand how the Merge sort works, consider the following sequence:

1 4 3 8 6 7 2 5

The Merge sort splits the sequence to produce

1 4 3 8
6 7 2 5

It then merges the two parts to yield

1 6 - 4 7 - 2 3 - 5 8

This is then split again to become

1 6 - 4 7
2 3 - 5 8

The next merge yields

1 2 3 6 - 4 5 7 8

The final split is

1 2 3 6
4 5 7 8

with the outcome

1 2 3 4 5 6 7 8

As you may have guessed, the Merge sort requires that each file be accessed

$\log_2 n$ times, where n is the number of total elements to sort.

Here is a simple version of the Merge sort. It assumes that the input file is twice as long as the information in it, so that only one file is actually needed; however, the Merge sort method is still the same. In this example **filtype** is defined as a file of type **DataItem**.

```
function Find(var fp:filtype;i:integer):DataItem;
var
    t:DataItem;
begin
    Seek(fp,i-1);
    Read(fp,t);
    Find:=t;
end; {Find}

procedure Mergesort(var fp: filtype; count:integer);
var
    i,j,k,l,t,h,m,p,q,r: integer;
    ch1,ch2:DataItem;
    up: boolean;

begin
    up:=TRUE;
    p:=1;
    repeat
        h:=1; m:=count;
        if up then
        begin
            i:=1; j:=count; k:=count+1; l:=2*count;
        end else
        begin
            k:=1; l:=count; i:=count+1; j:=2*count;
        end;
        repeat
            if m>=p then q:=p else q:=m;
            m:=m-q;
            if m>=p then r:=p else r:=m;
            m:=m-r;
            while (q<>0) and (r<>0) do
            begin
                if Find(fp,i) < Find(fp,j) then
                    begin
                        Seek(fp,i-1); Read(fp,ch2);
                        Seek(fp,k-1); Write(fp,ch2);
                        k:=k+h; i:=i+1; q:=q-1;
                    end else
                    begin
                        Seek(fp,j-1); Read(fp,ch2);
                        Seek(fp,k-1); Write(fp,ch2);
                        k:=k+h; j:=j-1; r:=r-1;
                    end ;
            end;
            while r<>0 do
            begin
                Seek(fp,j-1); Read(fp,ch2);
                Seek(fp,k-1); Write(fp,ch2);
                k:=k+h; j:=j-1; r:=r-1;
            end;
```

```
           while q<>0 do
           begin
              Seek(fp,i-1); Read(fp,ch2);
              Seek(fp,k-1); Write(fp,ch2);
              k:=k+h; i:=i+1; q:=q-1;
           end;
           h:=-1; t:=k;
           k:=l;
           l:=t;
        until m=0;
        up := not up;
        p:=p*2;
     until p>=count;
     if not up then
        for i:=1 to count do
        begin
           Seek(fp,i-1+count); Read(fp,ch2);
           Seek(fp,i-1); Write(fp,ch2);
        end;
end ; { Mergesort }
```

Searching

Databases of information exist so that from time to time, a user can locate and use the data in a given record, as long as its key is known. There is only one method of finding information in an unsorted file or array, and another for a sorted file or array.

Search Methods

Finding information in an unsorted array requires a *sequential search*, starting at the first element and stopping either when a match is found or when the end of the array is reached. This method must be used on unsorted data, but can also be applied to sorted data. If the data has been sorted, then a *binary search* can be used, which greatly speeds up any search.

THE SEQUENTIAL SEARCH   The sequential search is easy to code. The following function searches a character array of known length until a match is found with the specified key:

```
function SeqSearch(item: DataArray; count:integer;
                         key:DataItem):integer;
var
    t:integer;
begin
    t:=1;
    while (key<>item[t]) and (t<=count) t:=t+1;
    if t>count then SeqSearch:=0
    else Seqsearch:=t;
end ; { SeqSearch }
```

This function returns either the index number of the matching entry if there is one, or a 0 if there is not.

A straight sequential search will, on the average, test $n/2$ elements. In the best case, it will test only 1 element, and in the worst case, n elements. If the information is stored on disk, the search time can be very long. But if the data is unsorted, a sequential search is the only method available.

THE BINARY SEARCH   If the data to be searched is in sorted order, then a superior method called a *binary search* can be used to find a match. This method uses the "divide and conquer" approach. It first tests the middle element: if the element is larger than the key, it then tests the middle element of the first half; otherwise, it tests the middle element of the second half. The process is repeated until a match is found or until there are no more elements to test.

For example, to find the number 4 in the array 1 2 3 4 5 6 7 8 9, the binary search would first test the middle element, which is 5. Since this element is greater than 4, the search would continue with the first half, or

$$1\ 2\ 3\ 4\ 5$$

Here, the middle element is 3. This is less than 4, so the first half is discarded and the search continues with

$$4\ 5$$

This time, the match is found.

In the binary search, the number of comparisons in the worst case is $\log_2 n$. With average cases, the number is somewhat better, and with the best case, the number is 1.

You can use the following binary search function for character arrays to search any arbitrary data structure by changing the comparison portion of the routine and the type definition of **DataItem**:

```
function BSearch(item: DataArray; count:integer;
                        key:DataItem):integer;
var
   low, high, mid:integer;
   found:boolean;
begin
   low:=1; high:=count;
   found:=false;
   while (low<=high) and (not found) do
   begin
      mid:=(low+high) div 2;
```

```
      if key<item[mid] then high:=mid-1
      else if key>item[mid] then low:=mid+1
      else found:=true;    { found  }
   end;
   if found then b_search:=mid
   else BSearch:=0;    {not found}
end ; { BSearch }
```

The next chapter explores different approaches to data storage and retrieval, which in some cases can make sorting and searching a much easier job.

THREE

Queues, Stacks, Linked Lists, And Trees

Programs consist of *algorithms* and *data structures*. The good program is a blend of both. Choosing and implementing a data structure are as important as the routines that manipulate the data. How information is organized and accessed is usually determined by the nature of the programming problem. Therefore, as a programmer you must have in your "bag of tricks" the right storage and retrieval methods for any situation.

The actual representation of data in the computer is built "from the ground up," starting with the basic data types like **char**, **integer**, and **real**. At the next level are arrays, which are organized collections of the data types. Next, there are records, which are conglomerate data types accessed under one name. Transcending these physical aspects of the data, the final level concentrates on the sequence in which the data will be *stored* and *retrieved*. In essence, the physical data is linked to "data machines" that control the way your program accesses information. There are four of these machines:

- A queue
- A stack
- A linked list
- A binary tree.

Each method provides a solution to a class of problems; each is essentially a "device" that performs a specific storage and retrieval operation on the given information and request. The methods share two operations: *store an item* and *retrieve an item*, in which the item is one informational unit. This chapter shows you how to develop these methods for use in your own programs.

Queues

A *queue* is a linear list of information that is accessed in *first-in, first-out* order (sometimes called FIFO). The first item placed on the queue is the first item retrieved, the second item placed on the queue is the second item retrieved, and so on. This order is the only means of storage and retrieval; a queue does not allow random access of any specific item.

Queues are common in everyday life. For example, a line at a bank or at a fast food restaurant is a queue — except when patrons push their way to the front. To visualize how a queue works, consider the two routines **Qstore** and **Qretrieve**. **Qstore** places an item onto the end of the queue, and **Qretrieve** removes the first item from the queue and returns its value. Figure 3-1 shows the effect of a series of these operations. Keep in mind that a retrieval operation removes an item from the queue and, if the item is not stored elsewhere, effectively destroys it — the item cannot be accessed again.

Queues are used in many types of programming situations, such as simulations (discussed later in their own chapter), event scheduling (as in a PERT or Gant chart) and I/O buffering.

As an example, consider a simple event-scheduler program that allows you to enter a number of events. As each event is performed, it is taken off the list and the next event is displayed. You might use a program like this to organize such events as a day's appointments. To simplify the examples, the program uses an array of strings to hold the events. It limits each event description to 80 characters and the number of events to 100. First, here are the procedure **Qstore** and the function **Qretrieve** that will be used in the scheduling program. They are shown here with the necessary global variables and type definitions.

```
const
   MAX_EVENT = 100;
type
   EvtType = string[80];

var
   event: array[1..MAX_EVENT] of EvtType;
   spos, rpos: integer;


procedure Qstore(q:EvtType);
begin
   if spos=MAX_EVENT then
      WriteLn('List full')
   else
   begin
      event[spos]:=q;
      spos:=spos+1;
```

Action	Contents of Queue
Qstore(A)	A
Qstore(B)	A B
Qstore(C)	A B C
Qretrieve returns **A**	B C
Qstore(D)	B C D
Qretrieve returns **B**	C D
Qretrieve returns **C**	D

Figure 3-1. A queue in action

```
   end;
end; { Qstore }

function Qretrieve:EvtType;
begin
   if rpos=spos then
   begin
      WriteLn('No events in the Queue');
      Qretrieve:='';
   end else
   begin
      rpos:=rpos+1;
      Qretrieve:= event[rpos-1];
   end;
end;   { Qretrieve }
```

These functions require three global variables: **spos**, which holds the index of the next free storage location; **rpos**, which holds the index of the next item to retrieve; and **event**, which is the string array that holds the information. Before the program can call either **Qstore** or **Qretrieve**, the variables **spos** and **rpos** must be initialized to zero.

In this program the procedure **Qstore** places new events on the end of the list and checks if the list is full. The function **Qretrieve** takes events off the queue while there are events to perform. When a new event is scheduled, **spos** is incremented, and when an event is completed **rpos** is incremented. In essence, **rpos** "chases" **spos** through the queue. Figure 3-2 shows how this process appears in memory as the program executes. If **rpos** equals **spos**, then there are no events left in the schedule. Keep in mind that even though the information stored in the queue is not actually destroyed by the **Qretrieve** function, it can never be accessed again and is, in effect, gone.

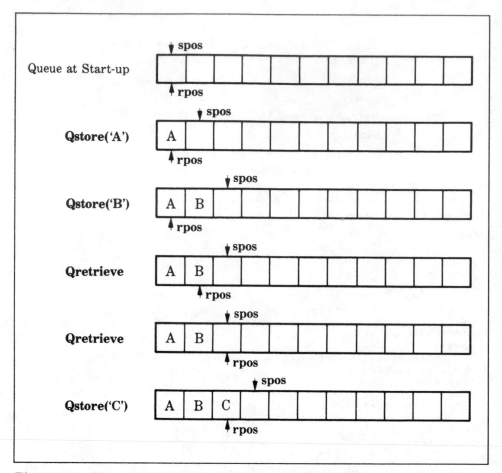

Figure 3-2.   The retrieval index chasing the storage index

Here is the entire program for this simple event scheduler. You may want to enhance this program for your own use.

```
program MiniScheduler;

const
   MAX_EVENT = 100;
type
   EvtType = string[80];

var
   event: array[1..MAX_EVENT] of EvtType;
   spos, rpos,t: integer;
   ch:char;
```

```
      done:boolean;

  procedure Qstore(q:EvtType);
  begin
      if spos=MAX_EVENT then
         WriteLn('List full')
      else
      begin
         event[spos]:=q;
         spos:=spos+1;
      end;
  end; { Qstore }

  function Qretrieve:EvtType;
  begin
      if rpos=spos then
      begin
         WriteLn('No events in the Queue');
         Qretrieve:='';
      end else
      begin
         rpos:=rpos+1;
         Qretrieve:= event[rpos-1];
      end;
  end;  { Qretrieve }

  procedure Enter;
  var
      s:string[80];

  begin
      repeat
         Write('Enter event ',spos+1,':');
         Read(s);
         WriteLn;
         if Length(s)<>0 then Qstore(s);
      until Length(s)=0;
  end; {Enter}

  procedure Review;
  var


    t:integer;
  begin
      for t:=rpos to spos-1 do WriteLn(t,':',event[t]);
  end; { Review }

  procedure Perform;
  var
      s:string[80];
  begin
      s:=Qretrieve;   { get next event }
      if Length(s)<>0 then WriteLn(s);
  end;  { Perform }

  begin   { scheduler }
    for t:=1 to MAX_EVENT do event[t]:='';  { init events }
    spos:=0; rpos:=0;  done:=FALSE;

    repeat
       Write('Enter, Review, Perform, Quit: ');
```

```
      Read(ch);
      WriteLn;
      case upcase(ch) of
         'E': Enter;
         'R': Review;
         'P': Perform;
         'Q': done:=TRUE;
      end;
   until done=TRUE;
end.
```

The Circular Queue

In the previous section, you may have thought of an improvement for the MiniScheduler program. Instead of having the program stop when it reaches the limit of the array used to store the queue, you could have both the storage index **spos** and the retrieval index **rpos** loop back to the start of the array. This method would allow any number of items to be placed on the queue, as long as items were also being taken off. This implementation of a queue is called a *circular queue* because it uses its storage array as if it were a circle instead of a linear list.

To create a circular queue in the MiniScheduler program, you should change the subprograms **Qstore** and **Qretrieve**, as shown here:

```
procedure Qstore(q:EvtType);
begin
   if spos+1=rpos then
      WriteLn('List full')
   else
   begin
      event[spos]:=q;
      spos:=spos+1;
      if spos=MAX_EVENT then spos:=1; { loop back }
   end;
end; { Qstore }

function Qretrieve:EvtType;
begin
   if rpos=MAX_EVENT then rpos:=1; { loop back }
   if rpos=spos then
   begin
      WriteLn('Queue empty');
      Qretrieve:=';';
   end else
   begin
      rpos:=rpos+1;
      Qretrieve:= event[rpos-1];
   end;
end;  { Qretrieve }
```

In essence, the queue is only full when both the storage index and the retrieval index are equal; otherwise, the queue still has room for another event. However, this means that when the program starts, the retrieval index **rpos** must not be set to 0 but rather to **MAX‗EVENT**, so that the first call to **Qstore** does not produce the message **list full**. You should note that the queue will hold only **MAX‗EVENT** −1 elements because **rpos** and **spos** must always be at least one element apart; otherwise, it would be impossible to know whether the queue was full or empty. Figure 3-3 shows the array used for the circular version of the MiniScheduler program. The most common use of a circular queue may be in operating systems that buffer the information read from and written to disk files or the console. Another common use is in real-time application programs in which, for example, the user may continue to input from the keyboard while the program performs another task. Many word processors do this when they reformat a paragraph or justify a line. There is a brief period in which what is being typed is not displayed until after the other process that the program is working on has been completed. To accomplish this, the application program must continue to check for keyboard entry during the other process's execution. If a key has been typed, it is placed quickly in the queue and the process continues. After the process is complete, the characters are retrieved from the queue and handled in the normal manner.

To see how this can be done with a circular queue, study the following simple program, which contains two processes. The first process counts to

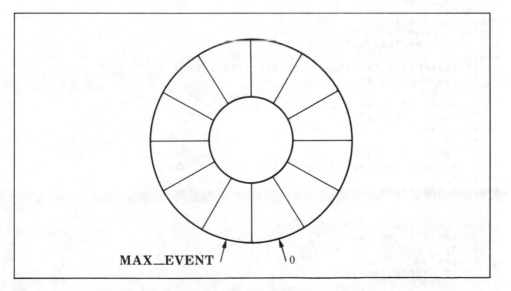

Figure 3-3. The circular array for the MiniScheduler program

32,000. The second process places characters into a circular queue as they are typed, without echoing them on the screen until it finds a semicolon. The characters you type will not be displayed, because the first process is given priority either until you type a semicolon or until the count finishes. Then the characters in the queue are retrieved and printed.

```pascal
program KeyBuffer;

const
   MAX_EVENT = 10;
type
   EvtType = char;
   dos_call = record
                al:char;
                ah:byte;
                bx,cx,dx,bp,si,di,ds,es,flags:integer
              end;

var
   event: array[1..MAX_EVENT] of EvtType;
   spos, rpos,t: integer;
   ch:char;
   dos:dos_call;

procedure Qstore(q:EvtType);
begin
   if spos+1=rpos then
      WriteLn('List full')
   else
   begin
      event[spos]:=q;
      spos:=spos+1;
      if spos=MAX_EVENT then spos:=1; { loop back }
   end;
end; { Qstore }

function Qretrieve:EvtType;
begin
   if rpos=MAX_EVENT then rpos:=1; { loop back }
   if rpos=spos then
   begin
      WriteLn('Queue empty');
      Qretrieve:=';';
   end else
   begin
      rpos:=rpos+1;
      Qretrieve:= event[rpos-1];
   end;
end;  { Qretrieve }


begin   { key buffer }
   dos.ah:=7;  dos.al:=' ';  { init }
   t:=1;
   repeat
      if KeyPressed then
      begin
```

```
      MsDos(dos); { Read with no echo }
      Qstore(dos.al);
    end;
    t:=t+1;
  until (t=32000) or (dos.al=';');
  repeat
      ch:=Qretrieve;
      if ch<>';' then Write(ch);
  until ch=';';
end.
```

The routine **KeyPressed** uses a function call to the operating system, which returns TRUE if a key has been pressed and returns FALSE if no key has been pressed. The **MsDos** call reads a key from the keyboard without echoing it to the screen. These calls work for the IBM PC only; if you have a different computer, you should consult the *Turbo Pascal User Manual* to find the right procedures to use. (In Chapter 5, you will learn how to use these and other operating-system calls in depth.)

Stacks

A *stack* is the opposite of a queue, because it uses *last-in, first-out* accessing (sometimes called LIFO). Imagine a stack of plates: the bottom plate in the stack is the last to be used, and the top plate (the last plate placed on the stack) is the first to be used. Stacks are used a great deal in system software, including compilers and interpreters.

For historical reasons, the two primary stack operations—*store* and *retrieve*—are usually called *push* and *pop*, respectively. Therefore, to implement a stack, you need two functions: **Push**, which places a value on the top of the stack; and **Pop**, which retrieves the top value from the stack. You also need a region of memory to use as the stack: you could use an array, or you could allocate a region of memory by using Turbo Pascal's dynamic memory allocation functions. Like the queue, the retrieval function takes a value off the list and if the value is not stored elsewhere, destroys it. Here are the general forms of **Push** and **Pop** that use an integer array:

```
const
   MAX = 100;

var
   stack:array [1..100] of integer;
   tos:integer;   { points to top of stack }
                  { must be initialized to 1 }

procedure Push(i:integer);
begin
   if tos>=MAX then WriteLn('Stack full')
```

```
   else
   begin
      stack[tos]:=i;
      tos:=tos+1;
   end;
end;  {Push}

function Pop:integer;
begin
   tos:=tos-1;
   if tos<1 then
   begin
      WriteLn('Stack underflow');
      tos:=tos+1;
      Pop:=0;
   end
   else Pop:=stack[tos];
end;  {Pop}
```

The variable **tos** is the index of the next open stack location. When implementing these functions, *always* remember to prevent overflow and underflow. In these routines, if **tos** is 0, the stack is empty; if **tos** is greater than or equal to the last storage location, the stack is full. Figure 3-4 shows how a stack works.

An excellent example of using a stack is a four-function calculator. Most calculators today accept a standard form of expression called *infix notation*, which takes the general form *operand-operator-operand*. For example, to add 100 to 200, you would enter **100**, press +, enter **200**, and press =. However, some calculators use an expression evaluation called *postfix notation*, in which both operands are entered before the operator is entered. For example, to add 100 to 200 using postfix you would first enter **100**, then enter **200**, and

Action	Contents of Stack
Push(A)	A
Push(B)	B A
Push(C)	C B A
Pop retrieves C	B A
Push(F)	F B A
Pop retrieves F	B A
Pop retrieves B	A
Pop retrieves A	*empty*

Figure 3-4.   A stack in action

then press +. As operands are entered, they are placed on a stack; when an operator is entered, two operands are removed from the stack and the result is pushed back onto the stack. The advantage of the postfix form is that very complex expressions can be evaluated easily by the calculator without much code.

The entire calculator program is shown here:

```pascal
program four_function_calc;
const
    MAX = 100;

var
    stack:array [1..100] of integer;
    tos:integer;  { points to top of stack }
    a,b:integer;
    s:string[80];

procedure Push(i:integer);
begin
    if tos>=MAX then WriteLn('Stack full')
    else
    begin
        stack[tos]:=i;
        tos:=tos+1;
    end;
end;  {Push}

function Pop:integer;
begin
    tos:=tos-1;
    if tos<1 then
    begin
        WriteLn('Stack underflow');
        tos:=tos+1;
        Pop:=0;
    end
    else Pop:=stack[tos];
end;  {Pop}

begin  { calculator }
    tos:=1;
    WriteLn('Four Function Calculator');
    repeat
        Write(': ');
        Read(s);
        WriteLn;
        Val(s,a,b);
        if (b=0) and ((Length(s)>1) or (s[1]<>'-')) then Push(a)
        else
        case s[1] of
                '+': begin
                        a:=Pop;
                        b:=Pop;
                        WriteLn(a+b);
                        Push(a+b);
                    end;
                '-': begin
                        a:=Pop;
```

```
                       b:=Pop;
                       WriteLn(b-a);
                       Push(b-a);
                 end;
          '*': begin
                       a:=Pop;
                       b:=Pop;
                       WriteLn(a*b);
                       Push(a*b);
                 end;
          '/': begin
                       a:=Pop;
                       b:=Pop;
                       if a=0 then WriteLn('divide by zero')
                       else begin
                             WriteLn(b div a);
                             Push(b div a);
                       end;
                 end;
          end;
   until UpCase(copy(s,1,1))='Q';
end.
```

Although this version is capable of integer arithmetic only, it would be simple to switch it to full floating-point operation by changing the data type of the stack and converting the **div** operator to the floating-point operator (/).

Linked Lists

Queues and stacks share two common traits. First, both have strict rules for referencing the data stored in them. Second, the retrieval operations are by nature *consumptive*; that is, accessing an item in a stack or queue requires its removal and, unless it is stored elsewhere, its destruction. Both stacks and queues also require, at least in concept, a contiguous region of memory in order to operate.

Unlike a stack or a queue, a *linked list* may access its storage in a random fashion, because each piece of information carries with it a *link* to the next data item in the chain. A linked list requires a complex data structure, whereas a stack or a queue can operate on both simple and complex data items. A linked-list retrieval operation does not remove and destroy an item from the list; a specific *deletion operation* must be added to do this.

Linked lists are used for two purposes. The first purpose is to create arrays of unknown size in memory. If you know the amount of storage in advance, then you can use a simple array; but if you do not know the actual size of a list, then you must use a linked list. The second purpose is for the disk-file storage of databases. The linked list allows you to insert and delete items quickly and easily without rearranging the entire disk file. For these reasons, linked lists are used extensively in database-management software.

Linked lists can be either singly linked or doubly linked. A *singly linked list* contains a link to the next data item. A *doubly linked list* contains links to both the next item and the previous item in the list. The type you use depends on your application.

Singly Linked Lists

A singly linked list requires that each item of information contain a link to the next item in the list. Each data item generally consists of a record that contains both information fields and a link pointer. The concept of a singly linked list is shown in Figure 3-5.

There are two ways to build a singly linked list. The first simply adds each new item to the beginning or the end of the list. The other adds items into specific places in the list (for example, by ascending sorted order).

The manner in which you build the list determines the way the *storage function* will be coded, as shown in the simple case of creating a linked list by adding items on the end. You need to define a record to hold the information and the links. Because mailing lists are common, this example uses one. The record type for each element in the mailing list is defined here. (It is similar to the element definition in Chapter 2.)

```
AddrPointer = ^address;
address = record
        name : string[30];
        street: string[40];
        city: string[20];
        state: string[2];
        zip: string[9];
        next: AddrPointer;    { pointer to next record }
end;

DataItem = address;
DataArray = array [1..100] of AddrPointer;
                            { hold pointers to }
                            { address records }
var
    start,last:AddrPointer;
```

The function **SL—Store** builds a singly linked list by placing each new element on the end. A pointer to a record of type **address** must be passed to **SL—Store**, as shown here:

```
procedure SL_Store(i:AddrPointer);
begin
    if last=nil then { first item in list }
```

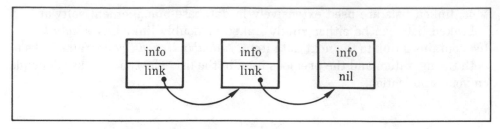

Figure 3-5.   A singly linked list in memory

```
   begin
      last:=i;
      start:=i;
      i^.next:=nil;
   end else
   begin
      last^.next:=i;
      i^.next:=nil;
      last:=i;
   end;
end;  { SL_Store }
```

Although you can sort the list created with **SL—Store** as a separate operation, it is easier to sort while building the list by inserting each new item in the proper sequence of the chain. In addition, if the list is already sorted, then it is advantageous to keep it sorted by inserting new items in their proper location. To do this, the list is scanned sequentially until the proper location is found; the new address is inserted at that point, and the links are rearranged as necessary.

Three possible situations can occur when inserting an item into a singly linked list. First, the item can become the new first item; second, it can be inserted between two other items; or third, it can become the last item. Figure 3-6 shows how the links are changed for each case.

If you change the first item in the list, you must update the entry point to the list elsewhere in your program. To avoid this you can use a *sentinel* as the first item. A sentinel is a special value that will always be first in the list. With this method you can keep the list's entry point fron changing. However, this method has the disadvantage of using an extra storage location to hold the sentinel, so it is not used here.

The function, **SLS—Store**, shown here, inserts addresses into the mailing list in ascending order based on the **name** field. It returns a pointer to the first element in the list and also requires that the pointers to both the beginning and end of the list be passed to it.

```
function SLS_Store(info,start:AddrPointer;
                   var last:AddrPointer):AddrPointer;
{ store entries in sorted order }

var
   old, top: ^ address;
   done:boolean;
begin
   top:=start;
   old:=nil;
   done:=FALSE;

   if start=nil then
   begin { first element in list }
      info^.next:=nil;
      last:=info;
      SLS_Store:=info;
   end else
   begin
```

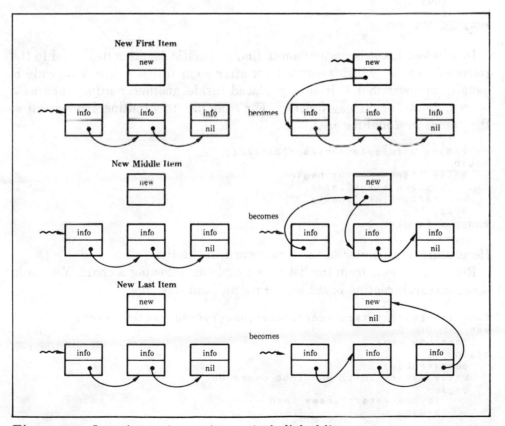

Figure 3-6. Inserting an item a into a singly linked list

```
      while (start<>nil) and (not done) do begin
          if start^.name < info^.name then begin
             old:=start;
             start:=start^.next;
          end else begin   { goes in middle }
             if old<>nil then begin
                old^.next:=info;
                info .next:=start;
                SLS_Store:=top;  { keep same starting point }
                done:=TRUE;
             end else begin
                info^.next:=start;  { new first element }
                SLS_Store:=info;
                done:=TRUE;
             end;
          end;
      end;  {while}
      if not done then
      begin
          last^.next:=info;  { goes on end }
          info^.next:=nil;
          last:=info;
          SLS_Store:=top;
      end;
   end;
end;  { SLS_Store }
```

In a linked list it is uncommon to find a specific function dedicated to the *retrieval process*, which returns item after item in list order. This code is usually so short that it is simply placed inside another routine, such as a search, delete, or display function. For example, this routine displays all of the names in a mailing list:

```
procedure Display(start:AddrPointer);
begin
   while start<>nil do begin
      WriteLn(start^.name);
      start:=start^.next;
   end;
end;  { Display }
```

Here, **start** is a pointer to the first record in the list.

Retrieving items from the list is as simple as following a chain. You could write a search routine based on the **name** field like this:

```
function Search(start:AddrPointer;name:str80):AddrPointer;
var
   done:boolean;
begin
   done:=FALSE;
   while (start<>nil) and (not done) do
   begin
      if name=start^.name then
      begin
```

```
        Search:=start;
        done:=TRUE;
      end else
        start:=start^.next;
   end;
   if start=nil then Search:=nil;  { not in list }
end;  { Search }
```

Because **Search** returns a pointer to the list item that matches the search name, **Search** must be declared as returning a record pointer of type **address**. If there is no match, a **nil** pointer is returned.

The process of deleting an item from a singly linked list is straightforward. As in insertion, there are three cases: deleting the first item, deleting a middle item, and deleting the last item. Figure 3-7 shows each case.

This function deletes a given item from a list of records of type **address**.

```
function SL_Delete(start,item,prior_item:AddrPointer)
               :AddrPointer;
begin
   if prior_item<>nil then
      prior_item^.next:=item^.next
   else start:=item^.next;
   SL_Delete:=start;
end;  {SL_Delete}
```

SL_Delete must be sent pointers to the deleted item, to the item before it in the chain, and to the start of the list. If the first item is to be removed, then the previous pointer must be **nil**. The function must return a pointer to

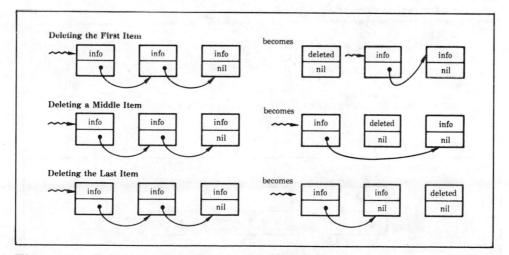

Figure 3-7. Deleting an item from a singly linked list

the start of the list because of the case in which the first item is deleted — the program must know where the new first element is located.

Singly linked lists have a major drawback that prevents their extensive use: the list cannot be followed in reverse order. For this reason, doubly linked lists are generally used.

Doubly Linked Lists

Doubly linked lists consist of data that is linked to both the next item and the preceding item. Figure 3-8 shows how the links are arranged. A list that has two links instead of one has two major advantages. First, the list can be read in either direction. This not only simplifies sorting the list but also, in the case of a database, allows a user to scan the list in either direction. Second, because either a forward link or a backward link can read the entire list, if one link becomes invalid, the list can be reconstructed using the other link. This is meaningful only in the case of equipment failure.

Three primary operations can be performed on a doubly linked list: inserting a new first item, inserting a new middle item, and inserting a new last item. These operations are shown in Figure 3-9.

Building a doubly linked list is similar to building a singly linked list, except that the record must have room to maintain two links. Using the mailing-list example again, you can modify **address** as shown here to accommodate this:

```
type
    str80 = string[80];
    AddrPointer = ^address;
    address = record
            name : string[30];
            street: string[40];
            city: string[20];
            state: string[2];
            zip: string[9];
            next: AddrPointer;    { pointer to next record }
```

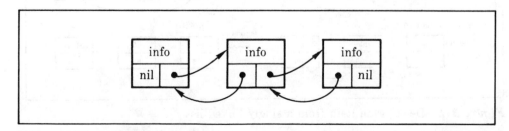

Figure 3-8.   A doubly linked list

```
        prior: AddrPointer;  { pointer to previous record}
end;

DataItem = address;
DataArray = array [1..100] of AddrPointer;
```

Using record **address** as the basic data item, the function **DL—Store**
builds a doubly linked list:

```
procedure DL_Store(i:AddrPointer);
begin
   if last=nil then { first item in list }
   begin
      last:=i;
      start:=i;
      i^.next:=nil;
      i^.prior:=nil;
   end
   else
```

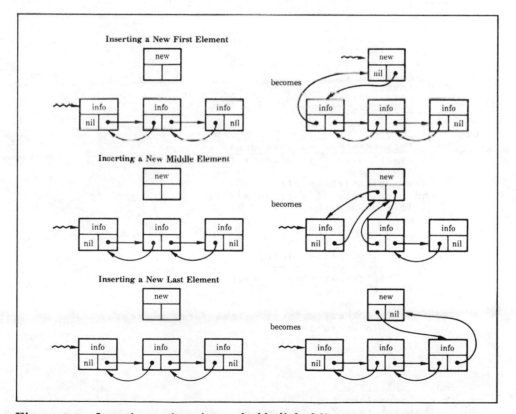

Figure 3-9. Inserting an item into a doubly linked list

```
      begin
      last^.next:=i;
      i^.next:=nil;
      i^.prior:=last;
      last:=i;
   end;
end;   { DL_Store }
```

This function places each new entry on the end of the list.

Like a singly linked list, a doubly linked list can have a function that stores each element in a specific location in the list as it is built, instead of always placing each new item on the end. The function **DSL—Store** creates a list that is sorted in ascending order based on the **name** field.

```
function DSL_Store(info,start:AddrPointer;
                   var last:AddrPointer):AddrPointer;
{ store entries in sorted order }

var
   old, top: ^ address;
   done:boolean;
begin
   top:=start;
   old:=nil;
   done:=FALSE;

   if start=nil then
   begin { first element in list }
      info^.next:=nil;
      last:=info;
      info^.prior:=nil;
      DSL_Store:=info;
   end else
   begin
      while (start<>nil) and (not done) do begin
         if start^.name < info^.name then begin
            old:=start;
            start:=start^.next;
         end else begin   { goes in middle }
            if old<>nil then
            begin
               old^.next:=info;
               info^.next:=start;
               start^.prior:=info;
               info^.prior:=old;
               DSL_Store:=top;   { keep same starting point }
               done:=TRUE;
            end else begin
               info^.next:=start;   { new first element }
               info^.prior:=nil;
               DSL_Store:=info;
               done:=TRUE;
            end;
         end;
      end;   {while}
      if not done then begin
         last^.next:=info;   { goes on end }
```

```
            info^.next:=nil;
            info^.prior:=last;
            last:=info;
            DSL_Store:=top;
        end;
    end;
end;   { DSL_Store }
```

Because an item may be inserted at the top of the list, this function must return a pointer to the first item so that other parts of the program will know where the list begins. As with the singly linked list, to retrieve a specific data item the program follows the links until the proper item is found.

There are three cases to consider when deleting an item from a doubly linked list: deleting the first item, deleting a middle item, and deleting the last item. Figure 3-10 shows how the links are rearranged.

The following function deletes an item of type **address** from a doubly linked list.

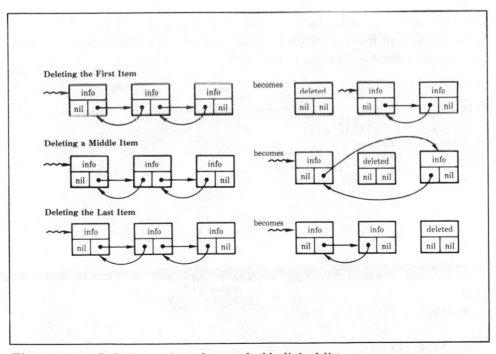

Figure 3-10.   Deleting an item from a doubly linked list

```
function DL_Delete(start,item:AddrPointer)
                              :AddrPointer;
begin
   if start=item then begin  { delete first in list }
      DL_Delete:=start^.next;
      if item^.next <> nil then begin
         item^.next^.prior:=nil;
      end;
      dispose(start);
   end else begin
      item^.prior^.next:=item^.next;
      item^.next^.prior:=item^.prior;
      DL_Delete:=start;    {still same starting point}
   end;
end; {DL_Delete}
```

This function requires one less pointer to be passed to it than the singly
linked list version required; the data item being deleted already carries a
link to the previous element and to the next element. Because the first item
in the list could change, the pointer to the top item is passed back to the
calling routine.

A Mailing List
That Uses a Doubly Linked List

Here is a simple mailing-list program that uses a doubly linked list. The
entire list is kept in memory while in use; however, the program can be modified to store the mailing list in a disk file.

```
program mlist;

type
   str80 = string[80];
   AddrPointer = ^address;
   address = record
            name : string[30];
            street: string[40];
            city: string[20];
            state: string[2];
            zip: string[9];
            next: AddrPointer;    { pointer to next record }
            prior: AddrPointer;   { pointer to previous record}
   end;

   DataItem = address;
   DataArray = array [1..100] of AddrPointer;
                                { hold pointers to }
                                { address records }
   filtype = file of address;

var
   test: DataArray;
```

```pascal
    t,t2: integer;
    mlist: FilType;
    start,last:AddrPointer;
    done: boolean;

function MenuSelect:char;  { returns the users selection }

var
    ch:char;

begin
    WriteLn('1. Enter names');
    WriteLn('2. Delete a name');
    WriteLn('3. Display the list');
    WriteLn('4. Search for a name');
    WriteLn('5. Save the list');
    WriteLn('6. Load the list');
    WriteLn('7. Quit');
    repeat
        WriteLn;
        Write('Enter your choice: ');
        Read(ch);  ch:=UpCase(ch); WriteLn;
    until (ch>='1') and (ch<='7');
    MenuSelect:=ch;
end;  { MenuSelect }

function DSL_Store(info,start:AddrPointer;
                      var last:AddrPointer):AddrPointer;
{ store entries in sorted order }

var
    old, top: ^ address;
    done:boolean;
begin
    top:=start;
    old:=nil;
    done:=FALSE;

    if start=nil then
    begin { first element in list }
        info^.next:=nil;
        last:=info;
        info^.prior:=nil;
        DSL_Store:=info;
    end else
    begin
        while (start<>nil) and (not done) do
        begin
            if start^.name < info^.name then
            begin
                old:=start;
                start:=start^.next;
            end else
            begin  { goes in middle }
                if old<>nil then
                begin
                    old^.next:=info;
                    info^.next:=start;
```

```
                         start^.prior:=info;
                         info^.prior:=old;
                         DSL_Store:=top;  { keep same starting point }
                         done:=TRUE;
                  end else
                  begin
                         info^.next:=start;  { new first element }
                         info^.prior:=nil;
                         DSL_Store:=info;
                         done:=TRUE;
                  end;
             end;
       end;  {while}
       if not done then
       begin
            last^.next:=info;  { goes on end }
            info^.next:=nil;
            info^.prior:=last;
            last:=info;
            DSL_Store:=top;
       end;
    end;
end;  { DSL_Store }

function DL_Delete(start:AddrPointer;
                   key:str80):AddrPointer;
var
    temp,temp2:AddrPointer;
    done:boolean;
begin
    if start^.name=key then
    begin  { is first in list }
       DL_Delete:=start^.next;
       if temp^.next <> nil then begin
          temp:=start^.next;
          temp^.prior:=nil;
       end;
       dispose(start);
    end else
    begin
       done:=FALSE;
       temp:=start^.next;
       temp2:=start;
       while (temp<>nil) and (not done) do
       begin
          if temp^.name=key then
          begin
             temp2^.next:=temp^.next;
             if temp^.next<>nil then
                temp^.next^.prior:=temp2;
             done:=TRUE;
             dispose(temp);
          end else
          begin
             temp2:=temp;
             temp:=temp^.next;
          end;
       end;
       DL_Delete:=start;   {still same starting point}
       if not done then WriteLn('not found');
    end;
```

```
end; {DL_Delete}

procedure Remove;
var
   name:str80;
begin
   Write('Enter name to delete: ');
   Read(name); WriteLn;
   start:=DL_Delete(start,name);
end;  { Remove }

procedure Enter;
var
   info: AddrPointer;
   done: boolean;
begin
   done:=FALSE;
   repeat
      New(info);  { get a new record }
      Write('Enter name: ');
      Read(info^.name);  WriteLn;
      if Length(info^.name)=0 then done:=TRUE
      else
      begin
         Write('Enter street: ');
         Read(info^.street);  WriteLn;
         Write('Enter city: ');
         Read(info^.city);  WriteLn;
         Write('Enter state: ');
         Read(info^.state);  WriteLn;
         Write('Enter zip: ');
         Read(info^.zip);  WriteLn;
         start:=DSL_Store(info,start,last);  { store it }
      end;
   until done;
end;  { Enter }

procedure Display(start:AddrPointer);
begin
   while start<>nil do begin
      WriteLn(start^.name);
      WriteLn(start^.street);
      WriteLn(start^.city);
      WriteLn(start^.state);
      WriteLn(start^.zip);
      start:=start^.next;
   end;
end;  { Display }

function Search(start:AddrPointer;name:str80):AddrPointer;
var
   done:boolean;
begin
   done:=FALSE;
   while (start<>nil) and (not done) do begin
      if name=start^.name then begin
         search:=start;
         done:=TRUE;
      end else
         start:=start^.next;
   end;
   if start=nil then search:=nil;  { not in list }
```

```
end;  { Search }


procedure Find;
var
   loc:AddrPointer;
   name:str80;
begin
   Write('Enter name to find: ');
   Read(name); WriteLn;
   loc:=Search(start,name);
   if loc<>nil then WriteLn(loc^.name)
   else WriteLn('not in list');
end; {Find}
procedure Save(var f:FilType;start:AddrPointer);
begin
   WriteLn('saving file');
   Rewrite(f);
   while start<>nil do
   begin
      Write(f,start^);
      start:=start^.next;
   end;
end; {Save}

function Load(var f:FilType;start:AddrPointer):AddrPointer;
{ returns a pointer to the start of the list }
var
   temp,temp2:AddrPointer;
   first:boolean;
begin
   WriteLn('load file');
   reset(f);
   while start<>nil do
   begin  { free memory, if any }
      temp:=start^.next;
      dispose(start);
      start:=temp;
   end;

   start:=nil; last:=nil;
   if not eof(f) then
   begin
      New(temp);
      Read(f,temp^);
      temp^.next:=nil;  temp^.prior:=nil;
      load:=temp;   { pointer to start of list }
   end;

   while not eof(f) do
   begin
      New(temp2);
      Read(f,temp2^);
      temp^.next:=temp2;  { build list }
      temp2^.next:=nil;
      temp^.prior:=temp2;
      temp:=temp2;
   end;
   last:=temp2;
end;  {Load}
```

```
begin
   start:=nil;  { initially empty list }
   last:=nil;
   done:=FALSE;

   Assign(mlist, 'mlistd.dat');

   repeat
      case MenuSelect of
         '1': Enter;
         '2': Remove;
         '3': Display(start);
         '4': Find;
         '5': Save(mlist,start);
         '6': start:=load(mlist,start);
         '7': done:=TRUE;
      end ;
   until done=TRUE;

end.  { Mlist }
```

Binary Trees

The fourth data structure is the *binary tree*. Although there can be many types of trees, binary trees are special, because when they are sorted they lend themselves to rapid searches, insertions, and deletions. Each item in a binary tree consists of information with a link to the left member and a link to the right member. Figure 3-11 shows a small tree.

The special terminology needed to discuss trees is a classic case of mixed metaphors. The *root* is the first item in the tree. Each data item is called a *node* (or sometimes a *leaf*) of the tree, and any piece of the tree is called a *subtree*. A node that has no subtrees attached to it is called a *terminal node*. The *height* of the tree equals the number of layers deep that its roots grow. Throughout this discussion, think of binary trees as appearing in memory in the same way as they do on paper, but remember that a tree is only a way to structure data in memory, and memory is linear in form.

The binary tree is a special form of the linked list. Items can be inserted, deleted, and accessed in any order. In addition, the retrieval operation is not destructive. Although they are easy to visualize, trees present difficult programming problems that this section can only introduce.

Most functions that use trees are recursive, because the tree itself is a recursive data structure; that is, each subtree is a tree. Therefore, the routines that are developed here are recursive as well. Nonrecursive versions of these functions do exist, but their code is much more difficult to understand.

The order of a tree depends on how the tree is going to be referenced. The

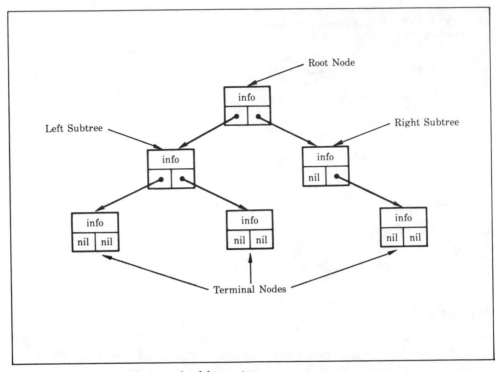

Figure 3-11. An example of a binary tree

process of accessing each node in a tree is called a *tree traversal*. Here is an example:

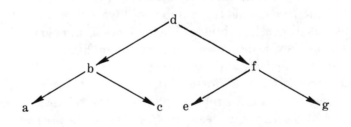

There are three ways to traverse this tree: *inorder, preorder,* and *postorder.* With inorder, you visit the left subtree, visit the root, and then visit the right subtree. In preorder, you visit the root, then the left subtree, and then the right subtree. With postorder, you visit the left subtree, then the right subtree, and then the root. The order of access for the tree just shown, using each method, is as follows:

inorder	a b c d e f g
preorder	d b a c f e g
postorder	a c b e g f d

Although a tree does not always need to be sorted, most uses require it. What constitutes a sorted tree depends on how you will traverse the tree. The examples in the rest of this chapter access the tree inorder. In a sorted binary tree, the subtree on the left contains nodes that are less than or equal to the root, while those on the right are greater than the root. The following function called **STree** builds a sorted binary tree.

```
type
    TreePointer = ^tree;
    tree = record
        data:char;
        left:TreePointer;
        right:TreePointer;
    end;
function STree(root,r:TreePointer;data:char):TreePointer;
begin
    if r=nil then
    begin
        New(r);   { get a new node }
        r^.left:=nil;
        r^.right:=nil;
        r^.data:=data;
        if data<root^.data then root^.left:=r
        else root^.right:=r;
        STree:=r;
    end else
    begin
        if data<r^.data then STree:=STree(r,r^.left,data)
        else STree:=STree(r,r^.right,data);
    end;
end;  { STree }
```

This algorithm simply follows the links through the tree, going left or right based on the **data** field. To use this function you need a global variable that holds the root of the tree. This global must be set initially to **nil**. A pointer to the root is assigned on the first call to **STree**. Since subsequent calls will not need to reassign the root, the variable **dummy** is used. If you assume that the name of this global is **rt**, then to call the **STree** function you would use

```
/* call STree */
if rt=nil rt:=STree(rt,rt,info) then
else dummy:=STree(rt,rt,info);
```

Using this call allows both the first and subsequent elements to be inserted correctly.

STree is a recursive algorithm, as are most tree routines. The same routine would be several times longer if straight iterative methods were used. The function must be called with a pointer to the root and to the subtree, and with the information that must be stored. Although for simplicity a single character is used here as the information, you could substitute any data type you like.

To traverse the tree built by using **STree** inorder and to print the **data** field of each node, you could use the function **InOrder**:

```
procedure InOrder(root:TreePointer);
begin
   if root<>nil then
   begin
      InOrder(root^.left);
      Write(root^.data);
      InOrder(root^.right);
   end;
end; {InOrder}
```

This recursive function returns when it encounters a terminal node (a **nil** pointer). The functions to traverse the tree in preorder and postorder are shown here:

```
procedure PreOrder(root:TreePointer);
begin
   if root<>nil then
   begin
      Write(root^.data);
      preorder(root^.left);
      preorder(root^.right);
   end;
end. {PreOrder}

procedure PostOrder(root:TreePointer);
begin
   if root<>nil then
   begin
      postorder(root^.left);
      postorder(root^.right);
      Write(root^.data);
   end;
end; {PostOrder}
```

You can write a short program that builds a sorted binary tree and prints that tree sideways on the screen of your computer. You need only a small modification to the **Inorder** procedure. The new program, called PrintTree, prints a tree inorder.

```
program PrintTree;

type

    TreePointer = ^tree;
    tree = record
           data:char;
           left:TreePointer;
           right:TreePointer;
       end;

var
    root,dummy: TreePointer;
    ch:char;

function STree(root,r:TreePointer;data:char):TreePointer;
begin
    if r=nil then
    begin
       New(r);   { get a new node }
       r^.left:=nil;
       r^.right:=nil;
       r^.data:=data;
       if data<root^.data then root^.left:=r
       else root^.right:=r;
       STree:=r;
    end else
    begin
        if data<r^.data then STree:=STree(r,r^.left,data)
        else STree:=STree(r,r^.right,data);
    end;
end;   { STree }

procedure PrintTree(r:TreePointer;n:integer);
var
    i:integer;

begin
    if r<>nil then
    begin
        PrintTree(r^.left,n+1);
        for i:=1 to n do Write('      ');
        WriteLn(r^.data);
        PrintTree(r^.right,n+1);
    end;
end;   { PrintTree }

begin   { main }
    root:=nil;
    repeat
       Write('enter a letter (Q to quit): ');
       Read(ch); WriteLn;
       if root=nil then root:=STree(root,root,ch)

       else dummy:=STree(root,root,ch);
       ch:=UpCase(ch);
    until ch='Q';

    PrintTree(root,0);

end.
```

The program actually sorts the information you give it. This process is a variation on the Insertion sort that was given in the previous chapter. For the average case, the Insertion sort's performance can be quite good, but Quick-Sort is still a better general-purpose sorting method, because it uses less memory and has less processing overhead. However, if you have to build a tree from scratch or if you have to maintain an already sorted tree, you should always insert new entries in sorted order by using the **STree** function.

If you have run the PrintTree program, you have probably noticed that some trees are *balanced*—each subtree is the same or nearly the same height as any other—and that other trees are far out of balance. If you were to enter the tree **abcd**, it would be built to look like this:

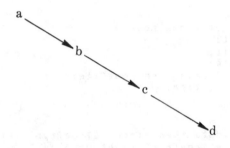

There would be no left subtrees. This is called a *degenerate tree* because it has degenerated into a linear list. In general, if the data you use to build a binary tree is fairly random, the tree produced will approximate a balanced tree. However, if the information used is already sorted, a degenerate tree will result. (It is possible to readjust the tree with each insertion to keep the tree in balance. The algorithms to do this are fairly complex; if you are interested in them, refer to books on advanced programming algorithms.)

Search functions are easy to implement for binary trees. This function returns a pointer to the node in the tree that matches the key; otherwise, it returns a **nil**:

```
function Search(root:TreePointer,
                key:DataItem):TreePointer;
begin
   if root<>nil then
   begin
      while (root^.data<>key) and (root<>nil) do
      begin
        if key < root^.data then root:=^.left
        else root:=root^.right;
      end;
```

```
      end;
    Search:=root;
end; {Search}
```

Unfortunately, deleting a node from a tree is not as simple as searching the tree. The deleted node may be either the root, a left node, or a right node. The node may also have from zero to two subtrees attached to it. Rearranging the pointers lends itself to a recursive algorithm, as shown here:

```
function DTree(root:TreePointer;key:char):TreePointer;
var
    temp,temp2:TreePointer;

begin
    if root^.data=key then
    begin {delete root}
       if root^.left=root^.right then
       begin {empty tree}
          Dispose(root);
          DTree:=nil;
       end
       else if root^.left=nil then
       begin
          temp:=root^.right;
          Dispose(root);
          DTree:=temp;
       end
       else if root^.right=nil then
       begin
          temp:=root^.left;
          Dispose(root);
          DTree:=temp;
       end
       else begin   {both leaves present}
          temp2:=root^.right;
          temp:=root^.right;
          while temp^.left<>nil do temp:=temp^.left;
          temp^.left:=root^.left;
          Dispose(root);
          DTree:=temp2;
       end;
    end
    else begin
       if root^.data<key then root^.right:=DTree(root^.right,key)
       else root^.left:=DTree(root^.left,key);
       DTree:=root;
    end;

end;  {DTree}
```

Remember to update the pointer to the root in the rest of your program, because the node deleted could be the root of the tree.

When used with database-management programs, binary trees offer power, flexibility, and efficiency. The information for these databases must reside on disk, and access times are important. Because a balanced binary tree has $\log_2 n$ comparisons as a worst case in searching, it performs far better than a linked list, which must rely on a sequential search.

FOUR

Dynamic Allocation

Designing a computer program can be somewhat like designing a building, with numerous functional and aesthetic considerations that contribute to the final outcome. For example, some programs are functionally rigid like a house, which has a certain number of bedrooms, a kitchen, two baths, and so on. Other programs must be open-ended like convention centers, which have movable walls and modular flooring that enable them to be adapted to various needs. This chapter presents the storage mechanisms that allow you to write flexible programs that can be adapted to the needs of the user and the capabilities of the computer.

There are two ways in which a Pascal program can store information in the main memory of the computer. The first is to use *global* and *local variables*—including arrays and records—that are defined by the Pascal language. With global variables, storage is fixed throughout the run time of your program. With local variables, storage is allocated from the stack space of the computer. Although global and local variables are efficiently implemented in Pascal, they require that the programmer know in advance the amount of storage needed for every situation. The second and more efficient way to store information is to use Pascal's dynamic allocation functions: **New** with either **Dispose** or the **Mark** and **Release** pair.

In both dynamic allocation methods, storage for information is allocated from the free memory area that lies between your program's permanent storage area and the stack (which Pascal uses to store local variables). This area is called the *heap*.

Figure 4-1 shows how a Pascal program would appear in memory. The stack grows downward as it is used; the amount of memory it needs is determined by the design of your program. For example, a program with many recursive functions makes greater demands on stack memory than a program that does not have recursive functions, because each recursive call allocates stack memory. The memory required for the program and global data

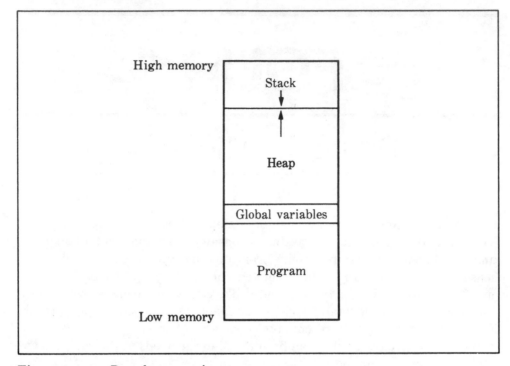

Figure 4-1.   A Pascal program's memory usage

is fixed during the execution of the program. Memory to satisfy a **New** request is taken from the free memory area, starting just above the global variables and growing toward the stack. In fairly extreme cases it is possible for the stack to run into the heap.

How the heap is managed depends upon whether you will be using **Dispose** to release memory back to the system or using the **Mark** and **Release** procedures instead. As the *Turbo Pascal User Manual* warns, **Dispose** and the **Mark** and **Release** pair can never be intermixed in a program. Therefore, you must decide in advance which procedure you are going to use. To help you understand how they differ, a quick review of **New**, with **Dispose** and with the **Mark** and **Release** pair, follows.

New

Using **New** allocates memory from the heap. This built-in procedure accepts a pointer argument and allocates enough memory from the heap to hold the type of variable that the pointer is declared as pointing to. After the call, the pointer argument points to the allocated memory. For example, to allocate room for a **real**, you could use this code format:

```
type
        rpntr = ^real;
var
        p:rpntr;
begin
        New(p);
        .
        .
        .
```

If there is no free memory left on the heap, the run-time error FF — *heap/stack collision* — is produced. To avoid this run-time error you should precede all calls to **New** with a call to **maxavail**, which returns the maximum number of bytes (for 8-bit systems) or paragraphs (for 16-bit systems) left in the heap. The examples in this chapter do not include this step, but you might need it in your applications.

Dispose

One reason applications usually use dynamic memory allocation is so that memory can be reused. One way to return memory back to the heap is to use **Dispose**. **Dispose** is called by using a pointer that was previously used in a call to **New** —that is, **Dispose** contains a pointer to a valid allocation region from the heap. After a call to **Dispose**, the memory that had been allocated to the pointer is freed and available for allocation. For example, the short program shown here allocates a pointer to a 40-element array of integers and returns them to the system prior to termination:

```
program Sample;   { Example of New and Dispose working
                    together }

type
    pntr = ^RecType;

    RecType = array[1..40] of integer;

var
    p:pntr;
    t:integer;

begin
    New(p);
    for t:=1 to 40 do p^[t]:=t*2;
    for t:=1 to 40 do Write(p^[t],' ');
```

```
    WriteLn;
    Dispose(p);
end.
```

Mark and Release

As an alternative to using **Dispose**, you can use **Mark** and **Release** to free heap memory after your program has finished using that memory. In essence, you call **Mark** prior to using **New**, and you call **Release** after using **New**, when it is time to deallocate the memory. **Release** then returns all memory allocated between the call to **Mark** and **Release**. This method returns a block of memory to the system, whereas **Dispose** only returns one pointer's worth.

   Mark is called with one pointer argument. This pointer may be of any type, because its only function is to store the starting point of a region of memory in the heap. **Release** must be called with the same pointer, which must not be modified. For example, the following program allocates an array of 40 integers and returns them to free memory by using **Mark** and **Release**:

```
program alloc;  { this version uses Mark and Release }

type
    pntr = ^RecType;

    RecType = array[1..40] of integer;

var
    p:pntr;
    t:integer;
    q:^integer;

begin
    Mark(q);
    New(p);
    for t:=1 to 40 do p^[t]:=t*2;
    for t:=1 to 40 do Write(p^[t],' ');
    WriteLn;
    Release(q);
    {At this point, all memory has been returned to the
     system.}
end.
```

   The choice of which system to use really depends on whether you always want your application to return a portion of allocated memory to the system. If you do, then you must use **Dispose**. If you always want your application to free all memory, then using **Mark** and **Release** is a better method. The examples in this book use **Dispose** instead of **Mark** and **Release** because **Dispose** offers more flexibility. Feel free to use **Mark** and **Release** if they suit your application better.

Sparse-Array Processing

A major use for dynamic allocation is *sparse-array processing*. In a sparse array not all of the elements are actually present. You may want to create an array like this when the array dimensions you need are larger than will fit in the memory of your machine and when not all array locations will be used. Multidimensional arrays can consume vast quantities of memory because their storage needs are exponentially related to their size. For example, a character array of 10×10 only needs 100 bytes of memory, and one that is 100×100 only needs 10,000, but a 1000×1000 character array needs 1,000,000 bytes of memory.

A spreadsheet program is a good example of a sparse array. Even though the matrix is large — say 999×999 — only a portion of it may be in use at any one time. Spreadsheets use the matrix to hold formulas, values, and strings associated with each location. In a sparse array, storage for each element is allocated from the pool of free memory as needed. Although only a small portion of the elements is actually in use, the array may appear to be large — larger than would normally fit in the memory of the computer.

There are three distinct techniques for creating a sparse array: a linked list, a binary tree, and a pointer array. All of these examples assume that the spreadsheet matrix is organized like this:

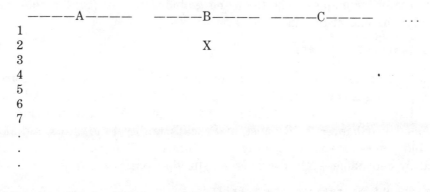

In this example, the X is located in cell B2.

The Linked-List Approach
To Sparse Arrays

When you implement a sparse array that was a linked list, a record is used to hold the information for each element in the array, including its logical position in the array and the links to both the previous element and next elements. Each record is placed in the list with the elements in sorted order, which is based on the array index. The array is accessed by following the links.

For example, you could use the following record to create a sparse array for use in a spreadsheet program:

```
str128 = string[128];
str9 = string[9];

CellPointer = ^cell;

cell = record
     CellName: str9;        { holds name of cell }
     formula: str128;
     next: CellPointer;     { pointer to next record }
     prior: CellPointer;    { pointer to previous record}
end;
```

In this example, the field **CellName** holds a string that contains the cell name, such as A1, B34, or Z19. The **formula** string holds the formula that is assigned to each spreadsheet location. Here are a few sample functions you would use in a spreadsheet program that uses a linked-list sparse array. (Remember that there are many ways to implement a spreadsheet program; the data record and routines used here should serve only as examples of sparse-array techniques.) The following global variables point to the beginning and the end of the linked array list:

```
start,last:CellPointer;
```

When you enter a formula into a cell of a typical spreadsheet, you are in effect creating a new element in the sparse array. If the spreadsheet uses a linked list, that new cell would be inserted by using **DLS_Store**, which was developed in Chapter 3. (Because of Pascal's ability to create stand-alone, reusable functions, you can use it with virtually no changes.) Here, the list is sorted by cell name—A12 precedes A13, and so on.

```
function DLS_Store(info,start:CellPointer;
                   var last:CellPointer):CellPointer;
{ store entries in sorted order - returns a pointer to
   start of the list. }
```

```
var
   old, top: ^ cell;
   done:boolean;
begin
   top:=start;
   old:=nil;
   done:=FALSE;

   if start=nil then begin { first element in list }
      info^.next:=nil;
      last:=info;
      info^.prior:=nil;
      DLS_Store:=info;
   end else
   begin
      while (start<>nil) and (not done) do
      begin
         if start^.CellName < info^.CellName then
         begin
            old:=start;
            start:=start^.next;
         end else
         begin  { goes in middle }
            if old<>nil then
            begin
               old^.next:=info;
               info^.next:=start;
               start^.prior:=info;
               info^.prior:=old;
               DLS_Store:=top;  { keep same starting point }
               done:=TRUE;
            end else
            begin
               info^.next:=start;  { New first element }
               info^.prior:=nil;
               DLS_Store:=info;
               done:=TRUE;
            end;
         end;
      end;  {while}
      if not done then
      begin
         last^.next:=info;  { goes on end }
         info^.next:=nil;
         info^.prior:=last;
         last:=info;
         DLS_Store:=top;
      end;

   end;
end;  { DLS_Store }
```

To remove a cell from the spreadsheet, you must remove the proper record from the list and allow the memory it occupies to be returned to the system by using **Dispose**. The **DL—Delete** function removes a cell from the list when given the cell name.

```
function DL_Delete(start:CellPointer;
                      key:str9):CellPointer;
var
   temp,temp2:CellPointer;
   done:boolean;
begin
   if start^.CellName=key then
   begin   { is first in list }
      DL_Delete:=start^.next;
      if temp^.next <> nil then
      begin
         temp:=start^.next;
         temp^.prior:=nil;
      end;
      Dispose(start);
   end else
   begin
      done:=FALSE;
      temp:=start^.next;
      temp2:=start;
      while (temp<>nil) and (not done) do
      begin
         if temp^.CellName=key then
         begin
            temp2^.next:=temp^.next;
            if temp^.next<>nil then
               temp^.next^.prior:=temp2;
            done:=TRUE;
            last:=temp^.prior;
            Dispose(temp);
         end else   begin
            temp2:=temp;
            temp:=temp^.next;
         end;
      end;
      DL_Delete:=start;    {still same starting point}
      if not done then WriteLn('not found');
   end;
end; {DL_Delete}
```

The **Find** function locates any specific cell. It is an important function because many spreadsheet formulas have references to other cells; these cells must be found so that their values can be updated. **Find** requires the use of a linear search to locate each item and, as shown in Chapter 3, the average number of comparisons in a linear search is $n/2$, where n is the number of elements in the list. In addition, a significant loss of performance occurs because each cell may contain references to other cells in the formula, and each of these cells must be found. Here is an example of **Find**:

```
function Find(cell:CellPointer):CellPointer;
var
    c:CellPointer;
begin
    c:=start;
```

```
    while c<>nil do begin
        if c^.CellName=cell^.CellName then find:=c
        else c:=c^.next;
    end;
    WriteLn('cell not found');
    Find:=nil;
end; {Find}
```

The linked-list approach to creating, maintaining, and processing a sparse array has one major drawback—it must use a linear search to access each cell in the list. Without using additional information, which requires more memory overhead, you cannot perform a binary search to locate a cell. Even the store routine uses a linear search to find the proper location in order to insert a new cell into the list. You can solve these problems by using a binary tree to support the sparse array.

The Binary Tree Approach
To Sparse Arrays

The binary tree is essentially a modified doubly linked list. Its major advantage over a list is that it can be searched quickly so that insertions and look-ups can be very fast. In applications in which you want a linked-list record but need fast search times, the binary tree is perfect.

To use a binary tree to support the spreadsheet example, the record **cell** must be changed as shown here:

```
CellPointer = ^cell;
str9 = string[9];
str128 = string[128];

cell = record
    CellName:str9;
    formula: str128;
    left:CellPointer;
    right:CellPointer;
  end;
```

You can modify the **Stree** function from Chapter 3 so that it builds a tree based on the cell name. Notice that it assumes that the parameter **New** is a pointer to a new entry in the tree.

```
function Stree(root,r,New:CellPointer):CellPointer;
begin
    if r=nil then
    begin
        New^.left:=nil;
        New^.right:=nil;
```

```
          if New^.CellName<root^.CellName then root^.left:=New
          else root^.right:=New;
          Stree:=New;
       end else
    begin
         if New^.CellName<r^.CellName then
            Stree:=Stree(r,r^.left,New)
         else Stree:=Stree(r,r^.right,New);
    end;
    Stree:=root;
end;  { Stree }
```

Stree must be called with a pointer to the root node for the first two parameters and a pointer to the new cell for the third. **Stree** returns a pointer to the root.

To delete a cell from the spreadsheet, you should modify the **Dtree** function as shown here to accept the name of the cell as a key:

```
function Dtree(root:CellPointer;key:str9):CellPointer;
var
    temp,temp2:CellPointer;

begin
    if root^.CellName=key then
    begin {delete root}
       if root^.left=root^.right then
       begin {empty tree}
          Dispose(root);
          Dtree:=nil;
       end
       else if root^.left=nil then
       begin
          temp:=root^.right;
          Dispose(root);
          Dtree:=temp;
       end
       else if root^.right=nil then begin
          temp:=root^.left;
          Dispose(root);
          Dtree:=temp;
       end
       else
       begin  {both leaves present}
          temp2:=root^.right;
          temp:=root^.right;
          while temp^.left<>nil do temp:=temp^.left;
          temp^.left:=root^.left;
          Dispose(root);
          Dtree:=temp2;
       end;
    end
    else
    begin
       if root^.CellName<key then
          root^.right:=Dtree(root^.right,key)
       else root^.left:=Dtree(root^.left,key);
```

```
        Dtree:=root;
    end;
end;   {Dtree}
```

Finally, given a cell name, you can use a modified **Search** function to quickly locate that cell in the spreadsheet:

```
function Search(root:CellPointer;key:str9):CellPointer;
begin
    if root=nil then Search:=nil
    else begin
        while (root^.CellName<>key) and (root<>nil) do
        begin
            if root^.CellName<key then root:=root^.left
            else root:=root^.right;
        end;
    end;
    Search:=root;
end; {Search}
```

The most important aspect of using a binary tree rather than a linked list is that it results in much faster search times. Remember, a sequential search requires an average of $n/2$ comparisons, where n is the number of elements in the list; a binary search requires only $\log_2 n$ comparisons.

The Pointer-Array Approach
To Sparse Arrays

Suppose that your spreadsheet's dimensions were 26×100 (A1 through Z100), a total of 2600 elements. In theory, then, you could use the following array of records to hold the spreadsheet entries:

```
    str9 = string[9];
    str128 = string[128];

    CellPointer = ^cell;

    cell = record
        CellName:str9;
        formula:str128;
    end;
var
    pa:array[1..2600] of cell;
```

However, 2600 cells multiplied by 128 (the **formula** field alone) requires 332,800 bytes of memory for a fairly small spreadsheet. This approach is obviously not practical. As an alternative, you can create an array of pointers to records. This method would require significantly less permanent storage than would the creation of an entire array, and would also offer performance far superior to that of the linked-list and binary tree methods. The declaration for this technique is shown here:

```
type
    str9 = string[9];
    str128 = string[128];
    CellPointer = ^cell
    cell = record
        CellName:str9;
        formula:str128;
    end;

var
    sheet:array[1..10000] of CellPointer;
```

You can use this smaller array to hold pointers to the information actually entered by the user of the spreadsheet. As each entry is made, a pointer to the cell information is stored in the proper location in the array. Figure 4-2 shows how this process might appear in memory, with the pointer array providing support for the sparse array.

Before you can use the pointer array, you must initialize each element to **nil**, which indicates that there is no entry in that location. Use the following function:

```
procedure InitSheet;
var
    t:integer;

begin
    for t:=1 to 10000 do sheet[t]:=nil;
end; {InitSheet}
```

Before you can write the **Store** procedure, you need a function called **Find-Index**. **FindIndex** returns the proper pointer-array index when given the cell name. When computing the index, **FindIndex** assumes that all cell names consist of a capital letter followed by an integer — B34, C19, and so on. **FindIndex** is shown here:

```
function FindIndex(i:CellPointer):integer;
var
    loc,temp,code:integer;
    t:str9;

begin
    loc:=ord(i^.CellName[1]);
    t:=copy(i^.CellName,2,9);
    val(t,temp,code);
```

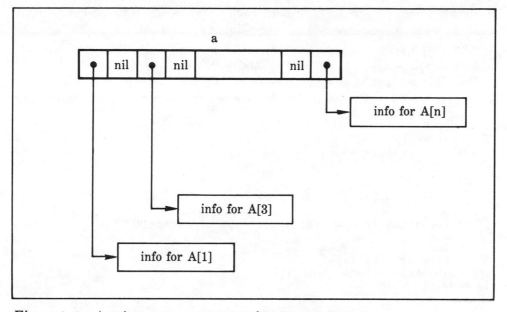

Figure 4-2.   A pointer array as support for a sparse array

```
    loc:=loc+(temp*26);
    FindIndex:=loc;
end; {FindIndex}
```

You need this function so that the **Store** procedure will know which pointer-array location to use for each cell. As you can see, finding the proper index is easy and fast because it is a simple computation—no search or lookup is needed. This type of process is sometimes referred to as a *direct hash*, because the item to be stored directly produces the index of the storage location. When the user enters a formula for a cell of the spreadsheet, the cell location (defined by its name) produces an index for the pointer array **sheet**. The index is derived from the cell name by converting the name into a number with **FindIndex**, and it is stored by using **Store**, as shown here:

```
procedure Store(New:CellPointer);
var
    loc:integer;

begin
    loc:=FindIndex(New);
    if loc>10000 then WriteLn('location out of bounds')
    else sheet[loc]:=New;
end; {Store}
```

Because each cell name is unique, each index is also unique; because the ASCII collating sequence is used, the pointer to each entry is stored into the proper array element. If you compare this procedure to the linked-list version, you will see how much shorter and simpler it is.

The **Delete** function also becomes short. When called with the index of the cell, **Delete** returns the pointer to the element and returns the memory to the system:

```
procedure Delete(r_cell:CellPointer);
var
   loc:integer;
begin
   loc:=FindIndex(r_cell);

   if loc>10000 then WriteLn('Cell out of bounds')
   else
   begin
      Dispose(r_cell);
      sheet[loc]:=nil;
   end;
end;  {Delete}
```

Again, when you compare this to the linked-list or tree version, you can see that this code is faster and simpler.

Remember that the pointer array itself uses some memory for every location, whether that location is used or not. This can be a serious limitation for some applications.

Deciding on an Approach
To Sparse Arrays

When deciding whether to use a linked-list approach, a binary tree approach, or a pointer-array approach for implementing a sparse array, you should always consider memory efficiency and speed.

When the array is very sparse, the most memory-efficient approaches are the linked-list and binary tree implementations, because only those array elements that are actually in use have memory allocated to them. The links themselves require little additional memory and generally have a negligible effect. The pointer-array design requires each array element to have a pointer allocated to it, whether or not its entry exists. Not only must the entire pointer array fit in memory, but there must be enough memory left over for the application's use. This could be a serious problem for certain applications, whereas it might not be a problem for others. You can usually decide this by calculating the approximate amount of free memory and determining whether it is sufficient for your program.

When the array is fairly full, however, the pointer-array approach makes better use of memory. Both the linked-list binary tree implementations need two pointers, whereas the pointer array only needs one. For example, if a 1000-element array is full, and if pointers are two bytes long, then both the linked-list and binary tree approaches use 4000 bytes for pointers—but the pointer-array approach needs only 2000, a savings of 2000 bytes.

The fastest-executing approach is the pointer array. As in the spreadsheet example, there is often an easy method that indexes the pointer array and links it with the sparse-array elements. This method makes accessing the elements of the sparse array nearly as fast as accessing the elements of a normal array. The linked-list version is very slow in comparison, because it must use a linear search to locate each element. Even if extra information were added to the linked list to allow faster accessing of elements, it would still be slower than the pointer array's direct accessing capability. The binary tree certainly speeds up the search time, but compared with the pointer array's direct indexing capability, it still seems sluggish.

Whenever possible, a pointer-array implementation is the best because it is much faster. If memory use is critical, however, then you have no choice but to use the linked-list or binary tree approach.

Reusable Buffers

When memory is scarce, dynamic allocation can be used in place of normal variables. As an example, imagine that there are two processes, A and B, inside one program. Assume that A requires 60% of free memory while executing and that B needs 55% of free memory while executing. If both A and B derive their storage needs from local variables, then A cannot call B, and B cannot call A, because more than 100% of memory would be required. If A never calls B, there is no trouble—until you *want* A to call B. The only way to do this is to use dynamic storage for both A and B and to free the memory before one process calls the other. In other words, if both A and B require more than one half of available free memory while executing, and if A must call B, then they must use dynamic allocation. In this way both A and B will have the memory they need when they need it.

Imagine that there are 100,000 bytes of free memory left in a computer that is running a program that has the following two functions:

```
procedure B; forward;
procedure A;
var
    a:array[1..60000] of char;
```

```
                begin
                       .
                       .
                       .
                   B;
                       .
                       .
                       .
                end;

                procedure B;
                var
                       b:array[1..55000] of char;
                begin
                       .
                       .
                       .
                end;
```

Here, **A** and **B** both have local variables, each requiring more than one half of free memory. There is no way that **B** can execute, because there is not enough memory available to allocate the 55,000 bytes needed for the local array **b**.

A situation like this is often insurmountable, but in certain instances you can work around it. If **A** did not need to preserve the contents of the array **a** while **B** was executing, then both **A** and **B** could share the memory. You can do this by allocating **A** and **B**'s array dynamically. Then **A** could free memory prior to the call to **B** and reallocate it later. The code would have this format:

```
          procedure B; forward;
          procedure A;
          var
                a: ^array[1..60000] of char;
          begin
          New(a);
                .
                .
                .
          Dispose(a); { Release memory for B }
          B;
          New(a); { get it back }
                .
                .
                .
          Dispose(a);
```

```
        end;

        procedure B;
        var
             b:^array[1..55000] of char;
        begin
             New(b);
             .
             .
             .
             Dispose(b);
        end;
```

Only the pointer **a** exists while **B** is executing. Although you only need to use this technique occasionally, you should master it anyway — it is often the only way around this type of problem.

The "Unknown Memory" Dilemma

If you are a professional programmer, you probably have faced the "unknown memory" dilemma. This occurs when you write a program that has some of its performance based on the amount of memory inside any and all computers that will run it. Examples of programs that can have this problem are spreadsheets, in-RAM mailing-list programs, and sorts. For example, an in-memory sort that can handle 10,000 addresses in a 256K machine may only be able to sort 5000 addresses in a 128K computer. If this program were to be used on computers of unknown memory sizes, it would be difficult to determine the optimum fixed-size array to hold the sort information for two reasons: either the program would not work on machines whose memory capabilities were too small to fit the array, or you would have to create an array for the worst case and not allow those users who have more memory to use it. The solution is to use dynamic allocation to hold the information.

A text-editor program is a good illustration of the memory dilemma and its solution. Most text editors do not have a fixed number of characters that they can hold; rather, they use all of the computer's available memory to store the text that the user types in. For example, as each line is entered, storage is allocated and a linked list is maintained. When a line is deleted, memory is returned to the system. One way to implement such a text editor would be to use the following record for each line:

```
line_pointer = ^line;
str80 = string[80];

line = record
```

```
        text: str80;    { holds each line }
        num: integer;
        next: line_pointer;    { pointer to next record }
        prior: line_pointer;   { pointer to previous record}
end;
```

For simplicity, this record always allocates enough memory for each line to be 80 characters long. In reality, only the exact length of the line would be allocated, and additional overhead would be incurred if the line were altered. The element **num** holds the line number for each line of text. This allows you to use the standard sorted, doubly linked list-storage function **DLS_Store** to create and maintain the text file as a linked list.

The entire program for a simple text editor is presented next. It supports the insertion and deletion of lines at any point, based on the line number specified. You may also list the text and store it in a disk file.

The general means of operation for the editor is based on a sorted, linked list of lines of text. The sort key is the line number of each line. Not only can you insert text easily at any point by specifying the starting line number, but you can also delete text easily. The only function that may not be intuitive is **PatchUp**: it renumbers the element **num** for each line of text when insertions or deletions make this necessary.

In this example, the amount of text that the editor can hold is directly based on the amount of free memory in the user's system. Thus, the editor automatically uses additional memory without having to be reprogrammed. This is probably the most important reason for using dynamic allocation when you are faced with the memory dilemma.

The program as shown is very limited, but the basic text-editing support is solid. You may enhance it to create a customized text editor.

```
program TextEd;

type
    str80 = string[80];
    LinePointer = ^line;
    line = record
            text: str80;    { holds each line }
            num: integer;
            next: LinePointer;    { pointer to next record }
            prior: LinePointer;   { pointer to previous record}
    end;
    DataItem = line;
    filtype = file of line;
var
    text: filtype;
    start,last:LinePointer;
    done: boolean;
    fname: str80;

function MenuSelect:char;   { returns the users selection }
var
    ch:char;
```

```
begin
   WriteLn('1. Enter text');
   WriteLn('2. Delete a linr');
   WriteLn('3. Display the file');
   WriteLn('4. Save the file');
   WriteLn('5. Load the file');
   WriteLn('6. Quit');
   repeat
      WriteLn;
      Write('Enter your choice: ');
      Read(ch);  ch:=UpCase(ch); WriteLn;
   until (ch>='1') and (ch<='6');
   MenuSelect:=ch;
end;  { MenuSelect }

function Find(lnum:integer):LinePointer;
var
   i:LinePointer;
begin
   i:=start;
   Find:=nil;
   while(i<>nil) do begin
      if lnum=i^.num then find:=i;
      i:=i^.next;
   end;
end;  {Find}

procedure PatchUp(lnum,incr:integer);
var
   i:LinePointer;

begin
   i:=Find(lnum);
   while(i<>nil) do begin
      i^.num:=i^.num+incr;
      i:=i^.next
   end;
end;  {PatchUp}


function DLS_Store(info,start:LinePointer;
                   var last:LinePointer):LinePointer;
{ store entries in sorted order }
var
   old, top: ^ line;
   done:boolean;
begin
   top:=start;
   old:=nil;
   done:=FALSE;

   if start=nil then
   begin { first element in list }
      info^.next:=nil;
      last:=info;
      info^.prior:=nil;
      DLS_Store:=info;
   end else
   begin
      while (start<>nil) and (not done) do
      begin
```

```
            if start^.num < info^.num then
              begin
          old:=start;
          start:=start^.next;
      end else
      begin  { goes in middle }
          if old<>nil then
          begin
              old^.next:=info;
              info^.next:=start;
              start^.prior:=info;
              info^.prior:=old;
              DLS_Store:=top;  { keep same starting point }
              done:=TRUE;
          end else
          begin
              info^.next:=start;   { New first element }
              info^.prior:=nil;
              DLS_Store:=info;
              done:=TRUE;
          end;
      end;
end;  {while}
if not done then
      begin
          last^.next:=info;  { goes on end }
          info^.next:=nil;
          info^.prior:=last;
          last:=info;
          DLS_Store:=top;
      end;
    end;
end;  { DLS_Store }

function DL_Delete(start:LinePointer;
                    key:integer):LinePointer;
var
    temp,temp2:LinePointer;
    done:boolean;
begin
    if start^.num=key then
    begin  { is first in list }
        DL_Delete:=start^.next;
        if temp^.next <> nil then
        begin
            temp:=start^.next;
            temp^.prior:=nil;
        end;
        Dispose(start);
    end else
    begin
        done:=FALSE;
        temp:=start^.next;
        temp2:=start;
        while (temp<>nil) and (not done) do
        begin
            if temp^.num=key then
            begin
            temp2^.next:=temp^.next;
            if temp^.next<>nil then
```

```
                 temp^.next^.prior:=temp2;
             done:=TRUE;
             last:=temp^.prior;
             Dispose(temp);
          end else
          begin
             temp2:=temp;
             temp:=temp^.next;
          end;
       end;
       DL_Delete:=start;    {still same starting point}
       if not done then WriteLn('not found')
       else PatchUp(key+1,-1);
    end;
end; {DL_Delete}


procedure Remove;
var

    num:integer;
begin
    Write('Enter line to delete: ');
    Read(num); WriteLn;
    start:=DL_Delete(start,num);
end;  { Remove }

procedure Enter;
var
    info: LinePointer;
    num: integer;
    done: boolean;
begin
    done:=FALSE;
    Write('Enter starting line number: ');
    Read(num); WriteLn;
    repeat
       New(info);  { get a New record }
       info^.num:=num;
       Write(info^.num,': ');
       Read(info^.text); WriteLn;
       if Length(info^.text)=0 then done:=TRUE
       else begin
          if Find(num)<>nil then PatchUp(num,1);
          start:=DLS_Store(info,start,last);
       end;
       num:=num+1;
    until done;
end;  { Enter }

procedure Display(start:LinePointer);
begin
    while start<>nil do
    begin
       Write(start^.num,': ');
       WriteLn(start^.text);
       start:=start^.next;
    end;
    WriteLn;
end;  { display }
```

```
procedure Save(var f:filtype;start:LinePointer);
begin
   WriteLn('saving file');
   ReWrite(f);
   while start<>nil do
   begin
      Write(f,start^);
      start:=start^.next;
   end;
end; {Save}

function Load(var f:filtype):LinePointer;
{ returns a pointer to the start of the list }



var
   temp:LinePointer;
begin
   WriteLn('load file');
   Reset(f);
   while start<>nil do
   begin  { free memory, if any }
      temp:=start^.next;
      Dispose(start);
      start:=temp;
   end;
   last:=nil; start:=nil;
   while not eof(f) do
   begin
      New(temp);
      Read(f,temp^);
      start:=DLS_Store(temp,start,last);
   end;
   Load:=start;
end;  {Load}

begin
    start:=nil;  { initially empty list }
    last:=nil;
    done:=FALSE;

    Write('Enter Filename: ');
    ReadLn(fname);
    assign(text, fname);

    repeat
      case MenuSelect of
          '1': Enter;
          '2': Remove;
          '3': Display(start);
          '4': Save(text,start);
          '5': start:=Load(text);
          '6': done:=TRUE;
      end ;
    until done=TRUE;
 end.
```

Fragmentation

Fragmentation occurs when pieces of free memory lie between blocks of allocated memory. Although the free memory is usually large enough to fill allocation requests, a problem develops when the individual pieces are too small to fill a request, even though there would be sufficient memory if they were added together. Figure 4-3 shows how a sequence of calls to **New** and **Dispose** can produce this situation.

Some types of fragmentation are avoided because the dynamic allocation functions combine adjacent regions of memory. For example, if memory regions A, B, C, and D (shown below) were allocated and then regions B and C were freed, B and C could theoretically be combined because they are next to each other. However, if B and D were freed, there would be no way to combine them, because C lies between them and is still in use.

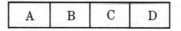

Since B and D were free while C was allocated, you might wonder why you couldn't just move C's contents to D and combine B and C. The problem is that your program would have no way of knowing that what was in C had been moved to D.

One way in which you may avoid excess fragmentation is to always allocate equal amounts of memory: then all deallocated regions can be reallocated to subsequent requests, and all of free memory can be used. If this is not possible, try to limit the different sizes to just a few. You can sometimes accomplish this by compacting several small requests into a large request. You should never allocate more memory than you need just to avoid fragmentation, because the amount of wasted memory will far outweigh any gains you may receive. Here is another solution: as the program runs, write all information out to a temporary disk file, free all memory, and then read the information back in. This eliminates gaps while reading the information back in.

Dynamic Allocation and Artificial Intelligence

Although Pascal is not a mainstream artificial intelligence (AI) language, you can use it to experiment. A common trait of many artificial intelligence

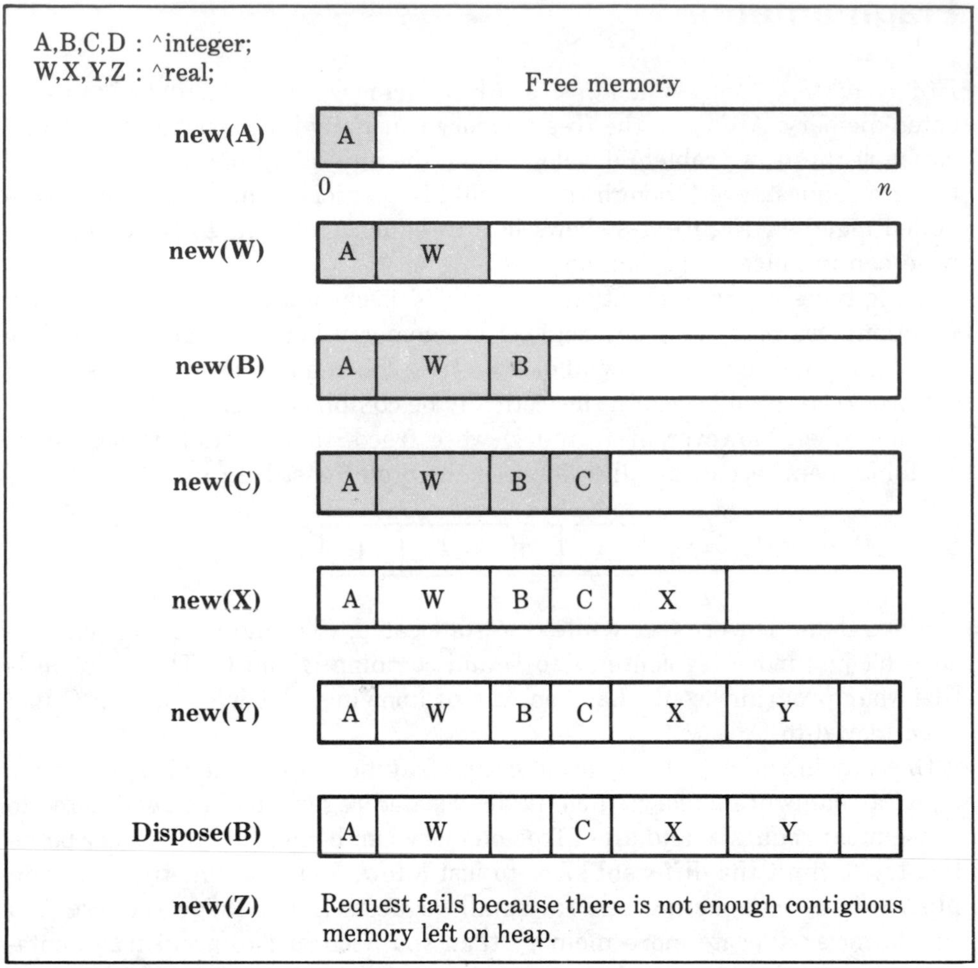

A,B,C,D : ^integer;
W,X,Y,Z : ^real;

Free memory

new(A)

| A | | | | | | |

0   n

new(W)

| A | W | | | | | |

new(B)

| A | W | B | | | | |

new(C)

| A | W | B | C | | | |

new(X)

| A | W | B | C | X | | |

new(Y)

| A | W | B | C | X | Y | |

Dispose(B)

| A | W | | C | X | Y | |

new(Z)   Request fails because there is not enough contiguous
memory left on heap.

Figure 4-3.   Fragmentation in dynamic allocation

programs is the existence of a list of information items that can be extended by the program automatically as it "learns" new things. In a language like LISP, considered to be the premier artificial intelligence language, the language itself performs list maintenance. In Pascal you have to program such procedures by using linked lists and dynamic allocation. Although the example here is very simple, the concepts can be applied to more sophisticated "intelligent" programs.

One interesting area of AI covers programs that seem to behave like people. The famous Eliza program, for example, appeared to be a psychiatrist.

It would be wonderful to have a computer program that would carry on a conversation about anything — it would be a great program to run when you were tired of programming and feeling lonely! The example used here is an extremely simple version of such a program. It uses words and their definitions to carry on a simple conversation with the user. One device common to many AI programs is the linking of an informational item with its meaning; in this case, the program links words with their meanings. The following record holds each word, its definition, its part of speech, and its connotation:

```
VocabPointer = ^vocab;
str80 = string[80];
str30 = string[30];

vocab = record
      typ:char;
      connotate:char;
      word:str30;
      def:str80;
      next: VocabPointer;      { pointer to next record }
      prior: VocabPointer;     { pointer to previous record}
end;
```

In the program that follows, you enter a word, its definition, the type of word it is, and its connotation of good, bad, or indifferent. To hold these dictionary entries, a linked list is then built, by using dynamic allocation. **DLS_Store** creates and maintains a sorted, doubly linked list of the dictionary. After you have entered a few words into the dictionary, you can begin to have a conversation with the computer. For example, you type in a sentence, such as "It is a nice day." The program scans the sentence for a noun that it knows. If it finds one, it makes a comment about the noun, based on its meaning. If the program encounters a word that it does not know, it prompts you to enter that word with its definition. You type **quit** to exit conversation mode.

The procedure **Talk** is the part of the program that carries on the conversation. A support function called **Dissect** looks at your input sentence a word at a time. The variable **sentence** holds your input sentence. **Dissect** removes a word at a time from **sentence** and returns it in **word**. Here are the functions **Talk** and **Dissect**:

```
procedure Dissect(var s:str80;var w:str30);
var
    t,x:integer;
    temp:str80;
begin
    t:=1;
    while(s[t]=' ') do t:=t+1;
    x:=t;
    while(s[t]<>' ') and (t<=Length(s)) do t:=t+1;
    if t<=Length(s) then t:=t-1;
```

```
    w:=Copy(s,x,t-x+1);
    temp:=s;
    s:=Copy(temp,t+1,Length(s));
end;  { Dissect }

procedure Talk;
var
    sentence:str80;
    word:str30;
    w:VocabPointer;
begin
    WriteLn('Conversation mode (quit to exit)');
    repeat
        Write(': ');
        Read(sentence); WriteLn;
        repeat
            Dissect(sentence,word);
            w:=Search(start,word);
            if w<>nil then
            begin
                if w^.typ='n' then
                begin
                    case w^.connotate of
                        'g': Write('I like ');
                        'b': Write('I do not like ');
                    end;
                    WriteLn(w^.def);
                end  { if }
                else WriteLn(w^.def);
            end
            else if word<>'quit' then
            begin
                WriteLn(word,' is unknown.');
                Enter(TRUE);
            end;
        until Length(sentence)=0;
    until word='quit';
end; { Talk }
```

The entire program is shown here:

```
program Smart;

type
    str80 = string[80];
    str30 = string[30];
    VocabPointer = ^vocab;
    vocab = record
            typ:char;
            connotate:char;
            word:str30;
            def:str80;
            next: VocabPointer;    { pointer to next record }
            prior: VocabPointer;   { pinter to previous record}
    end;

    DataItem = vocab;
    DataArray = array [1..100] of VocabPointer; { hold pointers to }
                                                { vocab records }
```

```
      filtype = file of vocab;
var
    test: DataArray;
    smart: filtype;
    start,last:VocabPointer;
    done: boolean;

function MenuSelect:char;  { returns the users selection }

var
    ch:char;

begin
    WriteLn('1. Enter words');
    WriteLn('2. Delete a word');
    WriteLn('3. Display the list');
    WriteLn('4. Search for a word');
    WriteLn('5. Save the list');
    WriteLn('6. Load the list');
    WriteLn('7. Converse\n');
    WriteLn('8. Quit');
    repeat
        WriteLn;
        Write('Enter your choice: ');
        Read(ch);   ch:=UpCase(ch); WriteLn;
    until (ch>='1') and (ch<='8');
    MenuSelect:=ch;
end;  { MenuSelect }

function DLS_Store(info,start:VocabPointer;
          var last:VocabPointer):VocabPointer;
{ store entries in sorted order }

var
    old, top: ^ vocab;
    done:boolean;
begin
    top:=start;
    old:=nil;
    done:=FALSE;

    if start=nil then
    begin { first element in list }
        info^.next:=nil;
        last:=info;
        info^.prior:=nil;
        DLS_Store:=info;
    end else
    begin
        while (start<>nil) and (not done) do
        begin
            if start^.word < info^.word then
            begin
                old:=start;
                start:=start^.next;
            end else
            begin  { goes in middle }
                if old<>nil then
                begin
                    old^.next:=info;
```

```
                    info^.next:=start;
                    start^.prior:=info;
                    info^.prior:=old;
                    DLS_Store:=top;  { keep same starting point }
                    done:=TRUE;
               end else
               begin
                    info^.next:=start;  { New first element }
                    info^.prior:=nil;
                    DLS_Store:=info;
                    done:=TRUE;
               end;
          end;
     end;  {while}
     if not done then
     begin
          last^.next:=info;  { goes on end }
          info^.next:=nil;
          info^.prior:=last;
          last:=info;
          DLS_Store:=top;
     end;
   end;
end;  { DLS_Store }

function DL_Delete(start:VocabPointer;
                   key:str80):VocabPointer;
var
   temp,temp2:VocabPointer;
   done:boolean;

   begin
      if start^.word=key then
      begin  { is first in list }
          DL_Delete:=start^.next;
          if temp^.next <> nil then
          begin
               temp:=start^.next;
               temp^.prior:=nil;
          end;
          Dispose(start);
      end else
      begin
          done:=FALSE;
          temp:=start^.next;
          temp2:=start;
          while (temp<>nil) and (not done) do
          begin
               if temp^.word=key then
               begin
                    temp2^.next:=temp^.next;
                    if temp^.next<>nil then
                         temp^.next^.prior:=temp2;
                    done:=TRUE;
                    if last=temp then last:=last^.prior;
                    Dispose(temp);
               end else
               begin
                    temp2:=temp;
                    temp:=temp^.next;
```

```
            end;
         end;
         DL_Delete:=start;    {still same starting point}
         if not done then WriteLn('not found');
      end;
   end; {DL_Delete}

   procedure Remove;
   var
      name:str80;
   begin
      Write('Enter word to delete: ');
      Read(name); WriteLn;
      start:=DL_Delete(start,name);
   end;  { Remove }


   procedure Enter(one:boolean);
   var
      info: VocabPointer;
      done: boolean;
   begin
      done:=FALSE;
      repeat
         New(info);  { get a New record }
         Write('Enter word: ');
         Read(info^.word);  WriteLn;
         if Length(info^.word)=0 then done:=TRUE
         else
         begin
            Write('Enter type (n,v,a): ');
            Read(info^.typ);  WriteLn;
            Write('Enter connotation (g,b,n): ');
            Read(info^.connotate);  WriteLn;
            Write('Enter definition: ');
            Read(info^.def);  WriteLn;
            start:=DLS_Store(info,start,last);  { store it }
         end;
      until done or one;
   end;  { Enter }


   procedure Display(start:VocabPointer);
   begin
      while start<>nil do begin
         WriteLn('word: ',start^.word);
         WriteLn('type: ',start^.typ);
         WriteLn('connotation: ',start^.connotate);
         WriteLn('definition');
         WriteLn(start^.def);
         WriteLn;
         start:=start^.next;
      end;
   end;  { Display }

   function Search(start:VocabPointer;word:str30):VocabPointer;
   var
      done:boolean;
   begin
      done:=FALSE;
      while (start<>nil) and (not done) do
```

```
    begin
        if word=start^.word then begin
            Search:=start;
            done:=TRUE;
        end else
            start:=start^.next;
    end;
    if start=nil then Search:=nil;  { not in list }
end;  { Search }


procedure Find;
var
    loc:VocabPointer;
    word:str30;
begin
    Write('Enter word to Find: ');
    Read(word); WriteLn;
    loc:=Search(start,word);
    if loc<>nil then
    begin
        WriteLn('word: ',loc^.word);
        WriteLn('type: ',loc^.typ);
        WriteLn('connotation: ',loc^.connotate);
        WriteLn('definition');
        WriteLn(loc^.def);
        WriteLn;
    end
    else WriteLn('not in list');
end; {Find}

procedure Save(var f:filtype;start:VocabPointer);
begin
    WriteLn('saving file');
    ReWrite(f);
    while start<>nil do
    begin
        Write(f,start^);
        start:=start^.next;
    end;
end;

function Load(var f:filtype;start:VocabPointer):VocabPointer;
{ returns a pointer to the start of the list }
var
    temp:VocabPointer;
begin
    WriteLn('load file');
    Reset(f);
    while start<>nil do
    begin  { free memory, if any }
        temp:=start^.next;
        Dispose(start);
        start:=temp;
    end;
    start:=nil; last:=nil;
    while not eof(f) do
    begin
```

```
        New(temp);
        Read(f,temp^);
        start:=DLS_Store(temp,start,last);
    end;
    Load:=start;
end;   {Load}

procedure Dissect(var s:str80;var w:str30);
var
    t,x:integer;
    temp:str80;
begin
    t:=1;
    while(s[t]=' ') do t:=t+1;
    x:=t;
    while(s[t]<>' ') and (t<=Length(s)) do t:=t+1;
    if t<=Length(s) then t:=t-1;
    w:=copy(s,x,t-x+1);
    temp:=s;
    s:=copy(temp,t+1,Length(s));
end;   { Dissect }

procedure Talk;

var
    sentence:str80;
    word:str30;
    w:VocabPointer;
begin
    WriteLn('Conversation mode (quit to exit)');
    repeat
        Write(': ');
        Read(sentence); WriteLn;
        repeat
            Dissect(sentence,word);
            w:=Search(start,word);
            if w<>nil then begin
                if w^.typ='n' then
                begin
                    case w^.connotate of
                        'g': Write('I like ');
                        'b': Write('I do not like ');
                    end;
                    WriteLn(w^.def);
                end { if }
                else WriteLn(w^.def);
            end
            else if word<>'quit' then
            begin
                WriteLn(word,' is unknown.');
                enter(TRUE);
            end;
        until Length(sentence)=0;
    until word='quit';
end; { Talk }

begin
    start:=nil;  { initially empty list }
```

```
    last:=nil;
    done:=FALSE;

    Assign(smart, 'smart.dic');
    repeat
       case MenuSelect of
          '1': Enter(FALSE);
          '2': Remove;
          '3': Display(start);
          '4': Find;
          '5': Save(smart,start);
          '6': start:=Load(smart,start);
          '7': Talk;
          '8': done:=TRUE;
       end ;
    until done=TRUE;
end.
```

This program is fun and easy to write. You should be able to make it appear quite a bit smarter. One way to do so would be to have the program scan your sentence for verbs and then have it substitute an alternate verb in its comment. You could also make it ask questions.

FIVE

Interfacing to Assembly Language Routines and the Operating System

As powerful as Turbo Pascal is, sometimes you must either write a routine using assembler or use a system call into the operating system. You may have to use these methods to achieve faster run-time execution or to interface to some special hardware device that is not directly supported by Turbo Pascal. Whatever the reason, Turbo Pascal was designed with the flexibility to support such assembly language additions.

Each processor has a different assembly language, and each operating system has a different interface structure. Also, the calling convention, which defines how information is passed to and from a subprogram, varies slightly between the CP/M, CP/M-86, and MS-DOS versions of Turbo Pascal. This chapter is based on the IBM PC-DOS operating system and the 8086 assembly language, because they are the most popular. Even if you have different equipment, you can use the following discussions as a guide.

Assembly Language Interfacing

There are several reasons to use a routine that is written in assembler:

- To enhance speed and efficiency.
- To perform a machine-specific function that is unavailable in Turbo Pascal.
- To use a general-purpose, packaged assembly language routine.

Although all Turbo Pascal compilers can produce fast, compact object code, no compiler consistently creates code that is as fast or compact as that written by a competent programmer using assembler. The small difference usually does not warrant the extra time needed to write a program in assembler. However, there are special cases in which a specific function or procedure must be coded in assembler so that it will run quickly. This is necessary for a function or procedure that is used frequently and therefore greatly affects the ultimate execution speed of a program. A good example is a floating-point math package. Also, special hardware devices sometimes need exact timing, and you must code in assembler to meet such a strict timing requirement.

Many computers, including 8086/8088-based machines, have useful capabilities that cannot be directly executed by Turbo Pascal. For example, you cannot change data segments with any Turbo Pascal instruction, and you cannot control the contents of specific registers by using the Turbo Pascal language.

In professional programming environments, subroutine libraries are often purchased for such commonly needed capabilities as graphics and floating-point math. Sometimes you must take these in object format because the developer will not sell the source code. Occasionally, you can simply link these routines with your Pascal program; at other times, you must write an interface module to correct any differences in the interface used by Turbo Pascal and the routines you purchased.

There are two ways to integrate assembly code modules into your Turbo Pascal programs. The first is to code the routine separately; assemble it with a stand-alone assembler; and link it with the rest of your program by using the **external** command. The second way is to use the in-line assembly code capabilities found in the Turbo Pascal compiler.

It is not within the scope of this book to teach assembly language programming. This chapter assumes that you are already familiar with your computer's assembly language. The examples presented serve only as guides.

Internal Data Formats and Calling Conventions of Turbo Pascal

Before you can link assembly code to a Turbo Pascal program you must know how data is stored in a program and how it is passed between subprograms. For the MS-DOS version, all global variables are stored in the data segment and are accessed by using the DS register. All local variables are stored on the stack; they are accessed by using the BP register. Typed constants, stored in the code segment, are referenced by using the CS register. Figure 5-1 shows how each data type is stored in memory. Remember, pointers are stored in reverse-byte format. Therefore a pointer that held an offset of $B000 and a segment of $0010 would be stored as follows:

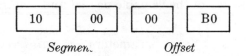

Segmen.   Offset

A *calling convention* is the method used by a Turbo Pascal compiler to pass information into subprograms and to return values from the functions. Turbo Pascal uses the stack to pass parameters into a subprogram and to return certain function results. (The AX register returns byte and word-sized function results.) Exactly what is on the stack when a subprogram is called

Type	Length	Comments
byte	1 byte	
char	1 byte	
integer	2 bytes	
real	6 bytes	The first byte is the mantissa; the next byte is the least-significant byte, and the last byte is the most-significant byte.
string	varies	The first byte holds the current length, and the next holds the first character.
set	varies	Since each element in a set uses one bit and the maximum number of elements is 256, the largest set will be 32 bytes long.
pointer	4 bytes	The two least-significant bytes hold the offset address, while the most-significant bytes hold the segment. They are stored by using reverse byte format. A **nil** value is 4 zero bytes.
arrays	varies	The lowest index values are at the lowest address in memory—the highest index value is at the highest address of the array in memory.
record	varies	The first field is in the lowest address; the last field is in the highest.

Figure 5-1. Built-in data types in memory

depends on both the type of the variable passed and whether it is declared as a *value* or *variable parameter.*

VALUE PARAMETERS   Value parameters are *unidirectional:* information is passed into a subprogram by using a value parameter, but any changes to that parameter do not affect the actual variable used to call the subprogram. Instead of operating on that variable, a copy of its value is made and is passed, thereby leaving the calling variable unchanged. In essence, only a *value* is passed to the procedure or function.

The **integer, char, byte**, and **boolean** value parameters are passed on the stack in one word. Also, any declared scalars other than **real** are passed by using one word on the stack. As in the case of **boolean** value variables, if only one byte is needed, the high-order half of the word is zero. A **real** uses six bytes. A string needs one byte more stack space than the length of the string. This extra byte holds the length of the string, and is the top byte of the string on the stack. All sets require 32 bytes of stack space when used as value parameters.

Pointers consist of two words: the segment and the offset. If the pointer is **nil** then both words are zero.

All arrays and records are passed as a two-word address—consisting of a segment and an offset—of the actual variable. If these variables will not be modified, then a copy must be made. (**NOTE**: this is an exception to the rule—unless your routine makes a copy, it will be operating directly on the calling variables.)

VARIABLE PARAMETERS   Unlike value parameters, variable parameters have their *addresses* passed on the stack. This means that a subprogram can operate on them directly. Variable parameters are *bidirectional:* they pass information into a subprogram; they can also return information back to the calling routine, because the value of the parameters can be modified. Two words are used on the stack to pass both the segment and the offset of the variable parameter, no matter what type it is.

FUNCTION RETURN VALUES   When a Turbo Pascal function terminates, it passes a return value back to the calling routine. For all scalar types except **real**, the value is returned in the AX register. Values that are **boolean** must also set the zero flag: set is TRUE, cleared is FALSE. Functions returning pointers place the segment in register DX and the offset in register AX.

When a function returns a multiple-byte type of variable, the variable must be placed into the *function result location* on the stack. Because the type of variable returned by a function is known at the time it is called, Turbo

Pascal allocates space on the stack that is large enough to hold it. With a **real** this space is six bytes wide, with the exponent at the lowest address. With arrays, strings, and records, the first byte of the variable is at the lowest address. The function result location is immediately below the return address of the calling function. Figure 5-2 shows how the stack looks when a function is called.

PRESERVING REGISTERS   All assembly language subprograms must preserve the BP, CS, DS, and SS registers. This can usually be done by using **push** and **pop** instructions.

When you write an assembly language module that must interface to Turbo Pascal code, you must follow all of the conventions that were defined earlier. Only by using these conventions can your assembly language routines correctly interface with your Turbo Pascal code.

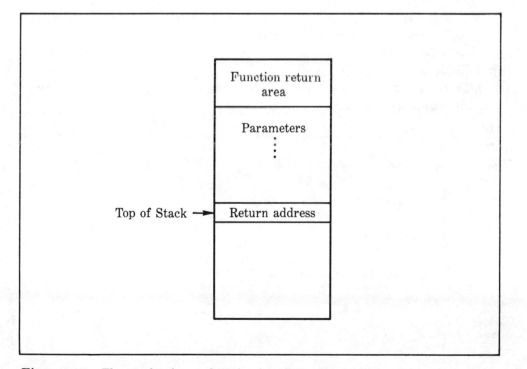

Figure 5-2.   The stack when a function is called

Creating an External Assembly Code Routine

Now that you know the basics, here is an actual external subprogram. For this example, assume that it is necessary to code the following function in assembler:

```
function mul(a,b:integer):integer;
begin
    a:=a*b;
    mul:=a;
end;
```

Since this function will be called from a Turbo Pascal program, you know that the two **integer** arguments will be passed on to the stack as two words. Therefore, if **mul** is called with

```
mul(10,20);
```

the value 20 will be pushed first and the value 10 will be pushed second, which is reverse order. Remember that if the calling arguments are scalar-type variables, their values are passed on the stack. For an array or a record, an address is passed on the stack.

The return value of **mul** must be placed in AX. Here is function **mul**, coded in assembly language:

```
code      segment 'code'
          assume cs:code
xmul      proc near   ; must be near because Turbo uses small
                      ; 8088 memory model
          push bp
          mov bp,sp

; get first parm
          mov ax,[bp]+4
; multiply by second
          mul [bp]+6
; restore bp and clear the stack
; return result is alReady in AX
          pop bp
          ret 4
xmul      endp
code      ends
          end
```

Notice that all appropriate registers are saved by using *push* and *pop*, and the arguments are accessed on the stack. If you are unfamiliar with 8086/8088 assembly code, consider the code that follows.

```
mov bp,sp

mov ax,[bp]+4

mul [bp]+6
```

This code puts the address of the top of the stack into register BP and then moves the fourth byte down on the stack, which is parameter **a**, into the AX register. Parameters are the fourth and sixth bytes down because the return address and the **push bp** use four bytes. Therefore, the parameters start at the fourth byte down from the top of the stack.

As the comment in the **external** function **mul** says, it is a *near procedure*. This is required to be compatible with the way Turbo Pascal handles the memory for the 8086/8088 system. If this function was *far*, it would have caused the stack to be invalid when the function returned to the Turbo Pascal program.

Before you can use the external function **mul**, it must be assembled, linked, and then transformed into a .COM file by using **exe2bin** —which is supplied by MS-DOS. The correct sequence is shown here:

```
masm mul;
link mul,,;
exe2bin mul.exe mul.com
```

The last steps transform the file containing **mul** into a .COM file, which is required by Turbo Pascal.

Your Turbo Pascal programs can now use the external function **mul**. For example,

```
program AsmTest;

var
    a,b,c:integer;

function mul(x,y:integer):integer; external 'mul.com';

begin
    a:=40;
    b:=20;
    c:=mul(a,b);    {multiply a by b and return result}
    WriteLn(c);
end.
```

can be used as long as **mul.com** is on the disk.

Remember that all of the examples are in 8086/8088 assembly language. If you use the CP/M version of Turbo Pascal, you must alter the examples according to the instructions in the *Turbo Pascal User Manual*.

In-line Assembly Code

Unlike standard Pascal, Turbo Pascal has an extension that allows in-line assembly code to become part of a Turbo Pascal program. Thus, you do not have to use a completely separate external subprogram. There are two advantages to this: first, the programmer is not required to write all of the interface code; second, all of the code is in "one place," making support easier. The only drawback is that the in-line assembly code is in a rather awkward format.

The **inline** statement allows assembly code to become part of a Turbo Pascal program. The general form of the statement is

inline(value/value/.../value);

where *value* is any valid assembly instruction or data. An * may be used to specify a location-counter reference. (In 8088 assembly code, this is specified as $. Because Turbo Pascal uses the $ to indicate a hexadecimal number, however, the * is substituted for the location counter.)

When the value is small enough to be contained in one byte, then only one byte is used; otherwise, two bytes are used to store the value. If you wish to override this, you can use the > or < directive. If a value starts with <, then only the low-order byte will be used. If a byte value is preceded by >, then a two-byte word will be generated, with the high-order byte being zero. For example, <$1234 generates only one byte with the value $34, while >$12 generates two bytes with the values $0012.

The following short program multiplies two integers together by using the function **mul**, which uses in-line assembly code to perform the actual multiplication. You should compare this **mul** to the external subprogram version from the previous section.

```
program AsmInline;    { this program shows an example of
                        inline assembly code }

var
   a,b,c:integer;

function mul(x,y:integer):integer;
begin
    inline($8B/$46/$04/    { mov ax,[bp]+4 }
           $F6/$66/$06/    { mul [bp]+6    }
           $89/$EC/        { mov sp,bp }
           $5D/            { pop bp }
           $C2/$06/$00);   { ret 6 }
end; {mul}
```

```
begin
   a:=10;
   b:=20;
   c:=mul(a,b);
   WriteLn(c);
end.
```

Here, the Turbo Pascal compiler automatically provides the code to return from the function. When the compiler compiles the **inline** code, the actual instructions are provided in the function at that place where the **inline** statement occurs.

A common use of in-line assembly code is to communicate with special hardware devices that are not supported by Turbo Pascal directly. For example, you could use this subprogram to turn on a fan when a temperature sensor reaches a target value. This subprogram assumes that sending a 1 out of port 200 turns on the fan:

```
procedure fan(temp:integer);
{ If temp >=100 degrees C, then turn on fan }
begin
   if temp>=100 then
      Inline($B8/00/01/   {mov AX,1}
             $E7/$C8);    {out 200,AX}
end;
```

Remember, the Turbo Pascal compiler provides all customary support for setting up and returning from a function call. All you have to do is provide the body of the function and follow the calling conventions to access the arguments.

Whatever method you use, you are creating machine dependencies that will make your program difficult to port to a new machine or operating system. However, for the demanding situations that require assembly code, it will usually be worth the effort.

When to Code in Assembler

Most programmers only code in assembler when absolutely necessary because such coding is difficult. As a general rule don't use it—it creates too many problems. However, there are two situations in which coding in assembler makes sense. The first situation is when there is absolutely no other way to do it—for example, when you need to interface directly to a hardware device that cannot be handled by using Turbo Pascal.

The second situation is when a program's execution time must be reduced.

In this situation, you should carefully choose the functions you code in assembler. If you code the wrong ones, you will see little increase in speed. If you choose the right one, your program will fly! To determine which subprograms need recoding, you must review the operational flow of your program. The routines used inside loops are generally the ones you should program in assembler because they are executed repeatedly. Using assembler to code a procedure or function that is used only once or twice may not offer significant improvement in speed, but using assembler to code a function that is used several times may. For example, consider the following procedure:

```
procedure ABC;
var
   t:integer;

begin
   init;
   for t:=0 to 1000 do begin
      phase1;
      phase2;
      if t=10 then phase3;
   end;
   byebye;
end;
```

Recoding **init** and **byebye** may not measurably affect the speed of this program, because they are executed only once. Both **phase1** and **phase2** are executed 1000 times, and recoding them will definitely have a major effect on the run time of this program; **phase3** is only executed once even though it is inside the loop, so recoding this subprogram into assembler probably would not be worth the effort.

With careful thought you can improve the speed of your program by recoding only a few subprograms in assembler.

Operating-System Interfacing

Because many Turbo Pascal programs fall into the category of system programs, it is often necessary to interface directly to the operating system, bypassing Turbo Pascal's normal interface, to perform certain operations. There may also be special operating-system functions, which cannot be accessed by your Turbo Pascal compiler, that you want to make use of. For these reasons, using the low-level resources of the operating system is a common occurrence in Turbo Pascal programming.

Several operating systems are currently supported by Turbo Pascal:

- PC-DOS or MS-DOS
- CP/M
- CP/M-86.

All operating systems have a set of functions that programs can use for such tasks as opening disk files, reading and writing characters to and from the console, and allocating memory for the program to run in. The way these functions are accessed varies from system to system, but they tend to use the general concept of a *jump table*. In an operating system like CP/M, the system calls are executed by using a CALL instruction to a specific region of memory with the desired function code in a register. In PC-DOS, a software interrupt is used. In either case, the jump table routes the proper function to your program. Figure 5-3 shows how an operating system and its jump table might appear in memory.

It is not possible to discuss all operating systems here. This chapter focuses only on PC-DOS because it is in widest use. However, the general techniques applied here are applicable to all operating systems.

Accessing System Resources
In PC-DOS

In PC-DOS the operating-system functions are accessed through software interrupts. Each interrupt has its own category of functions that it accesses, and the values of the AH register determine these functions. If additional information is needed, it is passed through the AL, BX , CX, and DX registers. The PC-DOS operating system is divided into BIOS (Basic I/O System) and DOS (Disk Operating System). The BIOS provides the lowest-level routines that DOS uses to provide the higher-level functions. However, there is overlap between the two systems. Fortunately, for the purposes of this chapter, they are accessed in basically the same way. A partial list of these interrupts is shown here:

Interrupt	Function
10h	Video I/O
13h	Disk I/O
16h	Keyboard
17h	Printer I/O
21h	High-level DOS calls

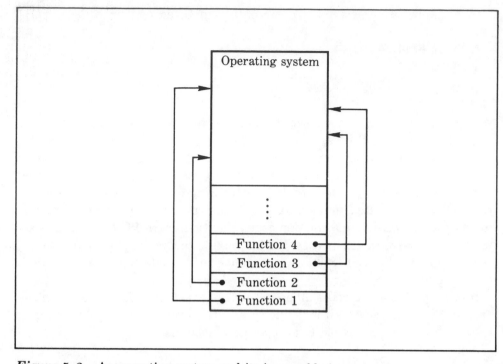

Figure 5-3.   An operating system and its jump table in memory

For a complete list and explanation, refer to the *IBM Technical Reference Manual.*

Each of these interrupts is associated with a number of options that can be accessed, depending upon the value of the AH register when called. Table 5-1 shows a partial list of the options available for each of these interrupts. There are two ways to access the functions found in Table 5-1. The first is by using a built-in system-call function called **MsDos** (for PC-DOS), which is supplied by Turbo Pascal. The second is by using assembly language interfacing.

Using the MsDos Procedure

The **MsDos** procedure performs an interrupt 21h call to access one of the higher-level functions in the operating system. **MsDos** takes the general

Table 5-1. System Routines Accessed Through Interrupts

AH register	Function
	Video I/O functions—Interrupt 10h
0	Set video mode
	if AL=0: 40×25 BW
	1: 40×25 color
	2: 80×25 BW
	3: 80×25 color
	4: 320×200 color graphics
	5: 320×200 BW graphics
	6: 340×200 BW graphics
1	Set cursor lines
	CH bits 0-4 contain start of line
	bits 5-7 are 0
	CL bits 0-4 contain end of line
	bits 5-7 are 0
2	Set cursor position
	DH: row
	DL: column
	BH: video page number
3	Read cursor position
	BH: video page number
	Returns
	DH: row
	DL: column
	CX: mode
4	Read light-pen position
	Returns
	if AH=0 pen not triggered
	if AH=1 pen triggered
	DH: row
	DL: column
	CH: raster line (0-199)
	BX: pixel column (0-319 or 0-639)
5	Set active video page
	AL may be 0-7
6	Scroll page up
	AL: number of lines to scroll, 0 for all
	CH: row of upper-left corner of scroll
	CL: column of upper-left corner of scroll
	DH: row of lower-right corner of scroll
	DL: column of lower-right corner of scroll
	BH: attribute to be used on blank line

Table 5-1.   System Routines Accessed Through Interrupts (*continued*)

AH register	Function
	Video I/O functions—Interrupt 10h
7	Scroll page down same as 6

8	Read character at cursor position
	  BH: video page
	Returns
	  AL: character read
	  AH: attribute

9	Write character and attribute at
	cursor position
	  BH: video page
	  BL: attribute
	  CX: number of characters to write
	  AL: character

10	Write character at cur-
	rent cursor position
	  BH: video page
	  CX: number of characters to write
	  AL: character

11	Set color palette
	  BH: palette number
	  BL: color

12	Write a dot
	  DX: row number
	  CX: column number
	  AL: color

13	Read a dot
	  DX: row number
	  CX: column number
	Returns
	  AL: dot read

14	Write character to screen and
	advance cursor
	  AL: character
	  BL: foreground color
	  BH: video page

15	Read video state
	Returns
	  AL: current mode
	  AH: number of columns on screen
	  BH: current active video page

Table 5-1.   System Routines Accessed Through Interrupts (*continued*)

AH register	Function
	BIOS disk I/O functions — Interrupt 13h
0	Reset disk system
1	Read disk status Returns AL: status (see *IBM Technical Reference Manual*)

2	Read sectors into memory
	    DL: drive number
	    DH: head number
	    CH: track number
	    CL: sector number
	    AL: number of sectors to read
	    ES:BX: address of buffer
	Returns
	    AL: number of sectors read
	    AH: 0 on success, otherwise status

3	Write sectors to disk (same as Read given earlier)
4	Verify (same as Read given earlier)

5	Format a track
	    DL: drive number
	    DH: head number
	    CH: track number
	    ES:BX: sector information

	BIOS keyboard I/O functions — Interrupt 16h

0	Read scan code
	Returns
	    AH: scan code
	    AL: character code

1	Get status of buffer
	Returns
	    ZF: 1 then buffer empty
	        0 then characters waiting
	        with next character in AX as
	        described earlier

2	Get status of keyboard (see *IBM Technical Reference Manual*)

Table 5-1.   System Routines Accessed Through Interrupts (*continued*)

AH register	Function
	BIOS printer I/O functions—Interrupt 17h

0	Print a character
	  AL: character
	  DX: printer number
	Returns
	  AH: status

1	Initialize printer
	  DX: printer number
	Returns
	  AH: status

2	Read status
	  DX: printer number
	Returns
	  AH: status

	High-level DOS function calls—Interrupt 21h (partial list)
1	Read character from the keyboard Returns AL: character
2	Display a character on the screen DL: character
3	Read a character from async port Returns AL: character
4	Write a character to async port DL: character
5	Print a character to list device DL: character
7	Read character from keyboard but do not display it. Returns AL: character
B	Check keyboard status Returns AL: 0FFH if key struck; 0 otherwise
D	Reset disk
E	Set default drive DL: Drive Number (0=A, 1=B,...)
11 (4E under 2.x)	Search for file name DX: Address of FCB

Table 5-1.   System Routines Accessed Through Interrupts (*continued*)

AH register	Function
	Video I/O functions—Interrupt 10h
	Returns
	AL: 0 if found, FFh if not
	with name in disk transfer address
12	Find next occurrence of file name
(4F under 2.x)	same as 11
1A	Set disk transfer address
	DX: disk transfer address
2A	Get system date
	Returns
	CX: year (1980-2099)
	DH: month (1-12)
	DL: day (1-31)
2B	Set system date
	CX: year (1980-2099)
	DH: month (1-12)
	DL: day (1-31)
2C	Get system time
	Returns
	CH: hours (0-23)
	CL: minutes (0-59)
	DH: seconds (0-59)
	DL: hundredths of seconds (0-99)
2D	Set system time
	CH: hours (0-23)
	CL: minutes (0-59)
	DH: seconds (0-59)
	DL: hundredths of seconds (0-99)

form

$$\textbf{MsDos}(registers);$$

where *registers* is a record of one of the following types:

```
reg_word = record
      AX,BX,CX,DX,BP,SI,DI,DS,ES,flags:integer;
end;

reg_byte = record
      AL,AH,BL,BH,DL,DH: byte;
      BP,SI,DI,DS,ES,flags:integer;
end;
```

The second form is used when byte values are needed. You can mix byte and register values or use a variant record type. You must decide what is the best record to use for your particular situation.

For the remainder of this chapter, the examples develop procedures that duplicate, in part, the standard procedures already built into Turbo Pascal. They are designed this way for three reasons. First, Turbo Pascal has included almost everything you need from the operating system for most situations. Second, it is important to illustrate as completely as possible how interfacing is done, so that special situations can be dealt with. Third, the examples provide some insight into the way Turbo Pascal procedures and functions work.

Here is a simple example. The following function determines whether a key has been pressed. It is similar to **keypressed**, which is built into Turbo Pascal. This function, **KbHit**, returns TRUE if a key has been hit and FALSE if not. It uses interrupt 21h, hex number $B, as shown here. Remember, hex numbers are preceded by $, which tells the compiler that a hex number follows. The program itself prints periods on the screen until a key is struck.

```
program kb;   {wait for keypress}
{$C-}
function KbHit:boolean;   { PCDOS specific }
type
   RegByte = record
   AL,AH,BL,BH,DL,DH: byte;
   BP,SI,DI,DS,ES,flags:integer;
   end;

var
   register:RegByte;
begin
   register.AH:=$B;
   MsDos(register);
   if register.AL=0 then KbHit:=FALSE
   else KbHit:=TRUE;
end;

begin
   repeat
      Write('.');
   until KbHit;
end.
```

Notice that the rest of the registers did not need to be set for this call, because only the function number, $B, was needed. In general, when a specific register is not used in the call, then it does not need a value assigned to it.

The $C− compiler directive is used in this program to disable CTRL-C, CTRL-S, and CTRL-Q checking. If this keyboard checking is not disabled, these keys would not be passed through to the program, but would be trapped by the Turbo Pascal run-time support system. CTRL-C would abort the program, CTRL-S would temporarily stop it, and CTRL-Q would restart it.

Using Assembly Interfacing
To BIOS and DOS Functions

Suppose that you wish to change the screen mode during the execution of a program. For PC-DOS, the seven modes that the color graphics adapter's screen can have are:

0	40	×	25 BW
1	40	×	25 color
2	80	×	25 BW
3	80	×	25 color
4	320	×	200 color graphics
5	320	×	200 BW graphics
6	640	×	200 BW graphics

The procedure **mode**, shown here, executes a BIOS call number 1—set mode—to switch the screen to 640×320 graphics, print the message **hi** on the screen, and wait for the user to press RETURN on the keyboard. After RETURN is pressed, the screen returns to 80×25 color mode. (This code only works for PC-DOS, and it requires a color graphics adapter.)

```
program mode;

procedure mode(ModeSet:integer); external 'mode.com';

begin
   mode(6);
   WriteLn('hi'); Read;
   mode(3);
end.
```

The **external** assembly code function called **mode** is shown here:

```
; this procedure will set the screen mode based on its
; single integer argument.
code      segment 'code'
          assume cs:code
mode      proc near  ; must be near because Turbo uses small
                     ; 8088 model
          push bp
          mov bp,sp

; get mode
          mov ax,[bp]+4
          mov ah,0    ; command to switch modes
          int 010h    ; call bios
```

```
; restore and exit
        pop bp
        ret 2
mode    endp
code    ends
        end
```

This function clears the screen by using the procedure **clr**:

```
program ClrScreen;

procedure clr; external 'clr.com';

begin
   WriteLn('strike any key to clear the screen');
   ReadLn;
   clr;
   WriteLn('screen clear complete');
end.
```

The assembly code **external** routine called **clr** is shown here:

```
; this routine clears the screen using the standard BIOS
; interrupt number 6.
cseg segment 'code'
        assume cs:cseg

clr proc near
; save registers used
        push ax
        push bx
        push cx
        push dx
        mov cx,0  ; start at 0,0
        mov dh,24 ; end at row 24
        mov dl,79 ; column 79
        mov ah,6  ; set scroll option
        mov al,0  ; clear the screen
        mov bh,7
        int 10h
; restore and exit
        pop dx
        pop cx
        pop bx
        pop ax
        ret
clr endp
cseg ends
        end
```

Another example of interfacing to BIOS through assembly language is the function **xy**, which locates the cursor at the specified x and y coordinates. This function is similar to the **GotoXY** procedure found in Turbo Pascal. For the IBM PC, 0,0 is the upper-left corner of the screen.

```
program gotoxy;

var
   t:integer;

procedure xy(x,y:integer); external 'xy.com';

begin
   for t:=0 to 24 do
   begin
      xy(t,t);
      Write(t);
   end;
end.
```

The assembly language **external** routine called **xy** is shown here:

```
code      segment 'code'
          assume cs:code
xy        proc near   ; must be near because Turbo uses small
                      ; 8088 model
          push bp
          mov bp,sp

; get first parm
          mov dh,[bp]+4 ; get x
          mov dl,[bp]+6 ; get y
          mov ah,2      ; tell bios to go there
          mov bh,0      ; page number
          int 10h    ;
;
          pop bp
          ret 4
xy        endp
code      ends
          end
```

Using the Scan Codes
From the PC Keyboard

One of the most frustrating experiences you can encounter while working with the IBM PC or a clone is trying to use the arrow keys (as well as INS, DEL, PGUP, PGDN, END, and HOME) and the function keys. These keys do not return the normal 8-bit (one byte) characters in the way that the rest of the keys do. When you press a key, the PC actually generates a 16-bit value called a *scan code*. The scan code consists of the low-order byte, which, if a normal key, contains the ASCII code for the key; and a high-order byte that contains the key's position on the keyboard. For most keys, these scan codes are converted into 8-bit ASCII values by the operating system. But for the function keys and the arrow keys, this is not done because the character code for a special key is 0. This means that you must use the position code to determine which key has been pressed. The routine to read a character from the keyboard, which is supported by DOS function call number 1, does not allow you to read the special keys. The problem becomes apparent when you want to use these special keys in a program.

The easiest way to access these keys when using Turbo Pascal is to write an assembly language routine that calls interrupt 16h to read the scan code:

```
; this routine returns a sixteen bit value from the keyboard
; the low order byte is either an ASCII character or 0.
; If it is 0, then the high order byte contains a scan.
; code.
code     segment 'code'
         assume cs:code
scan     proc near  ; must be near because Turbo uses small
                    ; 8088 model

         push bp
         mov bp,sp

; get first parm
         mov ah,0
         int 16h
         mov [bx+2],ax ; return value
; restore and exit
         pop bp
         ret 2
scan     endp
code     ends
         end
```

After the call, the scan code and the character code are already in AX, which is the correct register for returning information. After a call to interrupt 16h function 0, the position code is in AH and the character code is in AL.

The trick to using **scan** is knowing that when a special key is struck, the character code is 0. In such a case, you then decode the position code to determine which key was actually typed. Using **scan** to do all keyboard input requires that the calling routine make decisions based on the contents of AH and AL. Here is a short program that illustrates one way to do this:

```
program arrow;

var
   t:integer;

function scan:integer; external 'scan.com';

begin
   repeat
```

```
        t:=arrow;
        if Lo(t)=0 then WriteLn('scan code is ',Hi(t))
        else WriteLn(Chr(Lo(t)));
    until Chr(Lo(t))='q';
end.
```

Hi and **Lo** are used to access both halves of the 16-bit value returned by **scan**. You also need the function **Chr** to convert an integer into a character.

You can decode a scan code by looking in the *IBM Technical Reference Manual,* or by using the short program just given to determine the values experimentally (the latter method is more fun). To help you get started, here are the scan codes indicated for the arrow keys:

Left arrow	75
Right arrow	77
Up arrow	72
Down arrow	80

To completely integrate the special keys with the normal keys requires writing special input functions and bypassing the normal **read** and **readln** functions. While this is unfortunate, it is the only way. However, the reward is that your program can allow the user to work within the full IBM PC keyboard.

Final Thoughts on Operating-System Interfacing

This chapter has only scratched the surface of what you can do by using system resources creatively. To integrate your program with the operating system completely, you need to have access to information that describes all of the functions in detail.

There are several advantages to using operating-system functions. The first is that they can make better use of the special features of a given computer system, thus making your program look and feel more professional. Second, bypassing some of Turbo Pascal's built-in functions in favor of the operating-system functions can sometimes create programs that run faster and use less memory. Third, you have access to functions that are not available through Turbo Pascal's standard functions.

However, using the operating-system carries a price. You are creating more trouble for yourself when you use the operating-system functions instead of the standard functions and procedures, because your code is no longer portable. You may also become dependent on specific versions of a given operating system and a Turbo Pascal compiler, which will create compatibility problems when you distribute your programs. Only you can decide when and if you should introduce machine and operating-system dependencies into your programs.

SIX

Statistics

Most people who own or have frequent access to a computer use it at some point to perform *statistical analysis*. This analysis could take the form of monitoring or trying to predict the movement of stock prices in a portfolio, performing clinical testing to establish safe limits for a new drug, or even providing batting averages for the Little League team. The branch of mathematics that deals with the condensation, manipulation, and extrapolation of data is called *statistics*.

As a discipline, statistical analysis is quite young. It developed in the 1700s as an outgrowth of the study of games of chance. Indeed, probability and statistics are closely related. Modern statistical analysis began around the turn of this century when it became possible to sample and work with large sets of data. The computer made it possible to correlate and manipulate even larger amounts of data rapidly and to convert this data into a readily usable form. Today, because of the ever-increasing amount of information created and used by the government and media, every aspect of life is adorned with reams of statistical information. It is almost impossible to listen to the radio, watch the TV news, or read a newspaper article without being informed of some statistic.

Although Turbo Pascal was not designed specifically for statistical programming, it adapts to the task quite well. It even offers some flexibility that is not found in more common business languages such as COBOL or BASIC. One advantage of Turbo Pascal over COBOL is the speed and ease with which Turbo Pascal programs can interface to the graphics functions of the system to produce charts and graphs of data. Also, Turbo Pascal's math routines are much faster than those commonly found in interpretive BASIC.

This chapter focuses on various concepts of statistics, including

- The mean
- The median
- The standard deviation
- The regression equation (line of best fit)
- The coefficient of correlation.

It also explores some simple graphing techniques.

Samples, Populations, Distributions, And Variables

Before you use statistics, you must understand a few key concepts. Statistical information is derived by first taking a *sample* of specific data points and then drawing generalizations about them. Each sample comes from the *population*, which consists of all of the possible outcomes for the situation under study. For example, if you wished to measure the output of a box factory over a year by using only the Wednesday output figures and generalizing from them, then your sample would consist of a year's worth of Wednesday figures taken from the larger population of each day's output in the year.

It is possible for the sample to equal the population if the sample is exhaustive. In the case of the box factory, your sample would equal the population if you used the actual output figures—five days a week for the entire year. When the sample is less than the population, there is always room for error; however, in many cases you can determine the probability for this error. This chapter assumes that the sample is the same as the population; hence it does not cover the problem of sample error.

For election projections and opinion polls, a proportionally small sample is used to project information about the population as a whole. For example, you might use statistical information about Dow Jones stocks to make an inference about the stock market in general. Of course, the validity of these conclusions varies widely. In other uses of statistics, a sample that equals or nearly equals the population is used to summarize a large set of numbers for easier handling. For example, a board of education usually reports on the *average grade point* for a class, rather than on each student's individual grade.

Statistics are affected by the way that events are distributed in the population. Of the several common distributions in nature, the most important (and the only one used in this chapter) is the *normal distribution curve*, or the familiar "bell-shaped curve" as shown in Figure 6-1. As suggested by the graph in Figure 6-1, the elements in a normal distribution curve are found mostly in the middle. In fact, the curve is completely symmetrical around its peak—which is also the average for all of the elements. The further from the middle in either direction on the curve, the fewer elements there are. Many situations in real life have a normal distribution.

In any statistical process, there is always an *independent variable*, which is the number under study, and a *dependent variable*, which is the factor that determines the independent variable. This chapter uses *time*—the stepwise incremental passage of events—for the dependent variable. For example, when watching a stock portfolio, you may wish to see the movement of the stock on a daily basis. You would, therefore, be concerned with the movement of stock prices over a given period of time, not with the actual calendar date of each price.

Throughout this chapter, individual statistical functions will be developed and then assembled into a single menu-driven program. You can use this program to perform a wide variety of statistical analyses, as well as to plot information on the screen.

Whenever the elements of a sample are discussed, they will be called D and indexed from 1 to N, where N is the number of the last element.

The Basic Statistics

Three important values form the basis of many statistical analyses and are also useful individually. They are the *mean*, the *median*, and the *mode*.

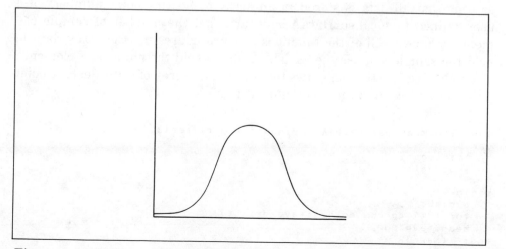

Figure 6-1.   The normal distribution curve

The Mean

The mean, or the arithmetic average, is the most common of all statistics. This single value can be used to represent a set of data—the mean can be called the set's "center of gravity." To compute the mean, all elements in the sample are added together and the result is divided by the total number of elements. For example, the sum of the set

$$1\ 2\ 3\ 4\ 5\ 6\ 7\ 8\ 9\ 10$$

equals 55. When that number is divided by the number of elements in the sample, which is 10, the mean is 5.5.

The general formula for finding the mean is

$$M = \frac{D_1 + D_2 + D_3 + \ldots + D_N}{N}$$

or

$$M = \frac{1}{N} \sum_{i=1}^{N} D_i$$

The symbol Σ indicates the summation of all elements between 1 and N.

As the statistical functions are developed in Turbo Pascal, you should assume that all data is stored in an array of floating-point numbers of a user-defined type called **DataArray**, and that the number of sample elements is known. All of the functions and procedures use the array **data** to hold the sample and use the variable **num** to hold the number of elements. The following function computes the mean of an array of **num** floating-point numbers and returns the floating-point average:

```
function Mean(data:DataArray;num:integer):real;
var
    t:integer;
    avg:real;

begin
    avg:=0;
    for t:=1 to num do avg:=avg+data[t];
    Mean:=avg/num;
end;  {Mean}
```

For example, if you called **Mean** with a 10-element array that contained the numbers 1 through 10, then **Mean** would return the result 5.5.

The Median

The median of a sample is the middle value, based on order of magnitude. For example, in the sample set

$$1\ 2\ 3\ 4\ 5\ 6\ 7\ 8\ 9$$

5 is the median, because it is in the middle. In the set

$$1\ 2\ 3\ 4\ 5\ 6\ 7\ 8\ 9\ 10$$

you could use either 5 or 6 as the median. In a well-ordered sample that has a normal distribution, the median and the mean are very similar. However, as the sample moves further from the normal distribution curve, the difference between the median and the mean increases. Calculating the mean of a sample is as simple as sorting the sample into ascending order and then selecting the middle element, which is indexed as $N/2$.

The function **Median**, shown here, returns the value of the middle element in a sample. A modified version of QuickSort (developed in Chapter 2) is used to sort the data array.

```
procedure  QuickSort(var item: DataArray; count:integer);
   procedure qs(l,r:integer; var it:DataArray);
      var
      i,j: integer;
      x,y: DataItem;
      begin
         i:=l; j:=r;
         x:=it[(l+r) div 2];
         repeat
            while it[i] < x do i:= i+1;
            while x < it[j] do j:=j-1;
            if i<=j then
            begin
               y:=it[i];
               it[i]:=it[j];
               it[j]:=y;
               i:=i+1; j:=j-1;
            end;
         until i>j;
         if l<j then qs(l,j,it);
         if l<r then qs(i,r,it)
      end;
begin
   qs(1,count,item);
end; {quick sort }

function Median(data:DataArray;num:integer):real;
var
   dtemp:DataArray;
   t:integer;

begin
   for t:=1 to num do dtemp[t]:=data[t];    {copy data for sort}
   QuickSort(dtemp,num);
   Median:=dtemp[num div 2];   {middle element}
end; {Median}
```

The Mode

The mode of a sample is the value of the most frequently occurring element. For example, in the set

$$1\ 2\ 3\ 3\ 4\ 5\ 6\ 6\ 6\ 7\ 8\ 9$$

the mode would be 6 because it occurs three times. There may be more than one mode; for example, the sample

$$10\ 20\ 30\ 30\ 40\ 50\ 60\ 60\ 70$$

has two modes—30 and 60—because they both occur twice.

The following function, **FindMode**, returns the mode of a sample. If there is more than one mode, then it returns the last one found.

```
function FindMode(data:DataArray;num:integer):real;
var
   t,w,count,oldcount:integer;
   md,oldmd:real;

begin
   oldmd:=0; oldcount:=0;
   for t:=1 to num do
   begin
      md:=data[t];
      count:=1;
      for w:=t+1 to num do
         if md=data[w] then count:=count+1;
      if count>oldcount then
      begin
         oldmd:=md;
         oldcount:=count;
      end;
   end;
   FindMode:=oldmd;
end; {FindMode}
```

Using the Mean, the Median, And the Mode

The mean, the median, and the mode share the same purpose: to provide one value that is the condensation of all values in the sample. However, each represents the sample in a different way. The mean of the sample is generally the most useful value. Because it uses all values in its computation, the mean reflects all elements of the sample. The main disadvantage to the mean is its sensitivity to one extreme value. For example, in an imaginary business called Widget, Inc., the owner's salary is $100,000 per year, while the salary of each of the nine employees is $10,000. The average wage at Widget is $19,500, but this figure does not fairly represent the actual situation.

In cases like the salary dispersion at Widget, the mode is sometimes used instead of the mean. The mode of the salaries at Widget is $10,000—a figure that reflects more accurately the actual situation. However, the mode can also be misleading. Consider a car company that makes cars in five different colors. In a given week, it made

> 100 green cars
> 100 orange cars
> 150 blue cars
> 200 black cars
> 190 white cars

Here, the mode of the sample is black, because 200 black cars were made, which is more than any other color. However, it would be misleading to suggest that the car company makes mostly black cars.

The median is interesting because its validity is based on the *hope* that the sample reflects a normal distribution. For example, if the sample is

> 1 2 3 4 5 6 7 8 9 10

then the median is 5 or 6 and the mean is 5.5. Hence, the median and mean are similar in this case. However, in the sample

> 1 1 1 1 5 100 100 100 100

the median is still 5, but the mean is about 46.

In certain circumstances, neither the mean, the mode, nor the median can be counted on to give a meaningful value. This leads to two of the most important numbers in statistics—the *variance* and the *standard deviation*.

The Variance and the Standard Deviation

Although the one-number summary (such as the mean, mode, or median) is very convenient, it can easily be misleading. Giving a little thought to this problem, you can see that the cause of the difficulty is not in the value itself, but due to the fact that it does not convey any information about the variations of the data. For example, in the sample

> 1 1 1 1 9 9 9 9

the mean is 5; however, there is no element in the sample that is close to 5. What you probably would like to know is *how close* each element in the sample is to the average; in other words, how variable the data is. Knowing the variability of the data helps you interpret the mean, median, and mode better. You can find the variability of a sample by computing its variance and its standard deviation.

The variance and its square root, the standard deviation, are numbers that tell you the average deviation from the sample mean. Of the two, the standard deviation is the most important. It can be thought of as the average of the distances that the elements are from the mean of the sample. The variance is computed as

$$V = \frac{1}{N} \sum_{i=1}^{N} (D_i - M)^2$$

where N is the number of elements in the sample, and M is the sample's mean. You must square the difference of the mean and each element in order to produce only positive numbers. If the numbers were not squared, they would by default always add up to 0.

The variance produced by this formula, V, is of limited value because it is difficult to understand. However, its square root, the standard deviation, is the number you are really looking for. The standard deviation is derived by first finding the variance and then taking its square root:

$$std = \sqrt{\frac{1}{N} \sum_{i=1}^{N} (D_i - M)^2}$$

where N is the number of elements in the sample and M is the sample's mean.

As an example, for the sample

$$11 \ 20 \ 40 \ 30 \ 99 \ 30 \ 50$$

you compute the variance as follows:

D	$D-M$	$(D-M)^2$
11	−29	−841
20	−20	−400
40	0	0

	D	$D{-}M$	$(D{-}M)^2$
	30	-10	-100
	99	59	3481
	30	-10	-100
	50	10	100
Sum	280	0	5022
Mean	40	0	717.42

Here the average of the squared differences is 717.42. To derive the standard deviation, you simply take the square root of that number; the result is approximately 26.78. To interpret the standard deviation, remember that it equals the *average distance that the elements are from the mean of the sample.*

The standard deviation tells you how nearly the mean represents the entire sample. If you owned a candy bar factory, and your plant supervisor reported that daily output averaged 2500 bars last month but that the standard deviation was 2000, you would know that the production line needed better supervision!

If your sample follows a standard normal distribution, then about 68% of the sample will be within one standard deviation from the mean, and about 95% will be within two standard deviations.

The following function computes and returns the standard deviation of a given sample:

```
function StdDev(data:DataArray;num:integer):real;
var
    t:integer;
    std,avg:real;

begin
    avg:=Mean(data,num);
    std:=0;
    for t:=1 to num do
        std:=std+((data[t]-avg)*(data[t]-avg));

    std:=std/num;
    StdDev:=Sqrt(std);

end;   {StdDev}
```

Simple Plotting on the Screen

The advantage of using graphs with statistics is that together they can convey the meaning clearly and accurately. A graph also shows at a glance how the sample is actually distributed and how the data varies. This discussion is limited to two-dimensional graphs, which use the X-Y coordinate system. (Creating three-dimensional graphs is a discipline unto itself and is beyond

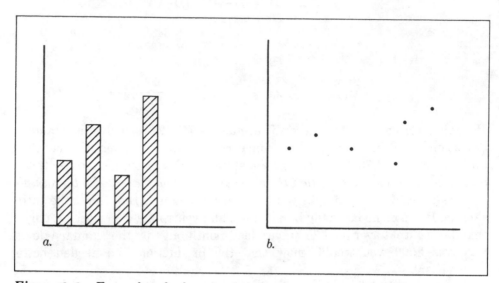

Figure 6-2.   Examples of a bar graph (*a*) and a scatter graph (*b*)

the scope of this book.)

There are two common forms of two-dimensional graphs: the *bar graph* and the *scatter graph*. The bar graph uses solid bars to represent the magnitude of each element; the scatter graph uses a single point per element, located at its X and Y coordinates. Figure 6-2 shows an example of each.

The bar chart is usually used with a relatively small set of information, as in the gross national product for the last ten years or the percentage output of a factory on a monthly basis. The scatter graph is generally used to display a large number of data points, as in the daily stock price of a company over a year. A modification of the scatter graph that connects the data points with a solid line is useful for plotting projections.

Here is a simple plotting function that creates a bar graph on the IBM PC. Through some Turbo Pascal library functions, the function uses the built-in graphics capabilities of the IBM PC. The functions **GraphColorMode**, **Palette**, **Draw**, and **Plot** are supplied by Turbo Pascal.

```
procedure SimplePlot(data:DataArray;num:integer);
{plots a bar graph of data using IBM PC graphics.}
var
   t,incr:integer;
   a:real;
   ch:char;

begin
   GraphColorMode;
   Palette(0);
```

```
GotoXY(1,25); Write(min);
GotoXY(1,1); Write(max);
GotoXY(38,25); Write(num);
Draw(0,190,200,190,1);   {base line}
for t:=1 to num do
begin
   a:=data[t];
   y:=trunc(a);
   incr:=10;
   x:=((t-1)*incr)+20;
   Draw(x,190,x,190-y,2);
end;
Read(ch);
TextMode;

end; {SimplePlot}
```

On the IBM PC, the maximum-resolution color graphics mode offers a resolution of 320×200 and is set by the call to **GraphColorMode**. The procedure **GotoXY** sets the cursor to the desired X-Y position. The **Draw** procedure has the general form

$$\textbf{draw}(start\_X, start\_Y, end\_X, end\_Y, color);$$

where all values must be integers. Refer to the *Turbo Pascal User Manual* for additional information.

This simple plotting routine has a serious limitation—it assumes that all data will be between 0 and 199, because the only valid numbers that can be used to call the **Draw** graphics function are within the range of 0 to 199. This assumption is fine in the unlikely event that your data elements consistently fit in that range. To make the plotting routine handle arbitrarily sized units, you must *normalize* the data before plotting it, in order to scale the data values to fit the required range. The process of normalization involves finding a ratio between the actual range of the data values and the physical range of the screen resolution. Each data element can then be multiplied by this ratio to produce a number that fits the range of the screen. The formula to do this for the Y-axis on the PC is

$$Y' = Y * \frac{200}{(max - min)}$$

where Y' is the value used when calling the plotting function. This same formula can be used to spread the scale when the data range is very small. This results in a graph that fills the screen as much as possible.

The function **BarPlot** scales the X and Y-axis and plots a bar graph of as many as 300 elements. The X-axis is assumed to be time and is in one-unit increments. Generally, the normalizing procedure finds the greatest value and the smallest value in the sample and then calculates their difference. This number, which represents the spread between the minimum and maximum, is used to divide the resolution of the screen. For the IBM PC, this number is 190 for the Y-axis and is 300 for the X-axis (because you need room for the borders and the base line). The ratio is then used to convert the sample data into the proper scale.

```
procedure BarPlot(data:DataArray;num:integer);
{Plots a bar graph of data using IBM PC graphics.}
var
    x,y,max,min,incr,t:integer;
    a, norm,spRead:real;
    ch:char;

begin
    GraphColorMode;
    Palette(0);
    { first, find min and max value to enable normalization}
    max:=GetMax(data,num);
    min:=GetMin(data,num);
    if min>0 then min:=0;
    spRead:=max-min;
    norm:=190/spRead;
    GotoXY(1,25); Write(min);
    GotoXY(1,1); Write(max);
    GotoXY(38,25); Write(num);
    for t:=1 to 19 do Plot(0,t*10,1);
    Draw(0,190,320,190,1);
    for t:=1 to num do
    begin
        a:=data[t]-min;
        a:=a*norm;
        y:=trunc(a);
        incr:=300 div num;
        x:=((t-1)*incr)+20;
        Draw(x,190,x,190-y,2);
    end;
    Read(ch);
    TextMode;
end; {BarPlot}
```

This version also prints hash marks along the Y-axis, which represent 1/20th of the difference between the minimum and maximum values. Figure 6-3 gives a sample of the output of **BarPlot** with 20 elements. By no means does **BarPlot** provide all of the features you may desire, but it will display a single sample accurately. You may find it easy to expand it to fit your needs.

Only a slight modification to **BarPlot** is required to make a procedure that plots a scatter graph. The major alteration changes the **Draw** function to one that plots only one point. This function is called **Plot**. Its general form is

$$\textbf{Plot}(x,y,color);$$

where x, y, and $color$ are integers. The function **ScatterPlot** is shown next.

```
procedure ScatterPlot(data:DataArray;num,ymin,ymax,xmax:integer);
var
    x,y,t,incr:integer;
    a,spRead,norm:real;

begin
    { first, find min and max value to enable normalization}
    if ymin>0 then ymin:=0;
    spread:=ymax-ymin;
    norm:=190/spread;
    GotoXY(1,25); Write(ymin);
    GotoXY(1,1); Write(ymax);
    GotoXY(38,25); Write(xmax);
    for t:=1 to 19 do Plot(0,t*10,1);
    Draw(0,190,320,190,1);
    for t:=1 to num do
    begin
        a:=data[t]-ymin;
        a:=a*norm;
        y:=trunc(a);
        incr:=300 div xmax;
        x:=((t-1)*incr)+20;
        Plot(x,190-y,2);
    end;
end; {ScatterPlot}
```

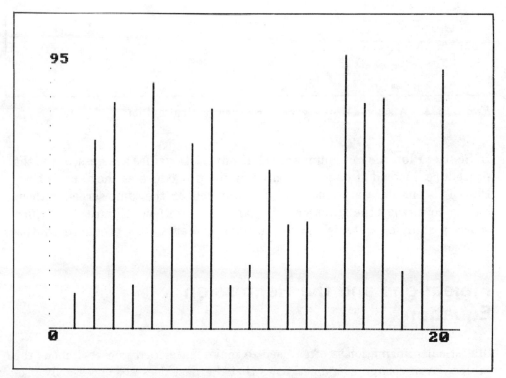

Figure 6-3.   A sample bar graph produced by **BarPlot**

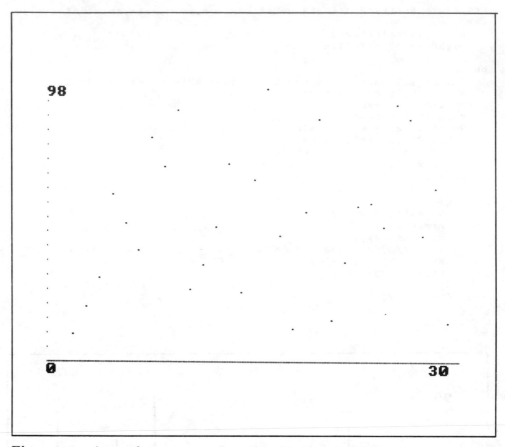

Figure 6-4.   A sample scatter graph produced by **ScatterPlot**

In **ScatterPlot**, the minimum and maximum data values are passed into the procedure, instead of being computed by the procedure as they are in **Bar-Plot**. This enables you to plot multiple data sets on the same screen without having to change the scale, creating an overlay effect. Figure 6-4, which shows a sample scatter graph of 30 data elements, was produced by this function.

Projections and the Regression Equation

Statistical information is often used to make "informed guesses" about the future. Even though everyone knows that the past does not necessarily predict the future and that there are exceptions to every rule, historical data is still used in this way. Very often, past and present trends do continue into the future. When they do, you can try to determine specific values at future points in time. This process is called making a *projection*, or *trend analysis*.

For example, consider a fictitious ten-year study of life spans, which collected the following data.

Year	Life Span
1970	69
1971	70
1972	72
1973	68
1974	73
1975	71
1976	75
1977	74
1978	78
1979	77

You might first ask yourself whether there is a trend here at all. If there is, you may want to know which way it is going. Finally, if there is indeed a trend, you might wonder what life expectancy will be in, say, 1985.

First look at the bar graph and scatter graph of this data, as shown in Figure 6-5. By examining these graphs, you can conclude that life spans are getting longer in general. Also, if you placed a ruler on the graphs to try to fit the data, and drew a line that extended into 1985, you could project that the 1985 life span would be about 82. However, while you might feel confident about your intuitive analysis, you would probably rather use a more formal and exact method to project life-span trends.

Given a set of historical data, the best way to make projections is to find the *line of best fit* in relation to the data. This is what you did with the ruler. A line of best fit most closely represents each point of the data and its trend. Although some or even all of the actual data points may not be on the line, the line best represents them. The validity of the line is based on how close the sample data points come.

A line in two-dimensional space has the basic equation

$$Y = a + bX$$

where Y is the independent variable, X is the dependent variable, a is the Y-intercept, and b is the slope of the line. Therefore, to find a line that best fits a sample, you must determine a and b.

Any number of methods can be used to determine the values of a and b, but the most common (and generally the best) is called the *method of least squares*. It attempts to minimize the distance between the actual data points and the line. The method involves two steps: the first step computes b, the slope of the line; the second finds a, the Y-intercept. To find b, use the formula

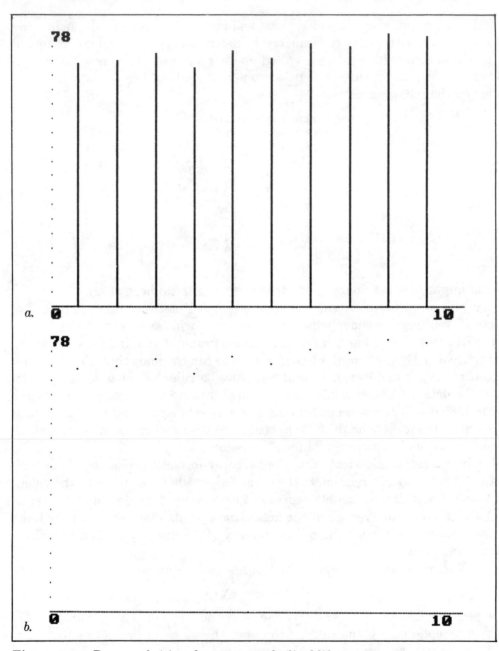

Figure 6-5. Bar graph (*a*) and scatter graph (*b*) of life expectancy

$$b = \frac{\sum\limits_{i=1}^{N} (X_i - M_x)(Y_i - M_y)}{\sum\limits_{i=1}^{N} (X_i - M_x)^2}$$

where M_x is the mean of the X coordinate and M_y is the mean of the Y coordinate. The derivation of this formula is beyond the scope of this book, but having found b, you can use it to compute a, as shown here:

$$a = M_y - bM_x$$

After you have calculated a and b, you can plug in any number for X and find the value of Y. For example, if you use the life-expectancy data, you find that the regression equation looks like this:

$$Y = 67.46 + 0.95 * X$$

Therefore, to find the life expectancy in 1985, which is 15 years from 1970, you will have

$$Life\ Expectancy = 67.46 + 0.95 * 15$$

$$\doteq 82$$

However, even with the line of best fit for the data, you may still want to know how well that line actually correlates with the data. If the line and data have only a slight correlation, then the regression line is of little use. However, if the line fits the data well, then it is a much more valid indicator. The most common way to determine and represent the correlation of the data to the regression line is to compute the *correlation coefficient*, which is a number between 0 and 1. The correlation coefficient is essentially a percentage that is related to the distance of each data point from the line. If the correlation coefficient is 1, then the data corresponds perfectly to the line; that is, each element of the sample is also on the regression line. A coefficient of 0 means that there are no points in the sample that are actually on the line—in fact, any line would be as good (or as bad) as the one used. The formula to find the correlation coefficient *cor* follows on the next page.

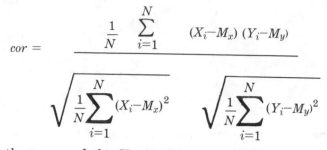

$$cor = \frac{\dfrac{1}{N} \sum_{i=1}^{N} (X_i - M_x)(Y_i - M_y)}{\sqrt{\dfrac{1}{N} \sum_{i=1}^{N} (X_i - M_x)^2} \ \sqrt{\dfrac{1}{N} \sum_{i=1}^{N} (Y_i - M_y)^2}}$$

Here M_x is the mean of the X coordinate and M_y is the mean of the Y coordinate. Generally, a value of 0.81 is considered a strong correlation. It indicates that about 66% of the data fits the regression line. To convert any correlation coefficient into a percentage, you simply square it.

Here is the function **Regress**. It uses the methods just described to find the regression equation and the coefficient of correlation, and it will also make a scatter plot of both the sample data and the line.

```
procedure Regress(data:DataArray;num:integer);
{compute the regression equation and the coefficient of
 correlation - then plot the data and regress line.}

var
    a,b,x_avg,y_avg,temp,temp2,cor:real;
    data2:DataArray;
    t,min,max:integer;
    ch:char;

begin
    {find Mean of y and y}
    y_avg:=0;   x_avg:=0;
    for t:=1 to num do
    begin
       y_avg:=y_avg+data[t];
       x_avg:=x_avg+t;    { because x is time}
    end;
    x_avg:=x_avg/num;
    y_avg:=y_avg/num;

    {find b factor in regress equation}
    temp:=0; temp2:=0;
    for t:=1 to num do
    begin
       temp:=temp+(data[t]-y_avg)*(t-x_avg);
       temp2:=temp2+(t-x_avg)*(t-x_avg);
    end;
    b:=temp/temp2;

    {find a in regress equation}
    a:=y_avg-(b*x_avg);

    {compute coefficent of correlation}
```

```
    for t:=1 to num do data2[t]:=t;   {copy data}
    cor:=temp/num;
    cor:=cor/(StdDev(data,num)*StdDev(data2,num));
    WriteLn('Regression equation is: Y = ',a:15:5,'+',b:15:5,'* X');
    WriteLn('Correlation Coefficient: ',cor:15:5);
    Write('Plot data and regression line? (y/n) ');
    Read(ch);WriteLn;
    ch:=UpCase(ch);
    if ch<>'N' then
    begin
        GraphColorMode;
        Palette(0);
        {do graphs}
        for t:=1 to num*2 do data2[t]:=a+(b*t);   {regression array}
        min:=GetMin(data,num)*2;
        max:=GetMax(data,num)*2;
        ScatterPlot(data,num,min,max,num*2);
        ScatterPlot(data2,num*2,min,max,num*2);
        Read;
        TextMode;
    end;

end; {Regress}
```

A scatter plot of both the sample data and the regression line is shown in Figure 6-6. The important point to remember while using projections like this is that the past does not necessarily predict the future—if it did, it wouldn't be fun!

Making a Complete Statistics Program

So far, this chapter has developed several functions that perform statistical calculations on single-variable populations. This section puts the functions together to form a complete program for analyzing data, printing bar graphs or scatter graphs, and making projections. Before you can design a complete program, you must define a record to hold the variable data information and a few necessary support routines.

First you need an array to hold the sample information. You can use a single-dimension, floating-point array called **data** of size MAX. MAX is defined so that it fits the largest sample you will need, which will be 100 in this case. The constant and type definitions and the global data are shown here:

```
program stats;

const
```

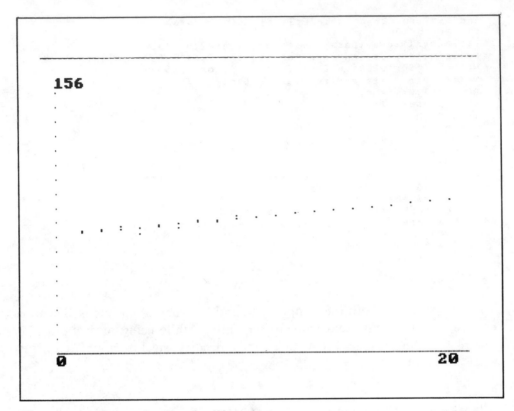

Figure 6-6. Regression line for life expectancy

```
    MAX = 100;

type
    str80 = string[80];
    DataItem = real;
    DataArray = array [1..MAX] of DataItem;
var
    data: DataArray;
    a,m,md,std:real;
    num:integer;
    ch:char;
    datafile: file of DataItem;
```

Besides the statistical functions developed already, you also need routines to save and load data. The **Save** routine must also store the number of data elements, and the **Load** routine must read back that number.

```
procedure Save(data:DataArray;num:integer);
var
    t:integer;
    fname:string[80];
    temp:real;
```

```
begin
   Write('enter filename: ');
   Read(fname); WriteLn;
   Assign(datafile,fname);
   Rewrite(datafile);
   temp:=num;    { change its type}
   Write(datafile,temp);
   for t:=1 to num do Write(datafile,data[t]);
   Close(datafile);
end; {Save}

procedure Load;
var
   t:integer;
   fname:string[80];
   temp:real;

begin
   Write('enter filename: ');
   Read(fname);WriteLn;
   Assign(datafile,fname);
   Reset(datafile);
   Read(datafile,temp);
   num:=trunc(temp);
   for t:=1 to num do Read(datafile,data[t]);
   Close(datafile);
end; {Load}
```

For your convenience, here is the entire statistics program:

```
program stats;

const
   MAX = 100;

type
   str80 = string[80];
   DataItem = real;
   DataArray = array [1..MAX] of DataItem;
var
   data: DataArray;
   a,m,md,std:real;
   num:integer;
   ch:char;
   datafile: file of DataItem;

procedure  QuickSort(var item: DataArray; count:integer);
   procedure qs(l,r:integer; var it:DataArray);
      var
      i,j: integer;
      x,y: DataItem;
      begin
         i:=l; j:=r;
         x:=it[(l+r) div 2];
         repeat
            while it[i] < x do i:= i+1;
            while x < it[j] do j:=j-1;
            if i<=j then
            begin
               y:=it[i];
```

```
                    it[i]:=it[j];
                    it[j]:=y;
                    i:=i+1; j:=j-1;
                end;
            until i>j;
            if l<j then qs(l,j,it);
            if l<r then qs(i,r,it)
        end;
begin
    qs(1,count,item);
end; { quick sort }

function IsIn(ch:char;s:str80):boolean;
var
    t:integer;

begin
    IsIn:=FALSE;
    for t:=1 to length(s) do
        if s[t]=ch then IsIn:=TRUE;
end;   {IsIn}



function Menu:char;
var
    ch:char;

begin
    WriteLn;
    repeat
        WriteLn('Enter data');
        WriteLn('Display data');
        WriteLn('Basic statistics');
        WriteLn('Regression line and scatter Plot');
        WriteLn('Plot a bar graph');
        WriteLn('Save');
        WriteLn('Load;');
        WriteLn('Quit');
        WriteLn;
        Write('choose one (E, D, B, k, P, S, L, D, Q): ');
        Read(ch); WriteLn;
        ch:=UpCase(ch);
    until IsIn(ch,'EBRPSLDQD');
    menu:=ch;
end; {Menu}

procedure Display(data:DataArray;num:integer);
var
    t:integer;

begin
    for t:=1 to num do WriteLn(t,': ',data[t]:15:5);
    WriteLn;
end;   {Display}

procedure Enter(var data:DataArray);
var
    t:integer;
```

```
begin
    Write('number of items?: ');
    Read(num); WriteLn;
    for t:=1 to num do begin
        Write('Enter item ',t,': ');
        Read(data[t]); WriteLn;
    end;
end;   {Enter}

function Mean(data:DataArray;num:integer):real;
var
    t:integer;
    avg:real;

begin
    avg:=0;
    for t:=1 to num do avg:=avg+data[t];
    Mean:=avg/num;
end;   {Mean}

function StdDev(data:DataArray;num:integer):real;
var
    t:integer;
    std,avg:real;

begin
    avg:=Mean(data,num);
    std:=0;
    for t:=1 to num do
        std:=std+((data[t]-avg)*(data[t]-avg));

    std:=std/num;
    StdDev:=Sqrt(std);
end;   {StdDev}

function FindMode(data:DataArray;num:integer):real;
var
    t,w,count,oldcount:integer;
    md,oldmd:real;

begin
    oldmd:=0; oldcount:=0;
    for t:=1 to num do
    begin
        md:=data[t];
        count:=1;
        for w:=t+1 to num do
            if md=data[w] then count:=count+1;
        if count>oldcount then
        begin
            oldmd:=md;
            oldcount:=count;
        end;
    end;
    FindMode:=oldmd;
end; {FindMode}


function Median(data:DataArray;num:integer):real;
```

```pascal
var
    dtemp:DataArray;
    t:integer;

begin
    for t:=1 to num do dtemp[t]:=data[t];    {copy data for sort}
    QuickSort(dtemp,num);
    Median:=dtemp[num div 2];    {middle element}
end; {Median}

function GetMax(data:DataArray;num:integer):integer;
var
    t:integer;
    max:real;

begin
    max:=data[1];
    for t:=2 to num do
        if data[t]>max then max:=data[t];
    GetMax:=trunc(max);
end;    {GetMax}

function GetMin(data:DataArray;num:integer):integer;
var
    t:integer;
    min:real;

begin
    min:=data[1];
    for t:=2 to num do
        if data[t]<min then min:=data[t];
    GetMin:=trunc(min);
end;    {GetMin}


procedure BarPlot(data:DataArray;num:integer);
{Plots a bar graph of data using IBM PC graphics.}
var
    x,y,max,min,incr,t:integer;
    a, norm,spread:real;
    ch:char;

begin
    GraphColorMode;
    Palette(0);
    { first, find min and max value to enable normalization}
    max:=GetMax(data,num);
    min:=GetMin(data,num);
    if min>0 then min:=0;
    spread:=max-min;
    norm:=190/spread;
    GotoXY(1,25); Write(min);
    GotoXY(1,1); Write(max);
    GotoXY(38,25); Write(num);
    for t:=1 to 19 do Plot(0,t*10,1);
    Draw(0,190,320,190,1);
    for t:=1 to num do
    begin
        a:=data[t]-min;
        a:=a*norm;
        y:=trunc(a);
```

```
    incr:=300 div num;
    x:=((t-1)*incr)+20;
    Draw(x,190,x,190-y,2);
end;
Read(ch);
TextMode;
end; {BarPlot}

procedure ScatterPlot(data:DataArray;num,ymin,ymax,xmax:integer);
var
    x,y,t,incr:integer;
    a,spread,norm:real;

begin
    { first, find min and max value to enable normalization}
    if ymin>0 then ymin:=0;
    spread:=ymax-ymin;
    norm:=190/spread;
    GotoXY(1,25); Write(ymin);
    GotoXY(1,1); Write(ymax);
    GotoXY(38,25); Write(xmax);
    for t:=1 to 19 do Plot(0,t*10,1);
    Draw(0,190,320,190,1);
    for t:=1 to num do begin
        a:=data[t]-ymin;
        a:=a*norm;
        y:=trunc(a);
        incr:=300 div xmax;
        x:-((t-1)*incr)+20;
        Plot(x,190-y,2);
    end;
end; {ScatterPlot}

procedure Regress(data:DataArray;num:integer);
{compute the regression equation and the coefficient of
 correlation - then Plot the data and regress line.}

var
    a,b,x_avg,y_avg,temp,temp2,cor:real;
    data2:DataArray;
    t,min,max:integer;
    ch:char;

begin
    {find Mean of y and y}
    y_avg:=0;  x_avg:=0;
    for t:=1 to num do
    begin
        y_avg:=y_avg+data[t];
        x_avg:=x_avg+t;    { because x is time}
    end;
    x_avg:=x_avg/num;
    y_avg:=y_avg/num;

    {find b fact in regress equation}
    temp:=0;  temp2:=0;
    for t:=1 to num do
    begin
        temp:=temp+(data[t]-y_avg)*(t-x_avg);
        temp2:=temp2+(t-x_avg)*(t-x_avg);
    end;
```

```
    b:=temp/temp2;

    {find a in regression equation}
    a:=y_avg-(b*x_avg);

    {compute coefficent of correlation}
    for t:=1 to num do data2[t]:=t;   {copy data}
    cor:=temp/num;
    cor:=cor/(StdDev(data,num)*StdDev(data2,num));
    WriteLn('Regression equation is: Y = ',a:15:5,'+',b:15:5,'* X');
    WriteLn('Correlation Coefficient: ',cor:15:5);
    Write('Plot data and regression line? (y/n) ');
    Read(ch);WriteLn;
    ch:=UpCase(ch);
    if ch<>'N' then begin
        GraphColorMode;
        Palette(0);
        {do graphs}
        for t:=1 to num*2 do data2[t]:=a+(b*t);   {regression array}
        min:=GetMin(data,num)*2;
        max:=GetMax(data,num)*2;
        ScatterPlot(data,num,min,max,num*2);
        ScatterPlot(data2,num*2,min,max,num*2);
        Read;
        TextMode;
    end;
end; {regress}

procedure Save(data:DataArray;num:integer);
var
    t:integer;
    fname:string[80];
    temp:real;
begin
    Write('Enter filename: ');
    Read(fname); WriteLn;
    Assign(datafile,fname);
    Rewrite(datafile);
    temp:=num;   { change its type}
    Write(datafile,temp);
    for t:=1 to num do Write(datafile,data[t]);
    Close(datafile);
end; {save}

procedure Load;
var
    t:integer;
    fname:string[80];
    temp:real;

begin
    Write('Enter filename: ');
    Read(fname);WriteLn;
    Assign(datafile,fname);
    Reset(datafile);
    Read(datafile,temp);
    num:=trunc(temp);
    for t:=1 to num do Read(datafile,data[t]);
    Close(datafile);
end; {Load;}
```

```
begin
   repeat
      ch:=UpCase(menu);
      case ch of
         'E': Enter(data);
         'B': begin
                 a:=Mean(data,num);
                 m:=Median(data,num);
                 std:=StdDev(data,num);
                 md:=FindMode(data,num);
                 WriteLn('Mean: ',a:15:5);
                 WriteLn('Median: ',m:15:5);
                 WriteLn('standard deviation: ',std:15:5);
                 WriteLn('mode: ',md:15:5);
                 WriteLn;
              end;
         'D': Display(data,num);
         'P': BarPlot(data,num);
         'R': Regress(data,num);
         'S': Save(data,num);
         'L': Load;
      end;
   until ch='Q';
end.
```

Using the Statistics Program

To give you an idea of how you can use the statistics program developed in this chapter, here is a simple stock-market analysis for Widget, Incorporated. As an investor, you will be trying to decide if it is a good time to invest in Widget by buying stock; if you should sell *short* (selling shares you do not have in the hope of a rapid price drop so that you can buy them later at a cheaper price); or if you should invest elsewhere.

Here is Widget's stock price for the past 24 months:

Month	Stock Price ($)
1	10
2	10
3	11
4	9
5	8
6	8
7	9
8	10
9	10
10	13
11	11
12	11
13	11
14	11

Month	Stock Price ($),
15	12
16	13
17	14
18	16
19	17
20	15
21	15
22	16
23	14
24	16

You should first find out if Widget's stock price has established a trend. After entering the figures, you find the following basic statistics:

Mean: 12.08
Median: 11

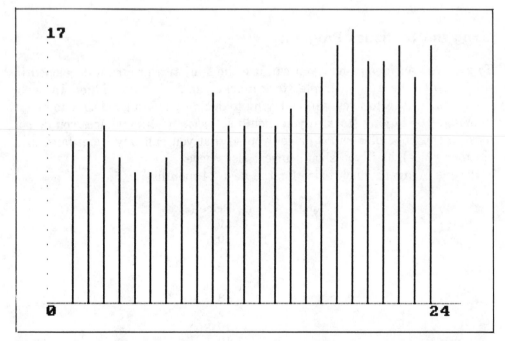

Figure 6-7. Graphs and statistical information on Widget's profits over the last 24 months

Standard deviation: 2.68
Mode: 11

Next you should plot a bar graph of the stock price, as shown in Figure 6-7. There may be a trend, but you should perform a formal regression analysis. The regression equation is

$$Y = 7.90 + 0.33 * X$$

with a correlation coefficient of 0.86, or about 74%. This is quite good — in fact, a definite trend is clear. Printing a scatter graph, as shown in Figure 6-8, makes this string growth readily apparent. Such results could cause an investor to throw caution to the wind and buy 1000 shares as quickly as possible.

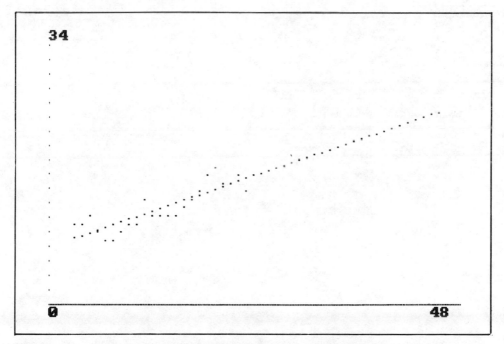

Figure 6-8. A scatter graph showing the growth of Widget, Incorporated

Final Thoughts

The correct application of statistical analysis requires a general understanding of how the results are derived and what they mean. As with the Widget example, it is easy to forget that past events cannot account for circumstances that can radically affect the final outcome. Blind reliance on statistical evidence can cause some very disturbing results. Statistics are used to reflect nature—but nature cannot be expected to reflect statistics.

SEVEN

Encryption and Data Compression

People who like computers and programming often like to play with codes and ciphers. Perhaps the reason for this is that all codes involve algorithms, just as programs do. Or perhaps these people simply have an affinity for cryptic things that most people cannot understand. All programmers seem to receive a great deal of satisfaction when a nonprogrammer looks at a program listing and says something like, "My God, that sure looks complicated!" After all, the act of writing a program is called "coding."

Closely associated with the topic of cryptography is *data compression.* Data compression means compacting information into a smaller space than is usually used. Because data compression can play a role in encryption and uses many of the same principles as encryption, it is included in this chapter.

Computer-based cryptography is important for two primary reasons. The most obvious is the need to keep sensitive data on shared systems secure. Although password protection is adequate for many situations, important, confidential files are routinely coded to provide a higher level of protection. The second use of computer-based codes is in data transmission. Not only are codes used for such matters as secret government information; they are also used by broadcasters to protect sky-to-earth station transmissions. Because these types of coding procedures are so complex, they are usually done by computer.

Data compression is commonly used to increase the storage capacity of various storage devices. Although the cost of storage devices has fallen sharply in the past few years, there can still be a need to fit more information into smaller areas.

A Short History of Cryptography

Although no one knows when secret writing began, a cuneiform tablet made around 1500 B.C. contains one of the earliest known examples. It contains a coded formula for making pottery glaze. The Greeks used codes as early as 475 B.C., and the upper class in Rome frequently used simple ciphers during the reign of Julius Caesar. During the Dark Ages, interest in cryptography (as well as many other intellectual pursuits) decreased, except among monks who occasionally used it. With the birth of the Italian Renaissance, the art of cryptography again flourished. By the time of Louis XIV of France, a code based on 587 randomly selected keys was used for government messages.

In the 1800s, two factors helped move cryptography forward. The first was Edgar Allan Poe's stories, such as "The Gold Bug," which featured coded messages and excited the imagination of many readers. The second was the invention of the telegraph and Morse code. Morse code was the first binary representation (dots and dashes) of the alphabet that received wide use.

By World War I, several nations had constructed mechanical "code machines" that permitted easy encoding and decoding of text by using sophisticated, complex ciphers. The story of cryptography changes slightly at this point to the story of code-breaking.

Before mechanical devices were used to encode and decode messages, complex ciphers were not frequently employed because of the time and effort required both for encoding and decoding. Hence, most codes could be broken within a relatively short period of time. However, the art of code-breaking became much more difficult when the code machines were used. Although modern computers would have made even those codes fairly easy to break, even computers cannot dwarf the incredible talent of Herbert Yardley, still considered the master code-breaker of all time. He not only broke the U.S. diplomatic code in 1915 in his spare time, but he also broke the Japanese diplomatic code in 1922—even though he did not know Japanese! He accomplished this by using frequency tables of the Japanese language.

By World War II, the major method used to break codes was to steal the enemy's code machine, thereby avoiding the tedious (if intellectually satisfying) process of code-breaking. In fact, the Allies' possession of a German code machine (unknown to the Germans) contributed greatly to the outcome of the war.

With the advent of computers—especially multiuser computers—the need for secure and unbreakable codes has become even more important. Not only do computer files occasionally need to be kept secret, but access to the computer itself must also be managed and regulated. Numerous methods of encrypting data files have been developed, and the DES (Data Encryption

Standard) algorithm, accepted by the National Bureau of Standards, is generally considered to be secure from code-breaking efforts. However, DES is very difficult to implement and may not be suitable for all situations.

Types of Ciphers

Of the more traditional coding methods, there are two basic types: *substitution* and *transposition*. A substitution cipher replaces one character with another, but leaves the message in the proper order. A transposition cipher scrambles the characters of a message according to some rule. These types of codes can be used at whatever level of complexity is desired, and they can even be intermixed. The digital computer adds a third basic encryption technique, called *bit manipulation*, that alters the computerized representation of data by some algorithm.

All three methods may make use of a *key*. A key is a string of characters needed to decode a message. Do not confuse the key with the method, however, because knowing the key is not enough to decode a message—the encryption algorithm must also be known. The key "personalizes" a coded message so that only those people who know the key can decode it, even though the method used to encode the message may be accessible.

Two terms that you should become familiar with are *plaintext* and *ciphertext*. The plaintext of a message is text you can read; the ciphertext is the encoded version.

This chapter presents computerized methods that use each of the three basic methods to code text files. You will see several short programs that encode and decode text files. With one exception, all of these programs have both a **code** and a **decode** function: the **decode** function always reverses the **code** process used to create the ciphertext. For the sake of simplicity, all letters in a message shown in the examples of this chapter are coded and decoded into uppercase.

Substitution Ciphers

One of the simplest substitution ciphers offsets the alphabet by a specified amount. For example, if each letter were offset by three, then

abcdefghijklmnopqrstuvwxyz

would become

defghijklmnopqrstuvwxyzabc

Notice that the letters *abc* were shifted off the front and were added to the end. To encode a message by using this method, you simply substitute the shifted alphabet for the real one. For example, the message

meet me at sunset

becomes

phhw ph dw vxqvhw

The program shown here enables you to code any text message by using any offset that you choose:

```
program subs1;  {A simple substitution cipher }
type
    str80 = string[80];

var
    inf,outf:str80;
    start:integer;
    ch:char;

procedure Code(inf,outf:str80;start:integer);
var
    infile,outfile:file of char;
    ch:char;
    t:integer;

begin
    Assign(infile, inf);
    Reset(infile);
    Assign(outfile,outf);
    Rewrite(outfile);

    while not EOF(infile) do
    begin
        read(infile,ch);
        ch:=UpCase(ch);
        if (ch>='A') and (ch<='Z') then
        begin
            t:=Ord(ch)+start;
            if t>Ord('Z') then t:=t-26; {wrap around}
            ch:=Chr(t);
        end;
        Write(outfile,ch);
    end;
    WriteLn('file coded');
    Close(infile); Close(outfile);
end;  {Code}

procedure Decode(inf,outf:str80;start:integer);
var
    infile,outfile:file of char;
    ch:char;
    t:integer;
```

```
begin
   Assign(infile, inf);
   Reset(infile);
   Assign(outfile,outf);
   ReWrite(outfile);

   while not EOF(infile) do
   begin
      read(infile,ch);
      ch:=UpCase(ch);
      if (ch>='A') and (ch<='Z') then
      begin
         t:=Ord(ch)-start;
         if t<Ord('A') then t:=t+26; {wrap around}
         ch:=Chr(t);
      end;
      Write(outfile,ch);
   end;
   WriteLn('file decoded');
   Close(infile); Close(outfile);
end;  {Decode}

begin
   Write('enter input file: ');
   ReadLn(inf);
   Write('enter output file: ');
   ReadLn(outf);
   Write('starting position (1-26): ');
   ReadLn(start);
   Write('Code or Decode (C or D): ');
   ReadLn(ch);
   if UpCase(ch)='C' then Code(inf,outf,start)
   else if UpCase(ch)='D' then Decode(inf,outf,start)
end.
```

Although a substitution cipher based on a constant offset will generally fool grade-schoolers, it is not suitable for most purposes because it is too easy to crack. After all, there are only 26 possible offsets, and it is easy to try all of them within a short period of time. An improvement on the substitution cipher is to use a scrambled alphabet instead of a simple offset.

A second failing of the simple substitution cipher is that it preserves the spaces between words, which makes it easier for code-breakers to crack. Another improvement would be to encode spaces. (Actually, all punctuation should be encoded, but for simplicity the examples will not do this.) For instance, you could map this random string containing every letter of the alphabet and a space

abcdefghijklmnopqrstuvwxyz<space>

onto this string:

qazwsxedcrfvtgbyhnujm ikolp

You may wonder if there is a significant improvement in the security of a message encoded by using a randomized version of the alphabet compared to the use of a simple offset version. The answer is yes—because there are 26 factorial (26!) ways to arrange the alphabet; with the space, that number becomes 27 factorial (27!) ways. The factorial of a number is that number times every whole number smaller than it, down to 1. For example, 6! is 6*5*4*3*2*1, which equals 720. Therefore, 26! is a very large number.

The program shown here is an improved substitution cipher that uses the randomized alphabet shown earlier. If you encoded the message

meet me at sunset

by using the improved substitution cipher program, it would look like

tssjptspqjpumgusj

which is definitely a harder code to break.

```
program subs2;   {Improved substitution cipher}
type
    str80 = string[80];

var
    inf,outf:str80;
    alphabet,sub:str80;
    start:integer;
    ch:char;

function Find(alphabet:str80;ch:char):integer;
{this function returns the index into the alphabet}
var
    t:integer;

begin
    Find:=-1;   {error Code}
    for t:=1 to 27 do if ch=alphabet[t] then Find:=t;
end;   {Find}

function IsAlpha(ch:char):boolean;
{returns TRUE if ch is a letter of the alphabet}
begin
     IsAlpha:= (UpCase(ch)>='A') and (UpCase(ch)<='Z');
end;   { IsAlpha }

procedure Code(inf,outf:str80);
var
    infile,outfile:file of char;
    ch:char;

begin
    Assign(infile, inf);
    Reset(infile);
    Assign(outfile,outf);
    ReWrite(outfile);
```

```
    while not EOF(infile) do
    begin
        Read(infile,ch);
        ch:=UpCase(ch);
        if IsAlpha(ch) or (ch=' ') then
        begin
            ch:=sub[Find(alphabet,ch)]; {Find substitution}
        end;
        Write(outfile,ch);
    end;
    WriteLn('file coded');
    Close(infile); Close(outfile);
end; {Code}


procedure Decode(inf,outf:str80);
var
    infile,outfile:file of char;
    ch:char;

begin
    Assign(infile, inf);
    Reset(infile);
    Assign(outfile,outf);
    ReWrite(outfile);

    while not EOF(infile) do begin
        Read(infile,ch);
        ch:=UpCase(ch);
        if IsAlpha(ch) or (ch=' ') then
        begin
            ch:=alphabet[Find(sub,ch)]; {replace with real
                                         alphabet again}
        end;
        Write(outfile,ch);
    end;
    WriteLn('file decoded');
    Close(infile); Close(outfile);
end; {Decode}


begin
    alphabet:='ABCDEFGHIJKLMNOPQRSTUVWXYZ ';
    sub      :='QAZWSXEDCRFVTGBYHNUJM IKOLP'; {substitution alphabet
    Write('enter input file: ');
    ReadLn(inf);
    Write('enter output file: ');
    ReadLn(outf);
    Write('Code or Decode (C or D): ');
    ReadLn(ch);
    if UpCase(ch)='C' then Code(inf,outf)
    else if UpCase(ch)='D' then Decode(inf,outf);
end.
```

Although code-breaking is examined later in this chapter, you should know that even this improved substitution code can still be broken easily by using a *frequency table* of the English language, in which the statistical information the use of each letter of the alphabet is recorded. (This type of substitution is used in the "cryptograms" next to the crossword puzzle given in many newspapers.) As you can easily see when you look at the coded message, "s" almost certainly has to be "e," the most common letter in the English language, and "p" must be a space. The rest of the message can be decoded with a little time and effort.

The larger a coded message is, the easier it is to crack with a frequency table. To impede the progress of a code-breaker who is applying frequency tables to a coded message, you can use a *multiple substitution cipher*. The same letter in the plaintext message will not necessarily have the same letter in the coded form. A multiple substitution cipher is made by adding a second randomized alphabet and switching between it and the first alphabet each time a letter is repeated. For the second string, use

poi uytrewqasdfghjklmnbvcxz

The program shown here will switch randomized alphabets after a letter is repeated twice. If you use it to code the message

meet me at sunset

this coded form will result:

tsslzsspplpumguuj

To see how this works, set up the ordered alphabet and the two randomized alphabets (called **sub** and **sub2**) over one another, as shown here:

alphabet: abcdefghijklmnopqrstuvwxyz<space>
     sub: qazwsxedcrfvtgbyhnujm ikolp
    sub2:   poi uytrewqasdfghjklmnbvcxz

When the program starts, the first random alphabet is used. The first letter in the message is "m," which corresponds to "t" in **sub**, and the "m" position in the array **count** is incremented to 1. The next letter is "e," and it becomes "s"; and the "e" position in the **count** array is incremented to 1. Then the second "e" in "meet" is encountered; at this time **sub** is still used to translate it, so it too becomes "s" and the "e" position in **count** is incremented to 2. This causes the program to change to the **sub2** alphabet and to zero the "e" position in the **count** array. The "t" in "meet" then becomes "l" and the space becomes "z." Then the "m" in "me" is encountered. After it is translated to "s," the **sub** alphabet is switched in, because a repeated letter has been encountered. This process of alternating alphabets continues until the message ends.

Here is a program that will create a multiple substitution cipher:

```
program subs3;   {Multiple substitution cipher}
type
    str80 = string[80];

var
    inf,outf:str80;
    alphabet,sub,sub2:str80;
    start,t:integer;
    ch:char;
    count:array[1..27] of integer;

function Find(alphabet:str80;ch:char):integer;
{this function returns the index into the alphabet}
var
    t:integer;

begin
    Find:=-1;   {error Code}
    for t:=1 to 27 do if ch=alphabet[t] then Find:=t;
end;   {Find}

function IsAlpha(ch:char):boolean;
{returns TRUE if ch is a letter of the alphabet}
begin
    IsAlpha:= (UpCase(ch)>='A') and (UpCase(ch)<='Z');
end;   { IsAlpha }

function Index(ch:char):integer;
begin
    if IsAlpha(ch) then Index:=Ord(UpCase(ch))-Ord('A')+1
    else Index:=27;   {the space on the end}
end; {Index}

procedure Code(inf,outf:str80);
var
    infile,outfile:file of char;
    ch:char;
    change:boolean;

begin
    Assign(infile, inf);
    Reset(infile);
    Assign(outfile,outf);
    ReWrite(outfile);

    change:=TRUE;
    while not EOF(infile) do
    begin
        Read(infile,ch);
        ch:=UpCase(ch);
        if IsAlpha(ch) or (ch=' ') then
        begin
        if change then
        begin
            ch:=sub[Find(alphabet,ch)]; {Find substitution}
            count[Index(ch)]:=count[Index(ch)]+1;
        end
        else
```

```pascal
        begin
            ch:=sub2[Find(alphabet,ch)]; {second sub}
            count[Index(ch)]:=count[Index(ch)]+1;
        end
    end;
    Write(outfile,ch);
    if count[Index(ch)]=2 then
    begin
        change:=not change;
        count[Index(ch)]:=0;
    end;
end;
WriteLn('file coded');
Close(infile); Close(outfile);
end; {Code}

procedure Decode(inf,outf:str80);
var
    infile,outfile:file of char;
    ch:char;
    change:boolean;

begin
    Assign(infile, inf);
    Reset(infile);
    Assign(outfile,outf);
    ReWrite(outfile);

    change:=TRUE;
    while not EOF(infile) do
    begin
        Read(infile,ch);
        ch:=UpCase(ch);
        if IsAlpha(ch) or (ch=' ') then
        begin
            if change then
            begin
                ch:=alphabet[Find(sub,ch)]; {Find substitution}
                count[Index(ch)]:=count[Index(ch)]+1;
            end
            else
            begin
                ch:=alphabet[Find(sub2,ch)]; {second sub}
                count[Index(ch)]:=count[Index(ch)]+1;
            end
        end;
        Write(outfile,ch);
        if count[Index(ch)]=2 then
        begin
            change:=not change;
            count[Index(ch)]:=0;
        end;
    end;
    WriteLn('file coded');
    Close(infile); Close(outfile);
end; {Decode}


begin
    alphabet:='ABCDEFGHIJKLMNOPQRSTUVWXYZ ';
    sub     :='QAZWSXEDCRFVTGBYHNUJM IKOLP'; {substitution alphabet}
```

```
   sub2    :='POI UYTREWQASDFGHJKLMNBVCXZ'; {substitution #2}
   for t:=1 to 27 do count[t]:=0; {init count array}
   Write('enter input file: ');
   ReadLn(inf);
   Write('enter output file: ');
   ReadLn(outf);
   Write('Code or Decode (C or D): ');
   ReadLn(ch);
   if UpCase(ch)='C' then Code(inf,outf)
   else if UpCase(ch)='D' then Decode(inf,outf);
end.
```

The use of multiple substitution ciphers makes it much more difficult to break a code by using frequency tables, because at different times different letters stand for the same thing. If you think about it, it would be possible to use several different randomized alphabets and a more complex switching routine to have all letters in the coded text occur with equal frequency. In this case, a frequency table would be useless in breaking the code.

Transposition Ciphers

One of the earliest-known uses of transposition codes was designed by the Spartans around 475 B.C. It used a device called a *skytale*, which is basically a strap that is wrapped around a cylinder, upon which a message is written crossways. The strap is then unwound and delivered to the recipient of the message, who also has a cylinder of equal size. Theoretically, it is impossible to read the strap without the cylinder, because the letters are out of order. In actual practice, however, this method leaves something to be desired because different-sized cylinders can be tried until the message begins to make sense.

You can create a computerized version of a skytale by placing the plain-text message into an array a certain way and writing it out a different way. To do this, a one-dimensional string is used to hold the message to be encoded, but the message is written to the disk file as a two-dimensional array. For this version, the plaintext, one-dimensional array is 100 bytes long and is written to disk as a 5×20 two-dimensional array. However, you could use any dimensions you wanted. Because a fixed-size array holds the message, it is likely that not every element of the array will be used. This makes it necessary to initialize the array before placing the plaintext into it. In actual practice, it is best to initialize the array with random characters; however, for simplicity, the # sign is used—but any other character would do.

If you placed the message

meet me at sunset

into the array **skytale** and viewed it as the two-dimensional array, it would look like this:

m	e	e	t	
m	e		a	t
	s	u	n	s
e	t	#	#	#
#	#	#	#	#

⋮

Then, if you wrote the array out by column, the message would look like this:

mm e...eest...e u...tan... ts...

where the periods indicate the appropriate number of # signs. To decode the message, columns are fed into **skytale**. Then the array **skytale** can be displayed in normal order. The "Skytale" program uses this method to code and decode messages.

```pascal
program skytale;  {skytale cipher}
{The largest message that can be coded is 100 characters}
type
    str100 = string[100];
    str80 = string[80];

var
    inf,outf:str80;
    skytale: str100;
    t:integer;
    ch:char;

function IsAlpha(ch:char):boolean;
{returns TRUE if ch is a letter of the alphabet}
begin
     IsAlpha:= (UpCase(ch)>='A') and (UpCase(ch)<='Z');
end;  { IsAlpha }

procedure Code(inf,outf:str80);
{Read in text file, output 2-dimensional array}
var
    infile,outfile:file of char;
    ch:char;
    t,t2:integer;

begin
    Assign(infile, inf);
```

```
    Reset(infile);
    Assign(outfile,outf);
    ReWrite(outfile);

    t:=1;
    while (not EOF(infile)) and (t<=100) do
    begin
        Read(infile,skytale[t]);
        t:=t+1;
    end;

    {now Write out the array as 5x20 2-dimensional}
    for t:=1 to 5  do
        for t2:=0 to 19 do
            Write(outfile,skytale[t+(t2*5)]);
    WriteLn('file coded');
    Close(infile); Close(outfile);
end; {Code}

procedure Decode(inf,outf:str80);
{Read in as 5x20 2-dimensional - output as 1-dimensional}
var
    infile,outfile:file of char;
    ch:char;
    t,t2:integer;

begin
    Assign(infile, inf);
    Reset(infile);
    Assign(outfile,outf);
    ReWrite(outfile);

    for t:=1 to 5 do
        for t2:=0 to 19 do
            Read(infile,skytale[t+(t2*5)]);

    {Write out normally}
    for t:=1 to 100 do Write(outfile,skytale[t]);

    WriteLn('file decoded');
    Close(infile); Close(outfile);
end; {Decode}


begin
    for t:=1 to 100 do skytale[t]:='#';
    Write('enter input file: ');
    ReadLn(inf);
    Write('enter output file: ');
    ReadLn(outf);
    Write('Code or Decode (C or D): ');
    ReadLn(ch);
    if UpCase(ch)='C' then Code(inf,outf)
    else if UpCase(ch)='D' then Decode(inf,outf);
end.
```

There are other methods of obtaining transposed messages. One method particularly suited for computer use swaps letters within the message as defined by some algorithm. For example, a program that transposes letters follows on the next page.

```
program transpose;   {transposition cipher}
{Up to 100 character messages may be coded.}
type
   str100 = string[100];
   str80 = string[80];

var
   inf,outf:str80;
   message: str100;
   ch:char;
   t:integer;

procedure Code(inf,outf:str80);
var
   infile,outfile:file of char;
   temp:char;
   t,t2:integer;

begin
   Assign(infile, inf);
   Reset(infile);
   Assign(outfile,outf);
   ReWrite(outfile);

   t:=1;
   while (not EOF(infile)) and (t<=100) do
   begin
      Read(infile,message[t]);
      t:=t+1;
   end;
   message[t-1]:='#';  {remove EOF}

   {now, transpose the characters}
   for t2:=0 to 4 do
       for t:=1 to 10 do
       begin
           temp:=message[t+t2*20];
           message[t+t2*20]:=message[t+10+t2*20];
           message[t+10+t2*20]:=temp;
       end;

   {now Write it out}
   for t:=1 to 100 do  Write(outfile, message[t]);

   WriteLn('file coded');
   Close(infile); Close(outfile);
end; {Code}

procedure Decode(inf,outf:str80);
var
   infile,outfile:file of char;
   temp:char;
   t,t2:integer;
   begin
       Assign(infile, inf);
       Reset(infile);
       Assign(outfile,outf);
       ReWrite(outfile);

       t:=1;
       while (not EOF(infile)) and (t<=100) do
```

```
begin
    Read(infile,message[t]);
    t:=t+1;
end;
message[t-1]:='#';  {remove EOF}

{now, transpose the characters}
for t2:=0 to 4 do
    for t:=1 to 10 do
    begin
        temp:=message[t+t2*20];
        message[t+t2*20]:=message[t+10+t2*20];
        message[t+10+t2*20]:=temp;
    end;

{now Write it out}
for t:=1 to 100 do Write(outfile, message[t]);

WriteLn('file decoded');
Close(infile); Close(outfile);
end; {Decode}

begin
    for t:=1 to 100 do message[t]:='#';
    Write('enter input file: ');
    ReadLn(inf);
    Write('enter output file: ');
    ReadLn(outf);
    Write('Code or Decode (C or D): ');
    ReadLn(ch);
    if UpCase(ch)='C' then Code(inf,outf)
    else if UpCase(ch)='D' then Decode(inf,outf);
end.
```

Although transposition codes can be effective, the algorithms become very complex if a high degree of security is needed.

Bit-Manipulation Ciphers

The digital computer has given rise to a new method of encoding through the manipulation of the bits that compose the actual characters of the plaintext. Although the real purist would claim that *bit manipulation* (or *alteration*, as it is sometimes called) is really just a variation of the substitution cipher, the concepts, methods, and options differ so significantly that it must be considered a cipher method in its own right.

Bit-manipulation ciphers are well-suited for computer use because they employ operations easily performed by the system. Also, the ciphertext tends to look completely unintelligible, which adds to security by making the data look like unused or crashed files, thereby confusing anyone who tries to gain access to the file.

Generally, bit-manipulation ciphers are only applicable to computer-based files and cannot be used to create hardcopy messages because the bit manipulations tend to produce nonprinting characters. For this reason, you should assume that any file coded by bit-manipulation methods will remain in a computer file.

Bit-manipulation ciphers convert plaintext into ciphertext by altering the actual bit pattern of each character through the use of one or more of the following logical operators:

AND
OR
NOT
XOR

Turbo Pascal is one of the best languages for creating bit-manipulation ciphers because it supports these operators for use on **byte** data types. When these operators are applied to **byte** variables, the operations occur on a bit-by-bit basis, making it easy to alter the state of bits within a byte.

The simplest and least-secure bit-manipulation cipher, uses only NOT, the 1's complement operator. (Remember that the **NOT** operator causes each bit within a byte to be inverted: a 1 becomes a 0 and a 0 becomes a 1.) Therefore, a byte complemented twice is the same as the original. The following program, called Complement, codes any text file by inverting the bits within each character. Because of Turbo Pascal's strong type-checking, the program must use **byte** variables instead of **char** variables, so that the bit-manipulation operators can be used.

```
program complement;   {1's complement cipher}
type
   str80 = string[80];

var
   inf,outf:str80;
   ch:char;
   t:integer;

procedure Code(inf,outf:str80);
var
   infile,outfile:file of byte;
   ch:byte;

begin
   Assign(infile, inf);
   Reset(infile);
   Assign(outfile,outf);
   ReWrite(outfile);

   while not EOF(infile) do
   begin
      Read(infile,ch);
      ch:=not ch;
```

```
      Write(outfile,ch);
   end;

   WriteLn('file coded');
   Close(infile); Close(outfile);
end; {Code}

procedure Decode(inf,outf:str80);
var
   infile,outfile:file of byte;
   ch:byte;

begin
   Assign(infile, inf);
   Reset(infile);
   Assign(outfile,outf);
   ReWrite(outfile);

   while not EOF(infile) do
   begin
      Read(infile,ch);
      ch:=not ch;
      Write(outfile,ch);
   end;

   WriteLn('file decoded');
   Close(infile); Close(outfile);
end; {Decode}
begin
   Write('enter input file: ');
   ReadLn(inf);
   Write('enter output file: ');
   ReadLn(outf);
   Write('Code or Decode (C or D): ');
   ReadLn(ch);
   if UpCase(ch)='C' then Code(inf,outf)
   else if UpCase(ch)='D' then Decode(inf,outf);
end.
```

It is difficult to show what the cipher text of a message would look like, because the bit manipulation used here generally creates nonprinting characters. Try it on your computer and examine the file—it will look quite cryptic.

There are two problems with this simple coding scheme. First, the encryption program does not use a key to decode, so anyone with access to the program can decode an encoded file. Second, and perhaps more importantly, this method would be easily spotted by any experienced computer programmer.

An improved method of bit-manipulation coding uses the **XOR** operator. The **XOR** operator has the following truth table:

XOR	0	1
0	0	1
1	1	0

The outcome of the **XOR** operation is TRUE if and only if one operand is TRUE and the other is FALSE. This gives the **XOR** a unique property: if you **XOR** a byte with another byte called the *key*, and then take the outcome of that operation and **XOR** it again with the key, the result will be the original byte, as show here:

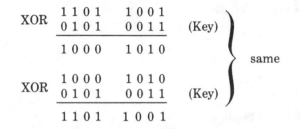

When used to code a file, this process solves the two inherent problems of the method that uses 1's complement. First of all, because it uses a key, the encryption program alone cannot decode a file; second, because using a key makes each file unique, what has been done to the file is not obvious to someone schooled only in computer science.

The key does not have to be just one byte long. For example, you could use a key of several characters and alternate the characters through the file. However, a single-character key is used here to keep the program uncluttered.

```pascal
program XorWithKey;  {xor with key for security}
type
    str80 = string[80];

var
    inf,outf:str80;
    ch:char;
    key:byte;
    t:integer;


procedure Code(inf,outf:str80;key:byte);
var
    infile,outfile:file of byte;
    ch:byte;

begin
    Assign(infile, inf);
    Reset(infile);
    Assign(outfile,outf);
    ReWrite(outfile);

    while not EOF(infile) do
    begin
        Read(infile,ch);
        ch:=key xor ch;
        Write(outfile,ch);
    end;

    WriteLn('file coded');
```

```
      Close(infile); Close(outfile);
end; {Code}

procedure Decode(inf,outf:str80;key:byte);
var
   infile,outfile:file of byte;
   ch:byte;

begin
   Assign(infile, inf);
   Reset(infile);
   Assign(outfile,outf);
   ReWrite(outfile);

   while not EOF(infile) do
   begin
      Read(infile,ch);
      ch:=key xor ch;
      Write(outfile,ch);
   end;

   WriteLn('file decoded');
   Close(infile); Close(outfile);
end; {Decode}

begin
   Write('enter input file: ');
   ReadLn(inf);
   Write('enter output file: ');
   ReadLn(outf);
   Write('enter one character key: ');
   ReadLn(ch);
   key:=Ord(ch);
   Write('Code or Decode (C or D): ');
   ReadLn(ch);
   if UpCase(ch)='C' then Code(inf,outf,key)
   else if UpCase(ch)='D' then Decode(inf,outf,key);
end.
```

Data Compression

Data-compression techniques essentially squeeze a given amount of information into a smaller area. It is often used in computer systems to increase the
storage of the system (by reducing the storage needs of the computer user), to
save transfer time (especially over phone lines), and to provide a level of
security. Although there are many data-compression schemes available, you
will be examining only two of them. The first is *bit compression*, where more
than one character is stored in a single byte, and the second is *character
deletion*, in which characters from the file are deleted.

Eight Into Seven

Most modern computers use byte sizes that are even powers of two because of
the binary representation of data in the machine. The upper- and lowercase

letters and the punctuation only require about 63 different codes needing only 6 bits to represent a byte. (A 6-bit byte could have values of 0 through 63.) However, most computers use an 8-bit byte; thus, 25% of the byte's storage is wasted in simple text files. You could, therefore, actually compact 4 characters into 3 bytes if you could use the last 2 bits in each byte. The only problem is that there are more than 63 different ASCII codes organized so that the uppercase and lowercase alphabet falls about in the middle. This means that some necessary characters require at least 7 bits. It is possible to use a non-ASCII representation (which is done on rare occasions), but it is not generally advisable. An easier option is to compact 8 characters into 7 bytes, exploiting the fact that no letter or common punctuation mark uses the eighth bit of a byte. Therefore, you can use the eighth bit of each of the 7 bytes to store the eighth character. This method still saves 12.5%.

However, many computers, including the IBM PC, do use 8-bit characters to represent special characters or graphics characters. Also, some word processors use the eighth bit to indicate text-processing instructions. Therefore, using this type of data compaction only works on "straight" ASCII files, which do not use the eighth bit.

To visualize how this works, consider the following 8 characters represented as 8-bit bytes:

byte 1	0 1 1 1	0 1 0 1
byte 2	0 1 1 1	1 1 0 1
byte 3	0 0 1 0	0 0 1 1
byte 4	0 1 0 1	0 1 1 0
byte 5	0 0 0 1	0 0 0 0
byte 6	0 1 1 0	1 1 0 1
byte 7	0 0 1 0	1 0 1 0
byte 8	0 1 1 1	1 0 0 1

As you can see, the eighth bit is always 0. This is always the case unless the eighth bit is used for parity checking. The easiest way to compress 8 characters into 7 characters is to distribute the 7 significant bits of byte 1 into the 7 unused eighth-bit positions of bytes 2 through 8. The 7 remaining bytes then appear as follows:

```
                              ┌──────────────────── byte 1—read down
             byte 2   │1 1 1 1   1 1 0 1
             byte 3    1 0 1 0   0 0 1 1
             byte 4    1 1 0 1   0 1 1 0
             byte 5    0 0 0 1   0 0 0 0
             byte 6    1 1 1 0   1 1 0 1
             byte 7    0 0 1 0   1 0 1 0
             byte 8    1 1 1 1   1 0 0 1
```

To reconstruct byte 1, you just put it back together again by taking the eighth bit off of each of the other 7 bytes.

This compression technique compresses any text file by 1/8, or 12.5%. This is quite a substantial savings. For example, if you were transmitting the source code for your favorite program to a friend over long-distance phone lines, then you would be saving 12.5% of the expense of transmission. (Remember, the object code, or executable version of the program, needs the full 8 bits.)

The following program compresses a text file by using the method just described:

```
program compress;   {fit characters into 7 bit words}
type
    str80 = string[80];

var
    inf,outf:str80;
    ch:char;
    t:integer;


procedure Compress(inf,outf:str80);
var
    infile,outfile:file of byte;
    ch,ch2:byte;
    done:boolean;

begin
    Assign(infile, inf);
    Reset(infile);
    Assign(outfile,outf);
    ReWrite(outfile);

    done:=FALSE;
    repeat
       Read(infile,ch);
       if EOF(infile) then
          done:=TRUE
       else
       begin
          ch:=ch shl 1; {shift off unused bit}
          for t:=0 to 6 do
          begin
             if EOF(infile) then
             begin
                ch2:=0;
                done:= TRUE;
             end else  Read(infile,ch2);
             ch2:=ch2 and 127; {turn off top bit}
             ch2:=ch2 or ((ch shl t) and 128); {pack bits}
             Write(outfile,ch2);
          end;
       end; {else}
    until done;
```

```
      WriteLn('file compressed');
      Close(infile); Close(outfile);
end; {Compress}

procedure Decompress(inf,outf:str80);
var
      infile,outfile:file of byte;
      ch,ch2:byte;
      s:array[1..7] of byte;
      done:boolean;

begin
      Assign(infile, inf);
      Reset(infile);
      Assign(outfile,outf);
      ReWrite(outfile);

      done:=FALSE;
      repeat
         ch:=0;
         for t:=1 to 7 do
         begin
            if EOF(infile) then
               done:=TRUE
            else
            begin
               Read(infile,ch2);
               s[t]:=ch2 and 127; {turn off top bit }
               ch2:=ch2 and 128; {clear lower bits}
               ch2:=ch2 shr t; {de-pack}
               ch:=ch or ch2; {build up 8th byte}
            end;
         end;
         Write(outfile,ch);
         for t:=1 to 7 do Write(outfile,s[t]);
      until done;

      WriteLn('file decompressed');
      Close(infile); Close(outfile);
end; {Decompress}

begin
      Write('enter input file: ');
      ReadLn(inf);
      Write('enter output file: ');
      ReadLn(outf);
      Write('Compress or Decompress (C or D): ');
      ReadLn(ch);
      if UpCase(ch)='C' then Compress(inf,outf)
      else if UpCase(ch)='D' then Decompress(inf,outf);
end.
```

This program's code is fairly complex because various bits must be shifted around. If you remember what is being done with the first byte out of each eight, then the code becomes easier to follow.

The 16-Character Language

Although unsuitable for most situations, an interesting method of data compression deletes unnecessary letters from words — in essence changing most words into abbreviations. Data compression is accomplished because the unused characters are not stored. Saving space by using abbreviations is very common — that is why "Mr." is used instead of "Mister." Instead of using actual abbreviations, the method presented in this section automatically removes certain letters from a message. To do this, a *minimal alphabet* is needed. A minimal alphabet is one in which several seldom-used letters have been removed, leaving only those necessary to form most words or to avoid ambiguity. Therefore, any character not in the minimal alphabet will be extracted from any word in which it appears. Exactly how many characters there are in a minimal alphabet is a matter of choice. However, this section uses the 14 most common letters, plus spaces and carriage-return characters.

Automating the abbreviation process requires that you know what letters in the alphabet are used most frequently so that you can create a minimal alphabet. In theory, you could count the letters of each word in a dictionary; however, different writers use different frequency mixes, so a frequency chart based just on the words available in English may not reflect the actual usage frequency of letters. (It would also take a long time to count the letters!) As an alternative, you can count the frequency of the letters in this chapter and use them as a basis for your minimal alphabet. To do so, you could use the following simple program. This program skips all punctuation except periods, commas, and spaces.

```
program count;
{count the number of each type of character in a file}
type
    str80 = string[80];

var
    inf:str80;
    t:integer;
    alpha:array[0..25] of integer;
    space,period,comma:integer;

function IsAlpha(ch:char):boolean;
{returns TRUE if ch is a letter of the alphabet}
begin
    IsAlpha:= (UpCase(ch)>='A') and (UpCase(ch)<='Z');
end;  { IsAlpha }

procedure Count(inf:str80);
var
    infile:file of char;
    ch:char;
```

```
begin
   Assign(infile, inf);
   Reset(infile);

   while not EOF(infile) do
   begin
      Read(infile,ch);
      ch:=UpCase(ch);
      if IsAlpha(ch) then
         alpha[Ord(ch)-Ord('A')]:=alpha[Ord(ch)-Ord('A')]+1
      else case ch of
         ' ': space:=space+1;
         '.': period:=period+1;
         ',': comma:=comma+1;
      end;
   end;
   Close(infile);
end; {Count}

begin
   Write('enter input file: ');
   ReadLn(inf);
   for t:=0 to 25 do alpha[t]:=0;
   space:=0; comma:=0; period:=0;
   Count(inf);
   for t:=0 to 25 do
      WriteLn(Chr(t+Ord('A')),': ',alpha[t]);
   WriteLn('space: ',space);
   WriteLn('period: ',period);
   WriteLn('comma: ',comma);
end.
```

By running the program on the text of this chapter, you get the following frequency:

A	2525	P	697
B	532	Q	62
C	838	R	1656
D	1145	S	1672
E	3326	T	3082
F	828	U	869
G	529	V	376
H	1086	W	370
I	2242	X	178
J	39	Y	356
K	94	Z	20
L	1103		
M	1140	Space	5710
N	2164	Period	234
O	1767	Comma	513

The frequency of letters in this chapter compares well with the standard

English mix and is offset only by the repeated use of the Turbo Pascal key-words in the programs.

To achieve significant data compression, you need to cut the alphabet sub-stantially by removing the letters used least frequently. Although there are many opinions about exactly what a workable minimum alphabet is, the 14 most common letters and the space account for about 85% of all characters in this chapter. Because the carriage-return character is also necessary to pre-serve word breaks, it must be included also. Therefore, this chapter uses a minimal alphabet consisting of 14 characters, a space, and a carriage return:

A B D E H I L M N O R S T U <space> <CR>

Here is a program that removes all characters except the 16 selected. The program actually writes the carriage-return/linefeed combination if it is present. This makes the output readable — it is not necessary to store the linefeed, because it could be reconstructed at a later time.

```
program Compres2;   {16-character language}
type
    str8U = string[80];

var
    inf,outf:str80;
    ch:char;
    t:integer;


procedure Comp2(inf,outf:str80);
var
    infile,outfile:file of char;
    ch:char;
    done:boolean;

begin
    Assign(infile, inf);
    Reset(infile);
    Assign(outfile,outf);
    ReWrite(outfile);

    done:=FALSE;
    repeat
      if not EOF(infile) then
      begin
          Read(infile, ch);
          ch:=UpCase(ch);
          if Pos(ch,'ABCDEJILMNORSTU ')<>0 then Write(outfile, ch);
          if Ord(ch)=13 then Write(outfile,ch); {cr}
          if Ord(ch)=10 then Write(outfile,ch); {lf}
      end
      else done:=TRUE;
    until done;

    WriteLn('file compressed');
    Close(infile); Close(outfile);
```

```
end; {Comp2}

begin
   Write('enter input file: ');
   ReadLn(inf);
   Write('enter output file: ');
   ReadLn(outf);
   Comp2(inf,outf);
end.
```

The program uses the built-in **Pos** function to determine if each character read is in the minimal alphabet. **Pos** returns 0 if there is no match, or the position of the first match if it is found.

If you use this program on the message

> Attention High Command:
> Attack successful. Please send additional supplies and
> fresh troops. This is essential to maintain our
> foothold.
> General Frashier

the compressed message would look like this:

> ATTENTION I COMMAND
> ATTAC SUCCESSUL LEASE SEND ADDITIONAL
> SULIES AND RES TROOS   TIS IS ESSENTIAL TO
> MAINTAIN OUR OOTOLD
> ENERAL RASIER

As you can see, the message is largely readable, although some ambiguity is present. Ambiguity is the chief drawback to this method of data compression. However, if you were familiar with the vocabulary of the writer of the message, you could probably select a better minimal alphabet that would remove some ambiguity.

In spite of the potential for ambiguity, quite a bit of space was saved. The original message was 168 bytes long, and the compacted message is 142 bytes long—a savings of about 16%.

If both character deletion and bit compression were applied to the message, then about 28% less storage would have been needed, which could be important. For example, if you were a submarine captain and wanted to send a message to headquarters but did not want to give away your position, you might want to compress the message by using both methods so that it would be as short as possible.

Both the bit-compression and character-deletion methods of data compression have uses in encryption. Bit compression further encrypts the information and makes decoding more difficult. If used before encryption, the character-deletion method has one wonderful advantage: it disguises the character frequency of the source language.

Code-Breaking

No chapter on encryption is complete without a brief look at code-breaking. The art of code-breaking is essentially one of trial and error. With the use of digital computers, relatively simple ciphers can easily be broken through exhaustive testing. However, the more complex codes either cannot be broken or require techniques and resources not commonly available. For simplicity, this section focuses on breaking the more straightforward codes.

If you wish to break a message that was ciphered using a simple substitution method with only an offset alphabet, then all you need to do is try all 26 possible offsets to see which one fits. A program to do this is shown here:

```
program brksub;   {Code breaker program for simple substitution
                   ciphers.  Messages can be as long as 1000
                   characters.}
type
   str80 = string[80];

var
   inf:str80;
   message:array[1..1000] of char; {holds input message}
   ch:char;

function IsAlpha(ch:char):boolean;
{returns TRUE if ch is a letter of the alphabet}
begin
   IsAlpha:= (UpCase(ch)>='A') and (UpCase(ch)<='Z');
end;  { IsAlpha }

procedure Break(inf:str80);
var
   infile:file of char;
   ch:char;
   done:boolean;
   sub,t,t2,l:integer;

begin
   Assign(infile, inf);
   Reset(infile);

   done:=FALSE;
   l:=1;
   repeat
     Read(infile,message[l]);
     message[l]:=UpCase(message[l]);
     l:=l+1;
   until EOF(infile);
   l:=l-1;   {clear EOF char}

   t:=0; sub:=-1;    {not Decoded}
```

```
   repeat
      for t2:=1 to l do
      begin
         ch:=message[t2];
         if IsAlpha(ch) then
         begin
            ch:=Chr(Ord(ch)+t);
            if ch>'Z' then ch:=Chr(Ord(ch)-26);
         end;
         Write(ch);
      end;
      WriteLn;
      WriteLn('Decoded? (Y/N): ');
      ReadLn(ch);
      if UpCase(ch)='Y' then sub:=t;
      t:=t+1;
   until (t=26) or (UpCase(ch)='Y');
   if sub<>-1 then Write('offset is ',sub);
   Close(infile);
end; {Break}

begin
   Write('enter input file: ');
   ReadLn(inf);
   Break(inf);
end.
```

With only a slight variation, you could use the same program to break ciphers that use a random alphabet. In this case, substitute manually entered alphabets as shown in this program:

```
program brksub2;   {Code breaker program for random substitution
                    ciphers.  Messages can be as long as 1000
                    characters.}
type
   str80 = string[80];

var
   inf:str80;
   sub:array[0..25] of char;
   message:array[1..1000] of char; {holds input message}
   ch:char;

function IsAlpha(ch:char):boolean;
{returns TRUE if ch is a letter of the alphabet}
begin
   IsAlpha:= (UpCase(ch)>='A') and (UpCase(ch)<='Z');
end;  { IsAlpha }

procedure Break2(inf:str80);
var
   infile:file of char;
   ch:char;
   done:boolean;
   t,l:integer;

begin
   Assign(infile, inf);
```

```
    Reset(infile);

    done:=FALSE;
    l:=1;
    repeat
       Read(infile,message[l]);
       message[l]:=UpCase(message[l]);
       l:=l+1;
    until EOF(infile);
    l:=l-1;   {clear EOF}

    repeat
       Write('enter substitution alphabet: ');
       ReadLn(sub);
       for t:=1 to l do
       begin
          ch:=message[t];
          if IsAlpha(ch) then begin
             ch:=sub[Ord(ch)-Ord('A')];
          end;
          Write(ch);
       end;
       WriteLn;
       WriteLn('Decoded? (Y/N): ');
       ReadLn(ch);
       if UpCase(ch)='Y' then done:=TRUE;
    until done;
    WriteLn('substitution alphabet is: ',sub);
    Close(infile);
end; {Break2}

begin
    Write('enter input file: ');
    ReadLn(inf);
    Break2(inf);
end.
```

Unlike substitution ciphers, the transposition and bit-manipulation ciphers are harder to break by using the trial-and-error methods shown here. If you have to break such complex codes, good luck!

Oh, and by the way —*hsaovbno wlymljapvu pz haahpuhisl, pa vjjbyz vusf hz hu hjjpklua.*

EIGHT

Random Number Generators
And Simulations

Random number sequences are used in a variety of programming situations, ranging from simulations (which are the most common) to games and other recreational software. Turbo Pascal contains a built-in function called **Random** that generates random numbers. As you will see in this chapter, **Random** is an excellent random number generator, but for some applications you may need two or more different generators to provide different sets of random numbers for different tasks. Also, certain simulations require a *skewed*, or unbalanced, random number generator, which produces a sequence that is weighted toward one end or the other. The first part of this chapter is devoted to constructing random number generators and to testing their quality.

The second half of this chapter shows how you can use random numbers in real-world simulations. The first is a grocery store check-out simulation, and the second is a "random-walk" stock portfolio manager. Both illustrate the fundamentals of simulation programming.

Random Number Generators

Technically, the term *random number generator* is absurd; numbers, in and of themselves, are not random. For example, is 100 a random number? Is 25? What is really meant by *random number generator* is something that creates a *sequence* of numbers that appear to be in random order. This raises a more complex question: What is a random sequence of numbers? The only correct answer is that a random sequence of numbers is a sequence in which all elements are completely unrelated. This definition leads to the paradox that any sequence can be both nonrandom and random, depending on the way the sequence was obtained. For example, this list of numbers

1 2 3 4 5 6 7 8 9 0

was created by typing the top row of keys, in order, on the keyboard, so the sequence certainly cannot be construed as having been randomly generated. But what if you happened to pull out this same sequence from a barrel of numbered tennis balls. Then it *would* be a randomly generated sequence. This discussion shows that the randomness of a sequence depends on *how it was generated*, not on what the actual sequence is.

Keep in mind that sequences of numbers generated by a computer are *deterministic:* each number other than the first depends on the number that precedes it. Technically, this means that only a *quasi-random* sequence of numbers can be created by a computer. However, this is sufficient for most problems and, for the purposes of this book, the sequences are simply called random.

Generally, it is best if the numbers in a random sequence are *uniformly* distributed. (Do not confuse this with normal distribution or the bell-shaped curve.) In a uniform distribution, all events are equally probable, so that a graph of a uniform distribution tends to be a flat line rather than a curve.

Before the widespread use of computers, whenever random numbers were needed they were produced by either throwing dice or pulling numbered balls from a jar. In 1955, the RAND Corporation published a table of 1 million random digits obtained with the help of a computer-like machine. In the early days of computer science, although many methods were devised to generate random numbers, most were discarded.

One particularly interesting method that almost worked was developed by John von Neumann, the father of the modern computer. Often referred to as the *middle-square method*, it squares the previous random number and then extracts its middle digits. For example, if you were creating three-digit numbers and the previous value was 121, you would square it to make 14641. Extracting the middle three digits would give you 464 as the next number. The problem with this method is that it tends to lead to a very short repeating pattern called a *cycle*, especially after a zero has entered the pattern. For this reason the method is not used today.

Currently, the most common way to generate random numbers is to use the equation

$$R_{n+1} = (aR_n + c) \bmod m$$

where the following conditions must be true.

$$R \quad >= 0$$
$$a \quad >= 0$$
$$c \quad >= 0$$
$$m \quad > \quad R_o, \ a, \text{ and } c$$

Note that R_n is the previous number, and R_{n+1} is the next number. This method is sometimes referred to as the *linear congruential method*. The formula is so simple that you might think that random number generation is easy. There is a catch, however: how well this equation performs depends heavily on the values of a, c, and m. Choosing these values is sometimes more of an art than a science. There are complex rules that can help you choose the values; however, this discussion will cover only a few simple rules and experiments.

The modulus (m) should be fairly large, because it determines the range of the random numbers. The modulus operation yields the remainder of a division that uses the same operands. Hence, 10 % 4 is 2, because 4 goes into 10 twice with a remainder of 2. Therefore, if the modulus is 12, then only the numbers 0 through 11 can be produced by the randomizing equation, whereas if the modulus is 21,425, the numbers 0 through 21,424 can be produced. Remember, a small modulus does not actually affect randomness — it only affects range. The choice of the multiplier, a, and the increment, c, is much harder. Usually the multiplier can be fairly large and the increment fairly small. A lot of testing is necessary to confirm that a good generator has been created.

As a first example, here is one of the more common random number generators. The equation shown in **Ran1** has been used as the basis for the random number generator in a number of popular languages.

```
var
    a1:integer;   {initialize to 1 prior to first call
                   to random}

function Ran1: real;
var
    t:real;
begin
    t:=(a1*32749+3) mod 32749;
    a1:=Trunc(t);
    Ran1:=Abs(t/32749);
end; {Ran1}
```

This function has three important features. First, the random number is actually an integer, even though the function returns a **real**. Integers are needed for the linear congruential method, but random number generators, by convention, are expected to return a number between 0 and 1, which means it is a floating-point value.

Second, the *seed*, or starting value, is set through the use of the global variable **a1**. Before the first call to **Ran1**, the variable **a1** must be initialized to 1.

Third, in **Ran1**, the random number is divided by the modulus before the function returns in order to obtain a number between 0 and 1. If you study this, you will see that the value of **a1** prior to the return line must be between 0 and 32748. Therefore, when **a1** is divided by 32749, a number is obtained that is equal to or greater than 0 but less than 1.

Many random number generators are not useful because they produce nonuniform distributions or have short, repeating sequences. Even when they seem to be very slight, these problems can produce biased results if the same random number generator is used over and over again. The solution is to create several different generators and to use them either individually or jointly to obtain more random numbers. Using several generators helps smooth the distribution of the sequence by reducing small biases in each generator. Therefore, here is another random number generating function, called **Ran2**, that produces a good distribution:

```
var
   a2:integer;    {initialize to 203 prior to first
                   call to Ran2}


function Ran2: real;
var
   t:real;
begin
   t:=(a2*10001+3) mod 17417;
   a2:=Trunc(t);
   Ran2:=Abs(t/17417);
end; {Ran2}
```

The global variable **a2** must be initialized to 203 before the first call to **Ran2**.

Each of these random number generators produces a good sequence of random numbers. Yet the questions remain: How "random" are the sequences? How good are these generators?

Determining the Quality
Of a Generator

You can use several tests to determine the randomness of a number sequence. None of these tests will tell you if a sequence is random; rather, they will tell you if it is not. The tests can identify a nonrandom sequence, but just because a specific test does not find a problem does not mean that a given sequence is indeed random. The test does, however, raise your confidence in the random number generator that produced the sequence. For the purposes of this book, the majority of these tests are either too complicated or too time-consuming in their most rigorous forms. Therefore, you will now look briefly at a few simple ways a sequence can be tested.

To begin, here is the way to find out how closely the distribution of the numbers in a sequence conforms to what you would expect a random distribution to be. For example, say that you are attempting to generate random sequences of the digits 0 through 9. The probability of each digit occurring is 1/10, because there are 10 possibilities for each number in the sequence, all of which are equally possible. Assume that the sequence

$$9\ 1\ 8\ 2\ 4\ 6\ 3\ 7\ 5\ 8\ 2\ 9\ 0\ 4\ 2\ 4\ 7\ 8\ 6\ 2$$

was actually generated. If you count the number of times each digit occurs, the result is

Digit	Occurrences
0	1
1	1
2	4
3	1
4	3
5	1
6	2
7	2
8	3
9	2

You should next ask yourself if this distribution is sufficiently similar to the expected distribution.

Remember: if a random number generator is good, it generates sequences randomly. In a truly random state, all sequences are possible. This seems to imply that any generated sequence should qualify as a valid random sequence. So how can you tell if the sequence just given is random? In fact, how could any sequence of the ten digits be nonrandom, since any sequence is possible? The answer is that some sequences are less likely to be random than others. You can determine the *probability* of a given sequence being random by using the *chi-square test*.

Basically, the chi-square test subtracts the expected number of occurrences from the observed number of occurrences for all numbers generated. This result is called *V*. You can use *V* to find a percentage in a table of chi-square values. This percentage represents the likelihood that a random sequence has been produced. A small chi-square table is given in Figure 8-1; you can find complete tables in most books on statistics.

The formula to obtain V is

$$V = \sum_{i=1}^{N} \frac{(O_i - E_i)^2}{E_i}$$

where O_i is the number of observed occurrences, E_i is the number of expected occurrences, and N is the number of discrete elements. The value for E_i is determined by multiplying the probability of that element's occurrence by the number of observations. In this case, because each digit is expected to occur one tenth of the time and 20 samples were taken, the value for E is 2 for all digits. N is 10 because there are 10 possible elements—the digits 0 through 9. Therefore,

$$V = \frac{(1-2)^2}{2} + \frac{(1-2)^2}{2} + \frac{(4-2)^2}{2} + \frac{(1-2)^2}{2} + \frac{(3-2)}{2} +$$

$$\frac{(1-2)^2}{2} + \frac{(2-2)^2}{2} + \frac{(2-2)^2}{2} + \frac{(3-2)^2}{2} + \frac{(2-2)^2}{2}$$

$$= \frac{1}{2} + \frac{1}{2} + \frac{4}{2} + \frac{1}{2} + \frac{1}{2} + \frac{1}{2} + 0 + 0 + \frac{1}{2} + 0$$

$$= 5$$

To determine the likelihood that the sequence is not random, find the row in the table shown in Figure 8-1 that equals the number of observations; in this case, it is 20. Then read across until you find a number that is greater than V. In this case, it is column 1. This means that there is a 99% likelihood that a sample of 20 elements will have a V greater than 8.260. Conversely, it means that there is only a 1% likelihood that the sequence tested was randomly generated. To "pass" the chi-square test, the probability for V must fall between 25% and 75%. (This range is derived by using mathematics beyond the scope of this book.)

However, you might counter this conclusion with the following question: Since all sequences are possible, how can this sequence have only a 1% chance of being legitimate? The answer is that it is just a probability—the chi-square test is actually not a test at all, only a confidence builder. In fact, if you use the chi-square test, you should obtain several different sequences and average the results to avoid rejecting a good random number generator. Any single sequence might be rejected, but several sequences averaged together should provide a good test.

On the other hand, a sequence can pass the chi-square test and still not be random. For example,

1 3 5 7 9 1 3 5 7 9

passes the chi-square test, but it does not appear to be very random. In this case, a *run* has been generated. A run is simply a strictly ascending or descending sequence of numbers that are at evenly spaced intervals. In this case, each group of five digits is in strictly ascending order, and as such (assuming it continued) would not be a random sequence. Runs can also be separated by "noise" digits: the digits that make up the run can be interspersed throughout an otherwise random sequence. It is possible to design tests to detect these situations, but they are beyond the scope of this book.

Another feature to test for is the length of the *period;* that is, how many numbers can be generated before the sequence begins to repeat—or worse, degenerates into a short cycle. All computer-based random number generators eventually repeat a sequence. The longer the period, the better the generator. Even though the frequency of the numbers within the period is uniformly distributed, the numbers do not constitute a random series, because a truly random series does not repeat itself consistently. Generally, a period of several thousand numbers is sufficient for most applications. (Again, a test for this can be performed.)

Several other tests can be applied to determine the quality of a random number generator. In fact, there probably has been more code written to test random number generators than to construct them. Here is yet another test that allows you to test random number generators "visually" by using a graph to show you how the sequence is generated.

	$p=99\%$	$p=95\%$	$p=75\%$	$p=50\%$	$p=25\%$	$p=5\%$
$n=5$	0.5543	1.1455	2.675	4.351	6.626	11.07
$n=10$	2.558	3.940	6.737	9.342	12.55	18.31
$n=15$	5.229	7.261	11.04	14.34	18.25	25.00
$n=20$	8.260	10.85	15.45	19.34	23.83	31.41
$n=30$	14.95	18.49	24.48	29.34	34.80	43.77

Figure 8-1. Selected chi-square values

Ideally, the graph should be based on the frequency of each number. However, since a random number generator can produce thousands of different numbers, that would be impractical. Instead, you will create a graph grouped by the "tenths" digit of each number; for example, since all random numbers produced are between 0 and 1, the number 0.9365783 is grouped under 9 and the number 0.34523445 is grouped under 3. This means that the graph of the output of the random number display program has 10 lines, with each line representing the number of times a particular number in the group occurred. The program also prints the mean of each sequence, which can be used to detect a bias in the numbers. Like the other graphics programs in this chapter, this program runs only on an IBM PC that has a color-graphics display adapter. Both the **Ran1** and **Ran2** functions developed earlier, as well as Turbo Pascal's built-in **Random** function, are displayed side by side for easy comparison:

```
program RanGenerator;    {Comparison of three random number
                         generators}

const
   COUNT = 1000;

var
   freq1,freq2,freq3: array[0..9] of integer;
   a2,a1:integer;
   f,f2,f3:real;
   r,r2,r3: real;
   y,x:integer;


procedure Display;
var
   t:integer;

begin
   for t:=0 to 9 do
   begin
      Draw(t*10,180,t*10,180-freq1[t],2);
      Draw(t*10+110,180,t*10+110,180-freq2[t],2);
      Draw(t*10+220,180,t*10+220,180-freq3[t],2);
   end;
end;  {Display}

function Ran1: real;
var
   t:real;
begin
   t:=(a1*32749+3) mod 32749;
   a1:=Trunc(t);
   Ran1:=Abs(t/32749);
end; {Ran1}

function Ran2: real;
var
   t:real;
begin
```

```
      t:=(a2*10001+3) mod 17417;
      a2:=Trunc(t);
      Ran2:=Abs(t/17417);
end; {Ran2}

begin
   Graphcolormode;
   Palette(0);    { setup for color graphics }

   Gotoxy(10,1);
   Write('Comparison of Random');
   GotoXY(12,2);
   Write('Number Generators');
   Draw(0,180,90,180,3);
   Draw(110,180,200,180,3);
   Draw(220,180,310,180,3);
   GotoXY(5,25);
   Write('Random            Ran1            Ran2');

   a1:=1; a2:=203; {initialize random generator variables }
   f:=0; f2:=0; f3:=0;

   for x:=0 to 9 do
   begin   { initialize frequency arrays }
      freq1[x]:=0;
      freq2[x]:=0;
      freq3[x]:=0;
   end;
   for x:=1 to COUNT do
   begin
      r:=Random;    { get a random number }
      f:=f+r;         { add for computation of mean }
      y:=Trunc(r*10); { convert to an integer between 0 and 9}
      freq1[y]:=freq1[y]+1;   { increment frequency count}

      r2:=Ran1;    { get a random number }
      f2:=f2+r2;        { add for computation of mean }
      y:=Trunc(r2*10); { convert to an integer between 0 and 9}
      freq2[y]:=freq2[y]+1;   { increment frequency count}

      r3:=Ran2;    { get a random number }
      f3:=f3+r3;        { add for computation of mean }
      y:=Trunc(r3*10); { convert to an integer between 0 and 9}
      freq3[y]:=freq3[y]+1;   { increment frequency count}

      Display;  { graph frequency counts }
   end;
   ReadLn;
   Textmode;

   Writeln('mean of Random is: ',f/COUNT);
   Writeln('mean of Ran1 is: ',f2/COUNT);
   Writeln('mean of Ran2 is: ',f3/COUNT);

end.
```

In this program, each function generates 1000 numbers, and based on the digit in the "tenths" position, the appropriate frequency array is updated. The procedure **Display** plots all three frequency arrays on the screen after each random number is generated, so you can watch the display grow.

Figure 8-2 shows the output from each random number generator at the end of the 1000 numbers. The mean is 0.489932 for **Ran1**, 0.4858311 for **Ran2**, and 0.500279 for **Random**. These are acceptable.

To use the display program effectively, you should watch both the shape of the graph and the way that it grows to check for any short, repeating cycles. For example, **Ran2** generates significantly fewer numbers between 0.9 and 0.999999 (the far-right bar) than does either **Random** or **Ran1**.

Of course this "test" is not conclusive, but it does give you insight into the way a generator produces its numbers, and it can speed up the testing process by allowing obviously poor generating functions to be rejected quickly. (It also makes a great program to run when someone asks you to show them your computer!)

Using Multiple Generators

One simple technique that improves the randomness of sequences produced by the three generators is to combine them under the control of one master function. This function selects between two of them, based on the result of the third. With this method you can obtain very long periods and diminish the effects of any cycle or bias. The function called **CombRandom**, shown here, combines **Ran1**, **Ran2**, and **Random**:

```
function CombRandom:real;
{ random selection of generators}
var
    f: real;

begin
    f:=Ran2;
    if f>0.5 then CombRandom:=Random
    else CombRandom:=Ran1;     {random selection of generators}
end; {CombRandom}
```

The result of **Ran2** is used to decide whether **Ran1** or **Random** becomes the value of the master function **CombRandom**. With this method the period of **CombRandom** is equal to or greater than the sum of the period of **Random** and **Ran1**. Thus, this method makes it possible to produce sequences with very long periods. Feel free to alter the mix between **Random** and **Ran1** by changing the constant in the **if** to obtain the exact distribution you want between **Random** and **Ran1**. You can also add additional generators and select between them for even longer periods.

Here is a program to display the graph of **CombRandom** and its mean. Figure 8-3 shows the final graph after 1000 random numbers have been computed. The mean of **CombRandom** is 0.496833.

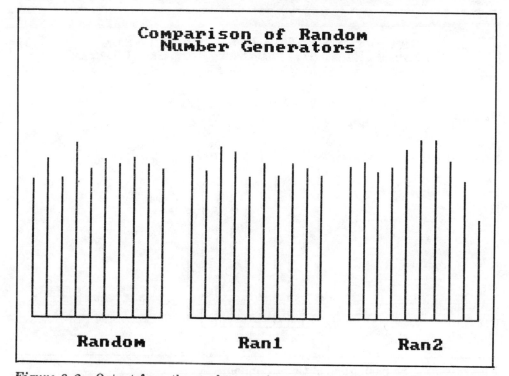

Figure 8-2. Output from the random number generator display program

```
program MultiRandom;   {combining three random generators into 1}

const
    COUNT = 1000;

var
    freq: array[0..9] of integer;
    a2,a1:integer;
    f,r:real;
    y,x:integer;


procedure Display;
var
    t:integer;

begin
    for t:=0 to 9 do
        Draw(t*10+110,180,t*10+110,180-freq[t],2);
end;  {Display}

function Ran1: real;
var
    t:real;
begin
    t:=(a1*32749+3) mod 32749;
```

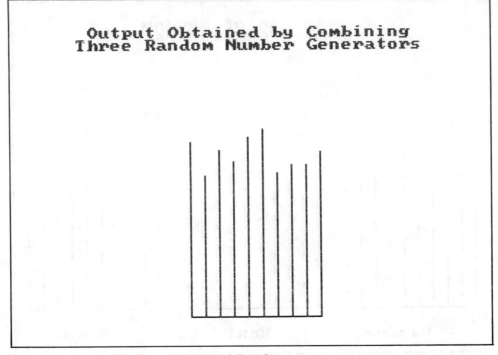

Figure 8-3. The final graph of **CombRandom**

```
    a1:=Trunc(t);
    Ran1:=Abs(t/32749);
end; {Ran1}

function Ran2: real;
var
    t:real;
begin
    t:=(a2*10001+3) mod 17417;
    a2:=Trunc(t);
    Ran2:=Abs(t/17417);
end;   {Ran2}

function CombRandom:real;
{ random selection of generators}
var
    f: real;

begin
    f:=Ran2;
    if f>0.5 then CombRandom:=Random
    else CombRandom:=Ran1;    {random selection of generators}
end; {CombRandom}

begin
    Graphcolormode;
```

```
Palette(0);   { setup for color graphics }
GotoXY(6,1);
Write('Output Obtained by Combining');
GotoXY(5,2);
Write('Three Random Number Generators');
Draw(110,180,200,180,3);

a1:=1; a2:=203; {initialize random generator variables }
f:=0;

for x:=0 to 9 do  freq[x]:=0; {initialize frequency array}

for x:=1 to COUNT do
begin
   r:=CombRandom;   { get a random number }
   f:=f+r;       { add for computation of mean }
   y:=Trunc(r*10); { convert to an integer between 0 and 9}
   freq[y]:=freq[y]+1;   { increment frequency count}

   Display;  { graph frequency count}
end;
ReadLn;
Textmode;

Writeln('mean of CombRandom is: ',f/COUNT);
end.
```

Simulations

The remainder of this chapter examines the application of random number generators to computer *simulations*. A simulation is a computerized model of a real-world situation. Anything can be simulated; the success of the simulation depends primarily on how well the programmer understands the event being simulated. Because real-world situations often have thousands of variables, many things are difficult to simulate effectively. However, there are several events that lend themselves very well to simulation.

Simulations are important for two reasons. First, they let you alter the parameters of a situation to test and observe the possible results, even though in reality such experimentation might be either too costly or dangerous. For example, a simulation of a nuclear power plant can be used to test the effects of certain types of failures without danger. Second, simulation allows you to create situations that cannot occur in the real world. For example, a psychologist might want to study the effects of gradually increasing the intelligence of a mouse to that of a human to find out at what point the mouse runs a maze the fastest. Although this cannot be done in real life, a simulation may provide insight into the nature of intelligence versus instinct. The first of two examples of simulations that use random generators follows next.

Simulating a Check-out Line

The first example simulates a check-out line in a grocery store. Assume that the store is open for 10 hours a day, with peak hours being from 12 noon to 1 P.M. and from 5 P.M. to 6 P.M. The 12 noon to 1 P.M. slot is twice as busy as normal, and the 5 to 6 P.M. slot is three times as busy. As the simulation runs, one random number generator "creates" customers, a second generator determines how long it will take one customer to check out, and a third generator decides which of the open lines the customers will go to. The goal of the simulation is to help management find the optimal number of check-out lines that need to be available on a typical shopping day so that the number of people in line at any time is limited to 10 or less, and cashiers do not have to wait for customers to serve.

The key to this type of simulation is to create multiple processes. Although Turbo Pascal does not support simultaneity directly, you can simulate multi-processing by having each function inside of a main program loop do some work and return—in essence, time-slicing the functions. For example, the function that simulated the check-out only checks out a part of each order each time it is called. In this way, each function inside the main loop continues to execute. The main program to the check-out program, without the supporting procedures and functions, is shown here with its global data:

```
program checkout;   {Simulation of grocery store check-out
                     lines}
                    {include extended graphics}
                    {$I GRAPH.P }
var
   queues,count: array[0..9] of integer;
   open: array[0..9] of boolean;
   cust,time:integer;
   a1,a2:integer;
   y,x:integer;
   change:boolean;

begin
   Graphcolormode;
   Palette(0);   { setup for color graphics }

   a1:=1; a2:=203; {initialize random generator variables }

   change:=FALSE;
   cust:=0;
   time:=0;

   for x:=0 to 9 do
   begin
      queues[x]:=0; {initialize queues}
      open[x]:=FALSE;   {no customers or check-outs at start of day}
      count[x]:=0; {line count}
   end;
```

```
    GotoXY(20,24); Write('1                10');
    GotoXY(1,24); Write('Check-out lines:');

    {now start day by opening up the first check-out station}
    open[0]:=TRUE;

    repeat
        AddCust;
        AddQueue;
        Display;
        CheckOut;
        Display;
        if (time>30) and (time<50) then AddCust;
        if (time>70) and (time<80) then begin
            AddCust;
            AddCust;
        end;
        time:=time+1;
    until time>100;   {end of day}
    ReadLn;
    Textmode;
end.
```

The file **GRAPH.P** has been included so that the program can use the extended graphics function **Circle**.

The main loop drives the entire simulation:

```
repeat
    AddCust;
    AddQueue;
    Display;
    CheckOut;
    Display;
    if (time>30) and (time<50) then AddCust;
    if (time>70) and (time<80) then
    begin
        AddCust;
        AddCust;
    end;
    time:=time+1;
until time>100;   {end of day}
```

The function **AddCust** uses either **Ran1** or **Random** to generate the number of customers arriving at the check-out lines at each request. **AddQueue** is used to place the customers into an open check-out line, according to the results of **Ran2**, and it also opens a new line if all of the currently open lines are full. **Display** shows a graph of the simulation. **CheckOut** uses **Ran2** to assign each customer a check-out count, and each call decrements that count by 1. When a customer's count is 0, the customer leaves the check-out line.

The variable **time** alters the rate at which customers are generated, in order to match the store's peak hours. Each pass through the loop represents one-tenth of an hour.

Figures 8-4, 8-5 and 8-6 show the state of the check-out lines when **time** = 28, **time** = 60, and **time** = 88, corresponding to normal time, the end of first peak, and the end of second peak, respectively. Notice that at the end of the second peak, a maximum of five check-out lines are needed. If the simulation was programmed properly, this means that the grocery store does not need to operate the remaining five lines.

You can directly control several variables in the program. First, you can alter the way customers arrive and the number of customers that arrive. You can also change **AddCust** to return gradually more or fewer customers as the peak hours approach or wane. The program assumes that customers will randomly choose which line to stand in. Although this may be true of some customers, others will obviously choose the shortest line. You can account for this by altering the **AddQueue** function to put customers into the shortest line at some times and to place customers randomly at other times. The simulation does not account for the occasional accident—such as a dropped ketchup bottle—or for an unruly customer at the check-out, both of which would cause a line to stall temporarily.

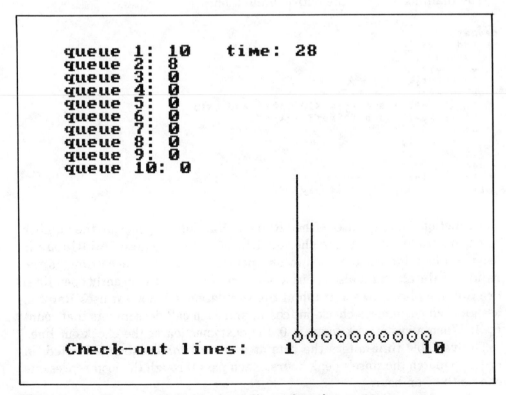

Figure 8-4. The state of the check-out lines when **time** = 28

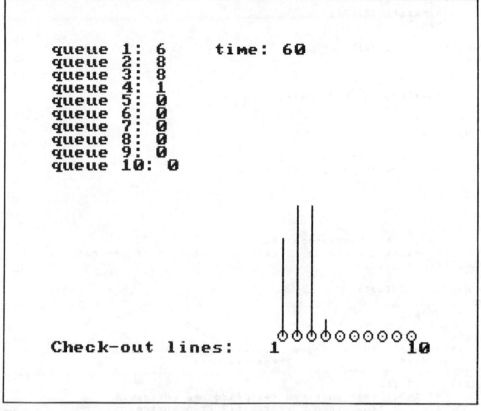

Figure 8-5. The state of the check-out lines when **time** = 60

The entire program is shown here:

```
program checkout;   {Simulation of grocery store check-out
                     lines}
                    {include extended graphics}
                    {$I GRAPH.P }
var
   queues,count: array[0..9] of integer;
   open: array[0..9] of boolean;
   cust,time:integer;
   a1,a2:integer;
   y,x:integer;
   change:boolean;


function Ran1: real;
var
   t:real;
begin
   t:=(a1*32749+3) mod 32749;
```

```pascal
      a1:=Trunc(t);
      Ran1:=Abs(t/32749);
end; {Ran1}

function Ran2: real;
var
   t:real;
begin
   t:=(a2*10001+3) mod 17417;
   a2:=Trunc(t);
   Ran2:=Abs(t/17417);
end;  {Ran2}

function CombRandom:real;
{ random selection of generators}
var
   f: real;

begin
   f:=Ran2;
   if f>0.5 then CombRandom:=Random
   else CombRandom:=Ran1;     {random selection of generators}
end; {CombRandom}

procedure AddCust;
var
   f,r:real;

begin
   if change then f:=Random  {alternate between two}
   else f:=Ran2;             {generators}

   if f>0.5 then
      if f<0.6 then cust:=cust+1  {add one customer}
      else if f<0.7 then cust:=cust+2 {two customers}
      else if f<0.8 then cust:=cust+3 {three customers}
      else cust:=cust+4;  {four customers}

end; {AddCust}

Procedure CheckOut;
var
   t:integer;

begin
   for t:=0 to 9 do
   begin
      if queues[t]<>0 then
      begin
         {get check-out time}
         while count[t]=0 count[t]:=Trunc(Ran1*5);
         {a new customer needs to get check-out time}
         count[t]:=count[t]-1;
         if count[t]=0 then queues[t]:=queues[t]-1;
         {remove the customer}
      end;
      if queues[t]=0 then open[t]:=FALSE; {close line down}
   end;
end; {CheckOut}
function AllFull:Boolean;
```

```
{See if there is any spare check-out capacity}
var
    t:integer;

begin
    AllFull:=TRUE;
    for t:=0 to 9 do
        if (queues[t]<10) and open[t] then AllFull:=FALSE;
end; {AllFull}

procedure AddQueue;
{open a check-out line}
var
    t,line:integer;
    done:Boolean;

begin
    done:=FALSE;
    while cust<>0 do
    begin
        if AllFull then
        begin
            t:=0;
            repeat
                if not open[t] then
                begin
                    open[t]:=TRUE;
                    done:=TRUE;
                end;
                t:=t+1;
            until done or (t=9);
        end
        else
        begin
            line:=Trunc(Ran2*10);
            if open[line] and (queues[line]<10) then
            begin
                queues[line]:=queues[line]+1;
                cust:=cust-1;
            end;
        end;
        if AllFull and open[9] then cust:=0; {all full}
    end;
end; {AddQueue}

procedure Display;
var
    t:integer;

begin
    GotoXY(15,1);
    Write('time: ',time);
    for t:=0 to 9 do
    begin
        Draw((t*10)+160,180,(t*10)+160,80,0);
        Circle((t*10)+160,180,3,3);
        Draw((t*10)+160,180,(t*10)+160,180-queues[t]*10,2);
        GotoXY(1,1+t);
        Write('queue ',t+1,': ',queues[t],' ');
    end;
```

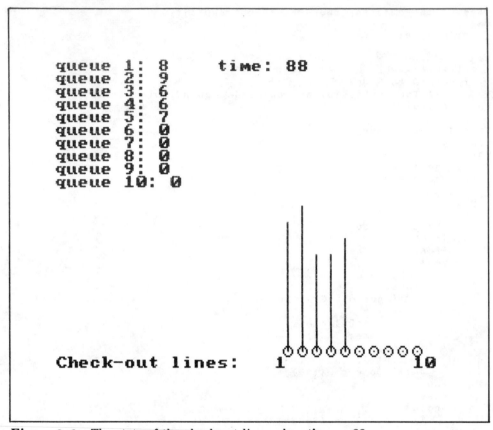

Figure 8-6.   The state of the check-out lines when **time** = 88

```
end; {Display}

begin
    Graphcolormode;
    Palette(0);   { setup for color graphics }

    a1:=1; a2:=203; {initialize random generator variables }

    change:=FALSE;
    cust:=0;
    time:=0;

    for x:=0 to 9 do
    begin
        queues[x]:=0; {initialize queues}
        open[x]:=FALSE;   {no customers or check-outs at start of day}
        count[x]:=0; {line count}
    end;
```

```
GotoXY(20,24); Write('1            10');
GotoXY(1,24); Write('Check-out lines:');

{now start day by opening up the first check-out station}
open[0]:=TRUE;

repeat
   AddCust;
   AddQueue;
   Display;
   CheckOut;
   Display;
   if (time>30) and (time<50) then AddCust;
   if (time>70) and (time<80) then
   begin
      AddCust;
      AddCust;
   end;
   time:=time+1;
until time>100;   {end of day}
ReadLn;
Textmode;
end.
```

Random-Walk Portfolio Management

The art of stock portfolio management is generally based on various theories and assumptions about many factors, some of which cannot be easily known unless you are an insider. There are buying and selling strategies based on statistical analyses of stock prices, PE ratios, the price of gold, the GNP, and even the cycles of the moon. The computer scientist's revenge is to use the computer to simulate the free marketplace—the stock exchange—without all of the real-life worry.

You may think that the stock exchange is simply too hard to simulate; that it has too many variables and too many unknowns; that it swings wildly at times and coasts smoothly at others. However, the problem itself is the solution: because the marketplace is so complex, it can be thought of as being composed of *randomly occurring events*. This means that you can simulate the stock exchange as a series of disconnected, random occurrences. This simulation is affectionately referred to as the *Random-walk method* of portfolio management. The term is derived from the classic experiment that involves a drunk wandering a street, weaving randomly from lamppost to lamppost. With the random-walk theory, you let chance be your guide, because it is as good as any other.

Before you go on, be warned: the random-walk method is generally discredited by professional money managers. It is presented here for your enjoyment only, not to help you make actual investment decisions.

To implement the random-walk method, first select ten companies from the *Wall Street Journal* by some chance method—for example, throw darts at it and use the companies whose names you hit. After you have selected ten companies, feed their names into the random-walk simulation program so that it can tell you what to do with them.

The program can tell you five things you can do with the stock of each company:

- Sell
- Buy
- Sell short
- Buy on margin
- Hold (do nothing).

The operations of selling, buying, and holding stock are self-explanatory. When you *sell short,* you sell stock that you do not own in the hopes that soon you can buy it cheaper and deliver it to the person you sold it to. Selling short is a way to make money when the market is going down. When you buy on *margin,* you use (for a small fee) the brokerage house's money to finance part of the cost of the stock that you purchased. The idea behind buying on margin is that if the stock increases enough, you make more money than you could have if you bought a smaller amount of stock with cash. This makes money only in a bull (rising) market.

The random-walk program is shown here. The built-in **KeyPressed** function checks for keyboard status and waits for a key-press. This allows you to use the sequence produced by the random number generator at a random point—in essence, creating a random seed value, which prevents the program from always producing the same advice.

```
program stock;   {Random-walk portfolio program}
type
   str80 = string[80];
   action = (buy, sell, hold, short, margin);
var
   t:integer;
   stock:array[1..10] of str80;
   ch:char;
   act:action;
   f:real;

procedure Enter;   {input the company names}
```

```
var
   t:integer;

begin
   for t:=1 to 10 do
   begin
      Write('Enter company name: ');
      ReadLn(stock[t]);
   end;
end;  {Enter}

function NextAction:action;
var
   f:real;

begin
   NextAction:=hold;
   case Trunc(Random*10) of
      1: NextAction:=sell;
      2: NextAction:=buy;
      3: NextAction:=short;
      4: NextAction:=margin
   end;
end; {NextAction}

begin

   Write('Wait a while, then strike any key ');
   repeat
      f:=Random;  {Randomize the generator}
   until KeyPressed;

   Writeln;
   Writeln('Enter New Companies? (Y/N) ');
   Read(kbd,ch);
   if UpCase(ch)='Y' then Enter;

   repeat
      for t:=1 to 10 do
      begin
         act:=NextAction;
         if Length(stock[t])>0 then
         begin
            Write(stock[t],': ');
            case act of
               buy: Writeln('buy');
               sell: Writeln('sell');
               short: Writeln('sell short');
               margin: Writeln('buy on margin');
               hold: Writeln('hold');
            end;
         end;
      end;
      Write('Again (Y/N) ');
      Read(kbd,ch);
   until UpCase(ch)='N';
end.
```

The program requires you to interpret its instructions in the following manner:

Instruction	Interpretation
buy	Buy as much of the specified stock as you can afford without borrowing.
sell	Sell all of the stock if any is owned. Then randomly select a new company for reinvesting your money.
sell short	Sell 100 shares of the specified company, even though you don't own it, in the hopes that you can buy it cheaper in the future.
buy on margin	Borrow money to buy shares of the specified stock.
hold	Do nothing.

For example, if you were to run this program using the fictitious company names Com1 through Com10, the first day's advice might look like this:

```
 Com1: sell
 Com2: buy
 Com3: buy on margin
 Com4: sell short
 Com5: hold
 Com6: hold
 Com7: hold
 Com8: buy
 Com9: hold
Com10: sell short
```

The second day's advice might be

```
 Com1: hold
 Com2: hold
 Com3: sell
 Com4: sell short
 Com5: hold
 Com6: hold
 Com7: buy
 Com8: buy on margin
 Com9: hold
Com10: sell
```

Remember, because the program waits for you to type a key, your output will differ from that shown here. You might prefer to run the program weekly or monthly instead of daily.

Feel free to alter the program in any way. For example, you could have the program give you amounts of stock to buy and sell, depending on your available investment dollars. Again, remember that this program is only for fun and is not recommended as a way to make actual investments in the market. However, it is interesting to create a portfolio on paper and to track its performance.

NINE

Expression Parsing
And Evaluation

How do you write a program that will take as input a string containing a numeric expression, for example, 10−5∗3, and return the answer, which in this case is −5? If a "high priesthood" still exists among programmers, then it must be made up of those few who know how to do this. Almost everyone who uses a computer is mystified by the way high-level language compilers, interpreters, and spreadsheet programs convert such complex expressions as 10∗3−(4+COUNT)/12 into instructions that a computer can execute. This conversion process is called *expression parsing*. It forms the backbone of all language compilers, interpreters, and spreadsheet programs. Few programmers know how to write an expression parser; this realm of programming is generally thought of as off-limits, except by the enlightened few.

However, this should not be so. Expression parsing is actually very straightforward and is similar to other programming tasks. In some ways it is easier, because it works with the strict rules of algebra. This chapter develops what is commonly referred to as a *recursive descent parser*, as well as all of the support routines that enable you to evaluate complex numeric expressions. All of these routines will be placed in one file that you use whenever you need it. After you have mastered the use of this file you can enhance and modify it to suit your needs—and join the "high priesthood" yourself.

Expressions

Although expressions can be made up of all types of information, you will be studying only one type: *numeric expressions*. For the purposes of this chapter, assume that numeric expressions can be made up of the following:

- Numbers
- The operators +, −, /, *, ^, and =
- Parentheses
- Variables.

The ^ symbol indicates exponentiation, as in BASIC, and the = symbol represents the assignment operator. All of these items follow the rules of algebra with which you are familiar. Some examples of expressions are

$$10-8$$
$$(100-5) * 14/6$$
$$a+b-c$$
$$10\char`^5$$
$$a=10-b$$

Assume the following precedence for each operator:

Highest:	^
	*/
	+ −
Lowest:	=

Operators of equal precedence evaluate from left to right.

For the examples in this chapter, the following assumptions have been made: All variables are single letters, which means that 26 variables—the letters A through Z—are available. All numbers are of type **integer**, although you could easily write the routines to handle floating-point numbers. Finally, only a minimal amount of error-checking is included in the routines to keep the logic clear and uncluttered.

Try to evaluate this sample expression:

$$10-2*3$$

This expression has a value of 4. Although you could easily create a program that would compute that specific expression, you may wonder how to create a computer program that will give the correct answer for any arbitrary expression. At first you might think that you could use a routine like this:

a := *get first operand*
while(*operands present*) **do**

```
begin
        op := get operator;
        b  := get second operand;
        a  := a op b
end;
```

According to this routine, you could get the first operand, the operator, and the second operand; perform the operation; then get the next operator and operand, if any; perform that operation; and so on. If you use this basic method, the expression 10−2*3 evaluates to 24 (that is, 8*3) instead of the correct answer, 4, because the procedure neglects the precedence of the operators. You cannot take the operands and operators in order from left to right, because the multiplication must be done before the subtraction. A beginner may think that this problem could be overcome easily—and sometimes, in very restrictive cases, it can—but the problem only gets worse when parentheses, exponentiation, variables, function calls, and the like are added in.

Although there are a few ways to write functions that evaluate expressions of this sort, you will study the one that is most easily written and is also the most common. (Some other methods used to write parsers employ complex tables that almost require another computer program to generate them. These are sometimes called *table-driven parsers*.) The method that you will examine is called a recursive descent parser, and in this chapter, you will see how it got its name.

Dissecting an Expression

Before you can develop a parser that evaluates expressions, you must get pieces of the expression easily. For example, given the expression

$$A*B-(W+10)$$

you must be able to get the operands A, B, W, and 10, the parentheses, and the operators *, +, and −. In general, you need a routine that returns each item in the expression individually. The routine also needs to skip over spaces and tabs, and it must know when the end of the expression has been reached.

Formally, each piece of an expression is called a *token*. Therefore, the function that returns the next token in the expression is called **GetToken**. A global string is needed to hold the expression string. In **GetToken**, this string is called **prog**. The **prog** variable is global because it must maintain its value between calls to **GetToken**, and it must allow other functions to use it. In addition to **prog**, the global integer **t** is used to index into **prog**, allowing **GetToken** to advance through the expression one token at a time. **GetToken** assumes that **prog** is terminated by a $. You must make sure that this is the case, because the $ signals the end of the expression.

Besides returning a token, you also need to know what type of token you are getting. For the parser developed in this chapter, you only need three types: **VARIABLE, NUMBER,** and **DELIMITER,** where **DELIMITER** is used for both operators and parentheses. Here is **GetToken** with its necessary globals, **#defines**, and support functions:

```pascal
type
    str80 = string[80];
    TType = (DELIMITER, VARIABLE, NUMBER);
var
    token,prog:str80;
    TokType: TType;
    code,t:integer;
    result:real;

function IsAlpha(ch:char):boolean;
{returns TRUE if ch is a letter of the alphabet}
begin
    IsAlpha:= (UpCase(ch)>='A') and (UpCase(ch)<='Z');
end; { IsAlpha }

function IsWhite(ch:char):boolean;
{True if newline, space or tab}
begin
    IsWhite:=(ch=' ') or (ch=chr(9)) or (ch=chr(13));
end; {IsWhite}

function IsDelim(ch:char):boolean;
{TRUE if is a delimiter}
begin
    if pos(ch,' +-/*%^=()$')<>0 then IsDelim:=TRUE
    else IsDelim:=FALSE;
end; {IsDelim}

function IsDigit(ch:char):boolean;
{TRUE if a digit between 0 and 9}
begin
    IsDigit:=(ch>='0') and (ch<='9');
end; {IsDigit}

procedure GetToken;
var
    temp:str80;
begin
    token:='';  {null string}
    while(IsWhite(prog[t])) do t:=t+1; {strip leading spaces}
    if prog[t]='$' then token:='$';
    if pos(prog[t],'+-*/%^=()')<>0 then
    begin
        TokType:=DELIMITER;
        token:=prog[t];  {is an operator}
```

```
      t:=t+1;
   end else if IsAlpha(prog[t]) then
   begin
      while(not IsDelim(prog[t])) do
      begin
         token:=concat(token,prog[t]);   {build variable}
         t:=t+1;
      end;
      TokType:=VARIABLE;
   end
   else if IsDigit(prog[t]) then
   begin
      while(not IsDelim(prog[t])) do
      begin
         token:=concat(token,prog[t]); {build number}
         t:=t+1;
         TokType:=NUMBER;
      end;
   end;
end; {GetToken}
```

Before this procedure can be used, the global variable t must be set to 1. Remember, this variable is used to index into the array **prog**, which holds the input expression. Upon entry into **GetToken**, the routine checks for the $ terminator, which indicates the end of the expression string. Next, leading spaces are skipped. Although spaces may be added into expressions to add clarity, the parser allows them but ignores them.

After the spaces have been skipped, **prog[t]** points to either a number, a variable, an operator, or a $ if trailing spaces end the expression. If the next character is an operator, that character is returned as a string in the global variable **token**, and the type of **DELIMITER** is placed in **TokType**. If that next character is a letter, it will be assumed to be one of the variables, and will be returned as a string in **token**; TokType is assigned the value **VARIABLE**. If that next character is a number, then the integer is returned as a string in **token** with a type of **NUMBER**. Finally, if the next character is none of these, you can then assume that the end of the expression has been reached, and **token** is a $.

To keep the code of this function clean, a certain amount of error-checking has been omitted and some assumptions have been made. For example, any unrecognized character is discarded. Also, in this version, variables may be any length, but only the first letter is significant. However, you can fill in these and other types of details, according to your specific application. You can modify or enhance **GetToken** easily to enable character strings, floating-point numbers, or whatever you want to return from an input string token.

To understand how **GetToken** works, study what it returns for each token and type for the following expression A+100−(B*C)/2.

Token	Token type
A	VARIABLE
+	DELIMITER
100	NUMBER
−	DELIMITER
(	DELIMITER
B	VARIABLE
*	DELIMITER
C	VARIABLE
)	DELIMITER
/	DELIMITER
2	NUMBER
$	$

Expression Parsing

Remember that there are several possible ways to parse and evaluate an expression. For the purposes of this chapter, think of expressions as *recursive data structures* that are defined in terms of themselves. If, for the moment, you restrict expressions to using only +, −, *, /, and parentheses, you could say that all expressions can be defined by using these rules:

> *Expression* => *term* [+ *term*] [− *term*]
> *term* => *factor* [* *factor*] [/ *factor*]
> *factor* => *variable*, *number*, or (*expression*)

where any part of these can be *nil*. The square brackets mean optional, and the => means "produces." In fact, the rules are called the *production rules* of the expression. Therefore, you would read the second rule as "Term produces factor times factor, or factor divided by factor." The precedence of the operators is implicit in the way an expression is defined.

The expression

$$10+5*B$$

has two terms: 10 and 5*B. However, it has three factors: 10, 5, and B. These factors consist of two numbers and one variable.

On the other hand, the expression

$$14*(7−C)$$

has two terms, 14 and (7−C), which is one number and one parenthesized expression. The parenthesized expression evaluates to one number and one variable.

This process forms the basis for a recursive descent parser, which is basically a set of mutually recursive routines that work in a chain-like fashion. At each appropriate step, the parser can perform the specified operations in the algebraically correct sequence. To see how this process works, follow the parsing of the input expression 9/3−(100+56) and perform the arithmetic operations at the right time:

Step 1. Get the first term: 9/3.

Step 2. Get each factor and divide integers. The resulting value is 3.

Step 3. Get the second term: (100+56). At this point, you must recursively analyze the second expression.

Step 4. Get each factor and add. The result is 156.

Step 5. Return from the recursive call and subtract 156 from 3, which yields an answer of −153.

If you are a little confused at this point, don't worry. This is a complex concept that takes some getting used to. There are two things to remember about this recursive view of expressions: first, the precedence of the operators is *implicit* in the way the production rules are defined; second, this method of parsing and evaluating expressions is very similar to the way you would do the same thing without a computer.

A Simple Expression Parser

In the remainder of this chapter, two parsers are developed. The first one parses and evaluates only constant expressions—that is, expressions with no variables. This is the parser in its simplest form. The second parser includes the 26 user-defined variables, A through Z, and allows assignments to those variables.

Here is the entire simple version of the recursive descent parser for integer expressions. It assumes the same global data shown for the **GetToken** procedure given earlier.

```
{ ********** Simple Expression Parser ************* }
procedure Level2(var result:real); forward;
procedure Level3(var result:real); forward;
procedure Level4(var result:read); forward;
procedure Level5(var result:real); forward;
procedure Level6(var result:real); forward;
procedure Primitive(var result:real); forward;
```

```
procedure GetExp(var result:real);
begin
   GetToken;
   if length(token)<>0 then
      Level2(result)
   else
      Serror(3);
end; {GetExp}

procedure Level2;
var
   op:char;
   hold:real;

begin
   Level3(result);
   op:=token[1];
   while((op='+') or (op='-') )do
   begin
      GetToken;
      Level3(hold);
      arith(op,result,hold);
      op:=token[1]
   end;
end; {Level2}

procedure Level3;
var
   op:char;
   hold:real;

begin
   Level4(result);
   op:=token[1];
   while ((op='*') or (op='/')) do
   begin
      GetToken;
      Level4(hold);
      arith(op,result,hold);
      op:=token[1];
   end;
end; {Level3}

procedure Level4;
var
   hold:real;

begin
   Level5(result);
   if token[1]='^' then
   begin
      GetToken;
      Level4(hold);
      arith('^',result,hold); {exponents}
   end;
end; {Level4}

procedure Level5;
var
   op:char;

begin
```

```
      op:=' ';
      if((TokType=DELIMITER) and ((token[1]='+') or (token[1]='-')))
      then
      begin   {unary plus or minus}
         op:=token[1];
         GetToken;
      end;
      Level6(result);
      if op='-' then result:=-result;
end; {Level5}

procedure Level6;
begin
   if(token[1]='(') and (TokType=DELIMITER) then
   begin   {Parenthesized expression}
      GetToken;
      Level2(result);
      if token[1]<>')' then Serror(2); {parentheses unbalanced}
      GetToken;
   end
   else Primitive(result);
end; {Level6}

procedure Primitive;
begin
   if TokType=NUMBER then
      val(token,result,code)
   else Serror(1);
   GetToken;
end; {Primitive}
```

The parser as shown can accept the operators: +, −, *, and /, as well as exponentiation (^), the unary minus, and parentheses. It has six levels, as well as the **Primitive** function, which returns the value of an integer number. The **forward** command is necessary because some of these routines are mutually recursive—hence, it is impossible to define all procedures prior to calling them.

In addition to the parser code just given, there are some special routines: **Serror**, which reports syntax errors, and **Pwr** and **Arith**, which perform the various arithmetic operations. These subprograms are shown here:

```
Procedure Serror(i:integer); {print error messages}
begin
   case i of
      1: WriteLn('Syntax Error');
      2: WriteLn('Unbalanced Parentheses');
      3: Writeln('No Expression Present');
   end;
end; {Serror}

function Pwr(a,b:real):real;
{raise a to b power}
var
   t: integer;
   temp:real;
begin
```

```
      if a=0 then Pwr:=1 else
      begin
         temp:=a;
         for t:=trunc(b) downto 2 do a:=a*temp;
         Pwr:=a;
      end;
end; {Pwr}

procedure Arith(op:char; var result,operand:real);
{perform arithmetic functions}
begin
   case op of
      '+':result:=result+operand;
      '-':result:=result-operand;
      '*':result:=result*operand;
      '/':result:=result/operand;
      '^':result:=Pwr(result,operand);
   end;
end; {Arith}
```

As shown earlier, the two globals, **token** and **TokType**, return the next token and its type from the expression string, and the **prog** string holds the expression.

Here is the entire parser and all support routines, along with a simple program that can be used to demonstrate it:

```
program parser;   {parser for reals and operators - no
                    variables }
type
    str80 = string[80];
    TType = (DELIMITER, VARIABLE, NUMBER);
var
    token,prog:str80;
    TokType: TType;
    code,t:integer;
    result:real;

function IsAlpha(ch:char):boolean;
{returns TRUE if ch is a letter of the alphabet}
begin
    IsAlpha:= (UpCase(ch)>='A') and (UpCase(ch)<='Z');
end; { IsAlpha }

function IsWhite(ch:char):boolean;
{True if newline, space or tab}
begin
    IsWhite:=(ch=' ') or (ch=chr(9)) or (ch=chr(13));
end; {IsWhite}

function IsDelim(ch:char):boolean;
{TRUE if is a delimiter}
begin
    if pos(ch,' +-/*%^=()$')<>0 then IsDelim:=TRUE
    else IsDelim:=FALSE;
end; {IsDelim}

function IsDigit(ch:char):boolean;
```

```
{TRUE if a digit between 0 and 9}
begin
   IsDigit:=(ch>='0') and (ch<='9');
end; {IsDigit}

procedure GetToken;
var
   temp:str80;

begin
   token:='';   {null string}
   while(IsWhite(prog[t])) do t:=t+1; {strip leading spaces}
   if prog[t]='$' then token:='$';
   if pos(prog[t],'+-*/%^=()')<>0 then
   begin
      TokType:=DELIMITER;
      token:=prog[t];   {is an operator}
      t:=t+1;
   end else if IsAlpha(prog[t]) then
   begin
      while(not IsDelim(prog[t])) do
      begin
         token:=concat(token,prog[t]);   {build token}
         t:=t+1;
         end;
         TokType:=VARIABLE;
      end
      else if IsDigit(prog[t]) then
      begin
         while(not IsDelim(prog[t])) do
         begin
            token:=concat(token,prog[t]); {build number}
            t:=t+1;
            TokType:=NUMBER;
         end;
      end;
   end; {GetToken}

Procedure Serror(i:integer); {print error messages}
begin
   case i of
      1: WriteLn('Syntax Error');
      2: WriteLn('Unbalanced Parentheses');
      3: Writeln('No Expression Present');
   end;
end; {Serror}

function Pwr(a,b:real):real;
{raise a to b power}
var
   t: integer;
   temp:real;
begin
   if a=0 then Pwr:=1 else
   begin
      temp:=a;
      for t:=trunc(b) downto 2 do a:=a*temp;
      Pwr:=a;
   end;
end; {Pwr}
```

```
procedure Arith(op:char; var result,operand:real);
{perform arithmetic functions}
begin
   case op of
      '+':result:=result+operand;
      '-':result:=result-operand;
      '*':result:=result*operand;
      '/':result:=result/operand;
      '^':result:=Pwr(result,operand);
   end;
end; {Arith}

{ ********** Expression Parser ************ }
procedure Level2(var result:real); forward;
procedure Level3(var result:real); forward;
procedure Level4(var result:real); forward;
procedure Level5(var result:real); forward;
procedure Level6(var result:real); forward;
procedure Primitive(var result:real); forward;


procedure GetExp(var result:real);
begin
   GetToken;
   if length(token)<>0 then
      Level2(result)
   else
      Serror(3);
end; {GetExp}

procedure Level2;
var
   op:char;
   hold:real;

begin
   Level3(result);
   op:=token[1];
   while((op='+') or (op='-') )do
   begin
      GetToken;
      Level3(hold);
      arith(op,result,hold);
      op:=token[1]
   end;
end; {Level2}

procedure Level3;
var
   op:char;
   hold:real;

begin
   Level4(result);
   op:=token[1];
   while ((op='*') or (op='/')) do
   begin
      GetToken;
      Level4(hold);
      arith(op,result,hold);
      op:=token[1];
   end;
```

```
end; {Level3}

procedure Level4;
var
    hold:real;

begin
    Level5(result);
    if token[1]='^' then
    begin
        GetToken;
        Level4(hold);
        arith('^',result,hold); {exponents}
    end;
end; {Level4}

procedure Level5;
var
    op:char;

begin
    op:=' ';
    if((TokType=DELIMITER) and ((token[1]='+') or (token[1]='-')))
    then
    begin    {unary plus or minus}
        op:=token[1];
        GetToken;
    end;
    Level6(result);
    if op='-' then result:=-result;
end; {Level5}

procedure Level6;
begin
    if(token[1]='(') and (TokType=DELIMITER) then
    begin    {Parenthesized expression}
        GetToken;
        Level2(result);
        if token[1]<>')' then Serror(2); {parentheses unbalanced}
        GetToken;
    end
    else Primitive(result);
end; {Level6}

procedure Primitive;
begin
    if TokType=NUMBER then
        val(token,result,code)
    else Serror(1);
    GetToken;
end; {Primitive}

begin   {main}
    repeat
        t:=1;   {initialize token counter}
        Write('enter an expression: ');
        ReadLn(prog);
        prog:=concat(prog,'$');
        GetExp(result);
        WriteLn(result);
    until prog='quit$'
end.
```

To understand exactly how the parser evaluates an expression, work through the following expression, which you can assume is contained in **prog**.

$$10-3*2$$

When **GetExp** (the entry routine into the parser) is called, it gets the first token and, if that token is **nil**, prints the message **no expression present** before it returns. If a token is present, then **Level2** is called. (**Level1** will be added to the parser later when the assignment operator is added, but it is not needed here.)

The token now contains the number 10. **Level2** calls **Level3**, and **Level3** calls **Level4**, which in turn calls **Level5**. **Level5** checks to see if the token is a unary + or −, which it is not in this case, so **Level6** is called. **Level6** either recursively calls **Level2** in the case of a parenthesized expression or calls **Primitive** to find the value of the integer. Finally, when **Primitive** is executed and the value 10 is placed in **result**, **GetToken** obtains another token. The functions then begin to return up the chain. At this time, the token is now the operator − and the functions return up to **Level2**.

The next step is very important. Because the token is a −, it is saved and **GetToken** obtains the new token 3; the descent down the chain begins again. Again, **Primitive** is entered, the integer 3 is returned in **result**, and the token * is read. This causes a return back up the chain to **Level3**, where the final token 2 is read. At this point, the first arithmetic operation occurs with the multiplication of 2 and 3. This result is then returned to **Level2**, and the subtraction is performed to yield an answer of 4.

Although the process may seem complicated at first, you should work through some other examples to verify for yourself that it functions correctly every time.

You could use this parser as a desktop calculator, as illustrated by the program used to show the use of the parser. You could also use it in a database or a simple spreadsheet application. Before it could be used in a language or a sophisticated calculator, the parser would have to be able to handle variables, which is the subject of the next section.

Adding Variables to the Parser

All programming languages and many calculators and spreadsheets use variables to store values for later use. The simple parser in the preceding section must be expanded to include variables before you can use it for this purpose. First you need the variables themselves. Since the parser is restricted to integer expressions, you can use integer variables. The parser will only recognize the variables A through Z, although you could expand it if you wanted to. Each variable uses one array location in a 26-element array. Therefore, you should add the following:

```
vars:array[0..25] of real;   {26 variables}
```

Before these variables are used, however, you should initialize them to 0.

You also need a routine to look up the value of a given variable. Because you are using the letters A to Z as variable names, you can easily index the array **vars** based on its name. Here is the function **FindVar**:

```
function FindVar(s:str80):real;
var
    t:integer;
begin
    FindVar:=vars[Ord(Upcase(s[1]))-Ord('A')];
end; {FindVar}
```

As written, this function actually accepts long variable names, but only the first letter is significant. You can modify this feature to fit your needs.

You must also modify the **Primitive** function to treat both numbers and variables as primitives, as shown here:

```
procedure Primitive;
begin
    if TokType=NUMBER then
        val(token,result,code)
    else if TokType=VARIABLE then
        result:=FindVar(token)
    else
        Serror(1);
    GetToken;
end; {Primitive}
```

Technically, this is all you need for the parser to use variables correctly; however, there is no way for these variables to be assigned values. You can often assign variables outside the parser, but, since it is possible to treat = as an assignment operator, you can make it part of the parser through various methods. One is to add a **Level1** to the parser, as shown here:

```
procedure Level1;
var
    hold:real;
    temp:TType;
    slot:integer;
    TempToken:str80;

begin
    if TokType=VARIABLE then
    begin
        {save old token}
        TempToken:=token;
```

```
      temp:=TokType;
      slot:=Ord(UpCase(token[1]))-Ord('A');
      GetToken;  {see if there is = for assignment}
      if token[1]<>'=' then
      begin
         PutBack;  {replace the token}
         {restore old token}
         token:=TempToken;
         TokType:=temp;
         Level2(result);
      end else
      begin {is assignment}
         GetToken;
         Level2(result);
         vars[slot]:=result;
      end;
   end {if}
   else Level2(result);
end; {Level1}
```

When a variable is encountered as the first token in an expression, the variable may be either the target of an assignment, as in

$$A=B*10$$

or it may simply be part of an expression, such as

$$A-123.23$$

For **Level1** to know what the variable is, a *look ahead* must be performed. "Look ahead" is the process of saving the current token and then obtaining the next token to see what it is. In this case, if the next token is =, then you know that an assignment is being made and the proper routines are executed. If it is not =, then the token must be put back into the expression string, and the previous token must be recovered. You can do this through the procedure **Putback,** which simply decrements the index t. As you can see, "look ahead" can be a time-consuming process and should generally be avoided except when it is absolutely necessary.

Here is the entire enhanced parser, support routines, and main program:

```
program parser2;  {Parser that includes variables}
type
    str80 = string[80];
    TType = (DELIMITER, VARIABLE, NUMBER);
var
   token,prog:str80;
   TokType: TType;
   code,t:integer;
   result:real;
   vars:array[0..25] of real;  {26 variables}

function IsAlpha(ch:char):boolean;
{returns TRUE if ch is a letter of the alphabet}
```

```
begin
   IsAlpha:= (UpCase(ch)>='A') and (UpCase(ch)<='Z');
end;  { IsAlpha }

function IsWhite(ch:char):boolean;
{True if newline, space or tab}
begin
   IsWhite:=(ch=' ') or (ch=chr(9)) or (ch=chr(13));
end;  {IsWhite}

function IsDelim(ch:char):boolean;
{TRUE if is a delimiter}
begin
   if pos(ch,' +-/*%^=()$')<>0 then IsDelim:=TRUE
   else IsDelim:=FALSE;
end; {IsDelim}

function IsDigit(ch:char):boolean;
{TRUE if a digit between 0 and 9}
begin
   IsDigit:=(ch>='0') and (ch<='9');
end; {IsDigit}

procedure GetToken;
var
   temp:str80;

begin
   token:='';  {null string}
   while(IsWhite(prog[t])) do t:=t+1; {strip leading spaces}
   if prog[t]='$' then token:='$';
   if pos(prog[t],'+-*/%^=()')<>0 then
   begin
      TokType:=DELIMITER;
      token:=prog[t];  {is an operator}
      t:=t+1;
   end else if IsAlpha(prog[t]) then
   begin
      while(not IsDelim(prog[t])) do
      begin
         token:=concat(token,prog[t]);  {build token}
         t:=t+1;
      end;
      TokType:=VARIABLE;
   end
   else if IsDigit(prog[t]) then
   begin
      while(not IsDelim(prog[t])) do
      begin
         token:=concat(token,prog[t]); {build number}
         t:=t+1;
         TokType:=NUMBER;
      end;
   end;
end; {GetToken}


procedure PutBack;  {put back unused token}
begin
   t:=t-length(token);
end; {PutBack}
```

```pascal
Procedure Serror(i:integer); {print error messages}
begin
   case i of
      1: WriteLn('Syntax Error');
      2: WriteLn('Unbalanced Parentheses');
      3: WriteLn('No Expression Present');
   end;
end; {Serror}

function Pwr(a,b:real):real;
{raise a to b power}
var
   t: integer;
   temp:real;
begin
   if a=0 then Pwr:=1 else
   begin
      temp:=a;
      for t:=trunc(b) downto 2 do a:=a*temp;
      Pwr:=a;
   end;
end; {Pwr}

function FindVar(s:str80):real;
var
   t:integer;
begin
   FindVar:=vars[Ord(Upcase(s[1]))-Ord('A')];
end; {FindVar}

procedure Arith(op:char; var result,operand:real);
{perform arithmetic functions}
begin
   case op of
      '+':result:=result+operand;
      '-':result:=result-operand;
      '*':result:=result*operand;
      '/':result:=result/operand;
      '^':result:=Pwr(result,operand);
   end;
end; {Arith}

{ ********** Expression Parser ************ }
{ **** with variables and assignment ****** }
procedure Level2(var result:real); forward;
procedure Level1(var result:real); forward;
procedure Level3(var result:real); forward;
procedure Level4(var result:real); forward;
procedure Level5(var result:real); forward;
procedure Level6(var result:real); forward;
procedure Primitive(var result:real); forward;


procedure GetExp(var result:real);
begin
   GetToken;
   if length(token)<>0 then
      Level1(result)
   else
      Serror(3);
```

```pascal
end; {GetExp}

procedure Level1;
var
   hold:real;
   temp:TType;
   slot:integer;
   TempToken:str80;

begin
   if TokType=VARIABLE then
   begin
      {save old token}
      TempToken:=token;
      temp:=TokType;
      slot:=Ord(UpCase(token[1]))-Ord('A');
      GetToken;   {see if there is = for assignment}
      if token[1]<>'=' then
      begin
         PutBack;   {replace the token}
         {restore old token}
         token:=TempToken;
         TokType:=temp;
         Level2(result);
      end else
      begin {is assignment}
         GetToken;
         Level2(result);
         vars[slot]:=result;
      end;
   end {if}
   else Level2(result);
end; {Level1}


procedure Level2;
var
   op:char;
   hold:real;

begin
   Level3(result);
   op:=token[1];
   while((op='+') or (op='-') )do
   begin
      GetToken;
      Level3(hold);
      arith(op,result,hold);
      op:=token[1]
   end;
end; {Level2}

procedure Level3;
var
   op:char;
   hold:real;

begin
   Level4(result);
   op:=token[1];
```

```
      while ((op='*') or (op='/')) do
      begin
         GetToken;
         Level4(hold);
         arith(op,result,hold);
         op:=token[1];
      end;
end; {Level3}

procedure Level4;
var
   hold:real;

begin
   Level5(result);
   if token[1]='^' then
   begin
      GetToken;
      Level4(hold);
      arith('^',result,hold); {exponents}
   end;
end; {Level4}

procedure Level5;
var
   op:char;

begin
   op:=' ';
   if((TokType=DELIMITER) and ((token[1]='+') or (token[1]='-')))
   then
   begin    {unary plus or minus}
      op:=token[1];
      GetToken;
   end;
   Level6(result);
   if op='-' then result:=-result;
end; {Level5}

procedure Level6;
begin
   if(token[1]='(') and (TokType=DELIMITER) then
   begin  {Parenthesized expression}
      GetToken;
      Level2(result);
      if token[1]<>')' then Serror(2); {parentheses unbalanced}
      GetToken;
   end
   else Primitive(result);
end; {Level6}

procedure Primitive;
begin
   if TokType=NUMBER then
      val(token,result,code)
   else if TokType=VARIABLE then
      result:=FindVar(token)
   else
      Serror(1);
   GetToken;
end; {Primitive}
```

```
begin  {main}
   for t:=0 to 25 do vars[t]:=0; {initialize variables}
   repeat
      t:=1;
      Write('enter an expression: ');
      ReadLn(prog);
      prog:=concat(prog,'$');
      GetExp(result);
      WriteLn(result);
   until prog='quit$';
end.
```

With the enhanced parser, you can now enter expressions such as

$$A=10/4$$
$$A-B$$
$$C=A*(F-21)$$

and they will be properly evaluated.

Syntax-Checking in a Recursive Descent Parser

In expression parsing, a syntax error is a situation in which the input expression does not conform to the strict rules required by the parser. Most of the time, a syntax error is caused by human error—usually in the form of typing mistakes. For example, the following expressions will not be parsed correctly by the parsers given in this chapter:

$$10**8$$
$$(10-5)*9)$$
$$/8$$

The first expression has two operators in a row, the second has unbalanced parentheses, and the last has a division sign starting an expression. Because syntax errors can confuse the parser and cause it to give erroneous results, it is important—indeed necessary—to guard against them.

As you studied the code for the parsers, you probably noticed the function **Serror**, which is called in certain situations. Unlike many other parsers, the recursive descent method makes syntax-checking very easy, because for the most part, it occurs in either **Primitive**, **FindVar**, or **Level6**, where parentheses are checked. The syntax-checking as it now stands has only one problem: the entire parser is not aborted on syntax error. This can cause multiple error messages to be generated.

To add complete error recovery, you must add a global variable that is checked at each level. The variable would initially be FALSE, and any call to

Serror would set it to TRUE, causing the parser to abort one function at a time.

If you leave the code the way it is, all that will happen is that multiple syntax error messages may be issued. While this could be an annoyance in some situations, it could be a blessing in others, because in some cases multiple errors will be caught. Generally, however, you will want to enhance the syntax-checking before using it in commercial programs.

TEN

Converting C and BASIC
To Turbo Pascal

Most programmers spend much of their time converting programs from one language into another. This is called *translating*. You may find the process to be either easy or difficult, depending on the methods you use to translate and on how well you know the source and destination languages. This chapter presents topics and techniques that will help you convert C and BASIC programs into Turbo Pascal.

Why would anyone want to translate a program written in one language into another? One reason is *maintainability*: a program written in an unstructured language like BASIC is difficult to maintain or enhance. Another reason is *speed and efficiency*: Turbo Pascal as a language is very efficient, and some demanding tasks have been translated into Turbo Pascal for better performance. A third reason is *practicality*: a user may see a useful program listed in one language but may own or use a compiler in a different language. You will probably find that you want to translate a program into Turbo Pascal for one or more of these reasons.

C and BASIC were chosen from the field of nearly a hundred computer languages because they are popular languages among microcomputer users and because they represent opposite ends of the programming-language spectrum. C is a structured language that has many similarities to Turbo Pascal, whereas BASIC is a nonstructured language and has virtually no similarities to Turbo Pascal. Although this chapter cannot cover the translation of these languages in every detail, it will examine several of the most important problems that you will confront. You must be already familiar with either C or BASIC; this chapter does not teach you either language.

Converting C to Turbo Pascal

C and Turbo Pascal have many similarities, especially in their control structures and their use of stand-alone subroutines with local variables. This makes it possible to do lots of *one-to-one translating*, which is the process of substituting Turbo Pascal's keyword or function for its equivalent keyword in C. With one-to-one translating you can use the computer to assist you with the translation process; a simple translation program will be developed later in the chapter.

Although C and Turbo Pascal are similar, there are several major differences between them. First, C does not use strong type-checking while Turbo Pascal does. Therefore, some types of routines written in C must be modified to make all operand types agree. For example, in C, character and integer types may be freely intermixed; in Turbo Pascal, they may not be intermixed without using certain type-conversion functions. (However, remember that strong type-checking—or the absence of it—does not necessarily make a language better or worse. It just changes the way a programmer thinks about a task.)

A second and more important difference is that C is not formally *block structured*, whereas Turbo Pascal is. The term *block structured* refers to a language's ability to create logically connected units of code that can be referenced together. The term also means that procedures can have other procedures nested inside them that will be known only to the outer procedure. Although C is commonly called block structured because it allows blocks of code to be created easily, it does not allow functions to be defined inside other functions. For example, the following code in C requires two functions:

```
A()
{
    printf("starting A\n");
    B();
}

B()
{
    printf("inside function B\n");
}
```

You would also have to make sure that there were no other functions called **B( )** anywhere else in the program. However, when this code is translated into Turbo Pascal, it looks like this:

```
procedure A;
var
```

```
   x:integer;

   procedure B;
   begin
      WriteLn('inside proc b');
   end;
begin
   WriteLn('starting A');
   B;
end;
```

Here, **procedure B** is defined inside of **procedure A**. This means that **procedure B** is known only to **procedure A** and may only be used by **procedure A**. Outside of **procedure A**, another **procedure B** could be defined without conflict.

A third difference between C and Turbo Pascal is that all C variables must be declared before they are used, but forward references to functions are not restricted and in fact are very common. But in Pascal, all variables, functions, and procedures must be declared before they are used. In standard Pascal, this means that if you must reference a function or procedure before it is declared, then you must use a **forward** declaration.

A fourth difference between C and Pascal is that *separate compilation* and linking are encouraged in C, whereas standard Pascal does not support them. Separate compilation is the process of compiling your program in pieces and then linking the pieces together with a linker. As discussed in Chapter 5, Turbo Pascal does allow external subroutines to be combined with a Pascal program, but not by separate compilation and linking, which is how most C compilers do it.

A Comparison of C and Turbo Pascal

Figure 10-1 compares Turbo Pascal keywords with C keywords and operators. As you can see, many Turbo Pascal keywords have no C equivalent. This is due in part to the fact that Turbo Pascal uses keywords in places where C uses operators to accomplish the same steps. At times, Turbo Pascal is simply "wordier" than C.

In addition to the keywords, Turbo Pascal has several built-in *standard identifiers* that can be used directly in a program. These identifiers may be functions (like **WriteLn**) or global variables (like **MaxInt**) that hold information about the state of the system. Also, Turbo Pascal uses standard identifiers to specify such data types as **real**, **integer**, **boolean**, and **character**. Figure 10-2 shows several of the more common C identifiers with their standard Pascal equivalents. In addition to these, any other C equivalents of

Turbo Pascal	C	Turbo Pascal	C
and	&&	mod	%
array		nil	(sometimes \0)
begin	{	not	!
case	switch	of	
const		or	||
div	/	packed	
do		procedure	
downto		program	
else	else	record	struct
end	}	repeat	do
file		set	
forward	extern (on occasion)	then	
for	for	type	
function		to	
goto	goto	until	while (as in do/while)
if	if	var	
in		while	while
label		with	

Figure 10-1.   A comparison of Turbo Pascal and C keywords

C	Turbo Pascal
char or int	boolean
char	byte
char	char
EOF	EOF
0	FALSE
flush (in library)	flush
integer	integer
scanf( ) and others	Read or ReadLn
float	real
any one-zero value	TRUE
printf( )	Write or WriteLn

Figure 10-2.   C equivalents of some standard Pascal identifiers

Pascal's built-in functions may be found in the C standard library; however, they may vary from compiler to compiler.

C also differs from Turbo Pascal in its operators. Figure 10-3 shows the C operators and their Turbo Pascal equivalents.

Converting C Loops Into Turbo Pascal Loops

Because program control loops are fundamental to most programs, this section compares C's loops to Turbo Pascal's loops. C has three built-in loops: **for**, **while**, and **do/while**.

C's **for** loop has the general form

for(*initialization; condition; increment*) *statement*;

The C **for** is much more general a statement than the Turbo Pascal **for/do**: the test condition does not have to be a target value, as in Turbo Pascal; rather it can be any Boolean expression. There is also no mechanism to tell you whether the loop is running positively or negatively, because C

C	Turbo Pascal	Meaning
+	+	Addition
−	−	Subtraction
*	*	Multiplication
/	/	Division
/	div	Integer division
%	mod	Modulus
	^	Exponentiation
=	:=	Assignment
==	=	Equals as a condition
<	<	Less than
>	>	Greater than
>=	>=	Greater than or equal to
<=	<=	Less than or equal to
!=	<>	Not equal

Figure 10-3.   C operators and their Turbo Pascal equivalents

does not use Turbo Pascal's **to** and **downto** convention. Another difference is that both the initialization and increment sections can be compound—something that has no parallel in Turbo Pascal. However, despite these differences, a C **for** loop will often have the form of the standard Pascal **for/do**, which makes translation a simple matter. For example, the C **for** loop

```
for(x=10;x<=100;++x) printf("%d\n",x);
```

can be translated into Pascal as

```
for x:=10 to 100 do WriteLn(x);
```

The C **while** and the Turbo Pascal **while/do** are virtually the same. However, C's **do/while** and Turbo Pascal's **repeat/until** require that you use different keywords and "reverse" the loop test. This is because the C **do/while** loops *while* the loop condition *is* true, whereas the Turbo Pascal **until** loops *until* something *becomes* true. A sample translation of both types of loops is shown here:

```
C                         Turbo Pascal

while(x<5)                while x<5 do
{                         begin
    printf("%d\n",x);        WriteLn(x);
    x=getnum();              Read(x);
}                         end;

do {                      repeat
    x=getnum();              Read(x);
    printf("%d\n",x);        WriteLn(x);
} while(x<=5);            until x>5;
```

Be careful when you translate **do/while** into **repeat/until**: you must reverse the sense of the test condition. (There have been some philosophical discussions concerning the **do/while** versus the **repeat/until**. The **do/while** is considered positive because it loops while the condition is TRUE; the **repeat/until** has been called a negative statement, because the loop executes as long as the condition is FALSE. It has been suggested that choosing the easiest loop to use is based on whether you are an optimist or a pessimist—but this is yet to be proved.)

A Sample Translation

To give you a sense of the translation process, follow the steps of converting a C program into Turbo Pascal. On the next page is a simple C program.

```
float qwerty;

main()
{
   qwerty=0;
   printf("%f",qwerty);
   printf("hello there\n");
   tom(25);
   printf("%f\n",ken(10));
   printf("%2.4f\n",qwerty):
}

tom(x)
int x;
{
   printf("%d", x*2);
}

float ken(w)
float w;
{
   qwerty=23.34;
   return w/3.1415;
}
```

This C program has three functions declared. (Keep in mind that all C sub-routines are functions, whether the return value is used or not.) The first step in translating this program into Turbo Pascal is to determine which C functions will become Turbo Pascal functions (that is, those that will return a value), and which will simply be procedures.

You can determine this by looking for the C keyword **return**. If it is present in a function, you can assume that a value is going to be returned. (Technically, this may not always be the case, but it is sufficient for this example.) The only function that uses a **return** is **ken**. Therefore, the Turbo Pascal equivalent of **ken** is

```
function ken (w: real): real;
begin
   ken:=w/3.1415;
   qwerty:=23.34
end;
```

The C function **tom** does not return a value, so it becomes a procedure in Turbo Pascal.

```
procedure tom (x: integer);
begin
   WriteLn(x*2);
end;
```

Next, the **main** function must be converted into the program code for the Turbo Pascal version shown on the following page.

```
begin
   qwerty:=0;
   WriteLn(qwerty);
   WriteLn('hello there');
   tom(25);
   WriteLn(ken(10));
   WriteLn(qwerty:2:4);
end.
```

Finally, you must declare the global variable **qwerty** as a **real**, and add the program header. When you do this and put the pieces together, the Turbo Pascal translation of the C program looks like this:

```
program test (input,output);
var qwerty: real;

procedure tom (x: integer);
begin
   WriteLn(x*2);
end;

function ken (w: real): real;
begin
   ken:=w/3.1415;
   qwerty:=23.34
end;

begin
   qwerty:=0;
   WriteLn(qwerty);
   WriteLn('hello there');
   tom(25);
   WriteLn(ken(10));
   WriteLn(qwerty:2:4);
end.
```

Using the Computer to Help You Convert C to Turbo Pascal

It is possible to construct a computer program that accepts source code in one language and outputs it in another. The best way to do this is to implement a complete language parser for the source language—but instead of generating code, it will output the destination language. You can occasionally find advertisements for such products in computer magazines, and their high prices reflect the complexity of the task.

A less ambitious approach is to construct a simple program to assist your program-conversion efforts by performing some of the simpler translation tasks. This "computer assist" can really make conversion jobs much easier.

A computer-assist translator accepts as input a program in the source language and performs all one-to-one translations into the destination language automatically, leaving the harder conversions up to you. For example, to assign **count** the value of 10, in C, you would write

```
count=10;
```

In Turbo Pascal, the statement is the same, except there is a colon next to the = sign. Therefore, the computer-assist translator can change the = assignment statement in C to the := in Turbo Pascal. Another example is the C **while** loop: the keyword **while** is used in the same way in Turbo Pascal.

However, C and Turbo Pascal access disk files in different ways, and there is no easy way to perform such a conversion automatically. Also, converting the C **do/while** into the Turbo Pascal **repeat/until** cannot easily be automated. Hence, these complicated translations are left to you.

Here are the steps to create a C-to-Turbo Pascal translator. First, a C-to-Turbo Pascal translator needs a function that returns one token at a time from the C program. The function **GetToken** developed in Chapter 9 can be modified for this use, as shown here:

```
procedure GetToken;
var
    temp:str80;

begin
    token:='';   {null string}
    While(IsWhite(prog[t])) do t:=t+1; {strip leading spaces}
    if prog[t]='$' then token:='$';
    if (pos(prog[t],'.#:;,+|<>&~-*/!%^=(){}')<>0)
        or (prog[t]=chr(39)) then
        begin
        if (prog[t]='{') or (prog[t]='}') then
        begin
            TokType:=NAME;
            if prog[t]='{' then
            begin
                token:='begin';
                indent:=indent+1;
            end else
            begin
                token:='end';
                indent:=indent-1;
            end;
        end
```

```
        else
        begin
            TokType:=DELIMITER;
            token:=prog[t];  {is an operator}
        end;
        t:=t+1;
    end else if IsAlpha(prog[t]) then
    begin
        while(not IsDelim(prog[t])) do
        begin
            token:=concat(token,prog[t]);  {build token}
            t:=t+1;
        end;
        TokType:=NAME;
    end
    else if IsDigit(prog[t]) then
    begin
        while(not IsDelim(prog[t])) do
        begin
            token:=concat(token,prog[t]); {build number}
            t:=t+1;
            TokType:=NUMBER;
        end;
    end else if prog[t]='"' then  {is string}
    begin
        t:=t+1;
        token:=chr(39);  { a ' }
        while prog[t]<>'"' do
        begin
            token:=concat(token,prog[t]);
            t:=t+1;
            TokType:=STR;
        end;
        t:=t+1;  {go past closing quotes}
        token:=concat(token,chr(39));
    end;
end; {GetToken}
```

C's { and } symbols are transformed into their Pascal equivalents **begin** and
end inside **GetToken** in order to simplify certain other areas of the program
later on.

The second step in creating the translator is to provide a routine that translates elements of the C language into their Turbo Pascal counterparts. The
function **translate** shown here is not the best way to code such a routine, but
it is sufficient for the translator's purposes.

```
procedure Translate;  {translate C into Pascal}
begin
    case token[1] of
        '~': token:='not';
        '=': {look ahead to see if double equals}
            begin
                GetToken;
                if token='=' then token:='=='
                else
                begin
                    PutBack;  {restore token to stream}
```

```
                    token:=':='; {assignment}
                 end;
            end;
        '!': {look ahead to see if <> or NOT}
             begin
                GetToken;
                if token='=' then token:='<>'
                else
                begin
                   PutBack;
                   token:='not';
                end;
             end;
        '%': token:='mod';
        '|': begin
                GetToken;
                if token<>'|' then PutBack; {not double or}
                token:='or';
             end;
        '&': begin
                GetToken;
                if token<>'&' then PutBack; {not double and}
                token:='and'
             end;
        '~': token:='xor';
    end;

    {now check for keywords}
    if token='switch' then token:='case'
    else if token='struct' then token:='record'
    else if token='int' then token:='integer'
    else if token='float' then token:='real'
    else if token='printf' then token:='Write'
    else if token='extern' then token:='forward'
    else if token='case' then token:='';
end;  {Translate}
```

Notice that in most cases, C keywords and operators are simply passed through, because they are the same in Turbo Pascal. However, in the case of the C **while** and **do/while** loops, it is impossible to know with this method whether you need a Pascal **while/do** loop or a **repeat/until** loop.

Here is the entire translation program:

```
program CToPascal;  { A simple C-to-Turbo Pascal convertor }
type
     str80 = string[80];
     TType = (DELIMITER, NAME, NUMBER,STR);
var
    inname,outname,token,prog:string[255];
    TokType: TType;
    infile,outfile: text;
    indent,t:integer;

function IsAlpha(ch:char):boolean;
{returns TRUE if ch is a letter of the alphabet}
begin
```

```
    IsAlpha:= (UpCase(ch)>='A') and (UpCase(ch)<='Z');
end; { IsAlpha }

function IsWhite(ch:char):boolean;
{True if newline, space or tab}
begin
    IsWhite:=(ch=' ') or (ch=chr(9)) or (ch=chr(13));
end; {IsWhite}

function IsDelim(ch:char):boolean;
{TRUE if is a delimiter}
begin
    if ch=chr(39) then IsDelim:=TRUE  {a ' }
    else if pos(ch,' #:.,;<>|&~+-/*%^=!()${}')<>0 then IsDelim:=TRUE
    else IsDelim:=FALSE;
end; {IsDelim}

function IsDigit(ch:char):boolean;
{TRUE if a digit between 0 and 9}
begin
    IsDigit:=(ch>='0') and (ch<='9');
end; {IsDigit}

procedure GetToken;
var
    temp:str80;

begin
    token:='';  {null string}
    while(IsWhite(prog[t])) do t:=t+1; {strip leading spaces}
    if prog[t]='$' then token:='$';
    if (pos(prog[t],'.#:,+|<>&~-*/!%^=(){}')<>0)
      or (prog[t]=chr(39)) then
        begin
        if (prog[t]='{') or (prog[t]='}') then
        begin
            TokType:=NAME;
            if prog[t]='{' then
            begin
                token:='begin';
                indent:=indent+1;
            end else
            begin
                token:='end';
                indent:=indent-1;
            end;
        end
        else
        begin
            TokType:=DELIMITER;
            token:=prog[t];  {is an operator}
        end;
        t:=t+1;
    end else if IsAlpha(prog[t]) then
    begin
        while(not IsDelim(prog[t])) do
        begin
            token:=concat(token,prog[t]);  {build token}
            t:=t+1;
        end;
        TokType:=NAME;
    end
```

```
   else if IsDigit(prog[t]) then
   begin
      while(not IsDelim(prog[t])) do
      begin
         token:=concat(token,prog[t]); {build number}
         t:=t+1;
         TokType:=NUMBER;
      end;
   end else if prog[t]='"' then   {is string}
   begin
      t:=t+1;
      token:=chr(39);   { a ' }
      while prog[t]<>'"' do
      begin
         token:=concat(token,prog[t]);
         t:=t+1;
         TokType:=STR;
      end;
      t:=t+1;  {go past closing quotes}
      token:=concat(token,chr(39));
   end;
end; {GetToken}

procedure PutBack;  {put back unused token}
begin
   t:=t-length(token);
end; {PutBack}

procedure Translate;  {translate C into Pascal}
begin
   case token[1] of
      '~': token:='not';
      '=': {look ahead to see if double equals}
           begin
              GetToken;
              if token='=' then token:='=='
              else
              begin
                 PutBack; {restore token to stream}
                 token:=':='; {assignment}
              end;
           end;
      '!': {look ahead to see if <> or NOT}
           begin
              GetToken;
              if token='=' then token:='<>'
              else
              begin
                 PutBack;
                 token:='not';
              end;
           end;
      '%': token:='mod';
      '|': begin
              GetToken;
              if token<>'|' then PutBack; {not double or}
              token:='or';
           end;
      '&': begin
              GetToken;
              if token<>'&' then PutBack; {not double and}
              token:='and'
```

```
                 end;
          '~': token:='xor';
     end;

     {now check for keywords}
     if token='switch' then token:='case'
     else if token='struct' then token:='record'
     else if token='int' then token:='integer'
     else if token='float' then token:='real'
     else if token='printf' then token:='Write'
     else if token='extern' then token:='forward'
     else if token='case' then token:='';
end;   {Translate}


procedure convert;
var
     count:integer;
begin
     GetToken;
     for count:=1 to indent do
        Write(outfile,'   ');
     while token<>'$' do
     begin
        case TokType of
           STR: Write(outfile,token);
           NAME: begin
               Translate;
               Write(outfile,token,' ');
               end;
           DELIMITER: begin
               Translate;
               Write(outfile,token);
               end;
           NUMBER: Write(outfile,token);
        end;
        GetToken;
     end;
     token:='';
     WriteLn(outfile, token);
end; {convert}


begin   {main}
     Write('Enter input file: ');
     ReadLn(inname);
     Write('Enter output file: ');
     ReadLn(outname);
     Assign(infile,inname);
     Assign(outfile,outname);
     Reset(infile);
     Rewrite(outfile);

     indent:=0;   {indentation counter for each BEGIN and END}
     while not EOF(infile) do
     begin
        t:=1;   { reset index each time }
        ReadLn(infile,prog);
        prog:=concat(prog,'$');
        convert;
```

```
      end;
      token:='.';
      WriteLn(outfile,token);
      close(infile); close(outfile);
end.
```

In this program, the global variable **indent** is used to indent the code automatically three spaces for each **begin** and to remove the three spaces for each **end**. This allows the pseudo-Pascal output to be properly formatted.

In essence, the C-to-Turbo Pascal conversion-assist program reads in a line of C source code, takes a token at a time from it, performs any translations it can, and writes out a Turbo Pascal version. To see how this simple program can make translating from C to Turbo Pascal easier, run this C program through the translator:

```
main()
{
    int t,a;

    t=getnum();
    if(t=10) then process(t);
    else {
        a=t-100;
        print("%d",a);
    }
}

process(x)
int x;
{
    int count;

    for(count=0;count;count++)
        printf("this is x*%d: %d\n",count,x*count);

}
```

After you run it through the translator program, the pseudo-Pascal output is as follows:

```
main ()
   begin
   integer t ,a ;

   t :=getnum ();
   if (t :=10)then process (t );
   else begin
       a :=t -100;
       print ('%d',a );
   end
end

process (x )
integer x ;
```

```
begin
integer count ;

for (count :=0;count ;count ++)
Write ('this is x*%d: %d\n',count ,x *count );
end.
```

As you can see, this is not Turbo Pascal code, but you have saved a lot of typing. All you need to do is edit this a line at a time to correct the differences.

Converting BASIC to Turbo Pascal

The task of converting BASIC to Turbo Pascal is much more difficult than that of converting C to Turbo Pascal. BASIC is not a structured language and bears little similarity to Turbo Pascal, which means that it does not have a complete set of control structures and, more importantly, it does not have stand-alone subroutines with local variables. The translation task is very tricky: generally, it requires extensive knowledge of both BASIC and Turbo Pascal, and an understanding of the program, because in essence you are rewriting the program in Turbo Pascal and using the BASIC version as a guide. Because of the complexity of the task, this section looks at some of the more troublesome translations and offers suggestions.

Converting BASIC Loops Into Turbo Pascal Loops

The **FOR/NEXT** loop is the only form of loop control in many versions of BASIC. The overall form of the **FOR/NEXT** loop in BASIC is generally similar to the **for/do** loop in Turbo Pascal: there is an initialization and a target value; but unlike BASIC's **STEP** option, the only increments allowed in the Turbo Pascal loop are 1 and −1. The Turbo Pascal **for/do** loop is much more sophisticated and flexible than the BASIC **FOR/NEXT** loop because it allows any scalar type to be used for loop control. You must recode any **FOR/NEXT** loops that use the **STEP** option as either **while/do** or **repeat/until** Pascal loops. However, for this discussion, the example uses only BASIC loops that do not use the **STEP** option. For example, the BASIC **FOR/NEXT** loop

```
10 FOR X=1 TO 100
20    PRINT X
30 NEXT
```

translates into Turbo Pascal as

```
for x:=1 to 100 do WriteLn(x);
```

As you can see, the conversion is essentially a one-to-one substitution. The real trick in converting the **FOR/NEXT** loop is making sure that the loop-control variable is not modified inside the loop. Many forms of BASIC allow the control variable to be altered by code inside the loop, as shown:

```
10 FOR COUNT=10 TO 0 STEP -1
20    INPUT A
30    PRINT A*COUNT
40    IF A=100 THEN COUNT = 0
50 NEXT
```

The **IF/THEN** statement in line 40 could cause the loop to exit early. To translate this properly into Turbo Pascal code, you must allow for this contingency. Although some other Pascal implementations may permit this, Turbo Pascal does not, because after the **for/do** statement has been compiled, the actual number of times the loop will repeat is fixed—even though you changed the loop control value in the body of the loop. Therefore, you must code BASIC **FOR/NEXT** loops of this type into either a Turbo Pascal **while/do** or **repeat/until** loop.

Some forms of BASIC have a **WHILE/WEND** loop available. In such a case, you would use a Turbo Pascal **while/do** loop and your translation would be straightforward. If the BASIC you are using does not have the **WHILE/ WEND** loop or if you choose not to use it, your job will be more difficult because you must recognize a *constructed loop* that uses **GOTO** statements. This will also be the case if a **repeat/until** type of loop has been constructed in BASIC. These types of translations become nightmarish, because you must actually understand how the code works in order to recognize the loop and translate it into one of Turbo Pascal's built-in loop control structures.

After you have found a constructed loop in BASIC, there is an easy way to tell whether that loop should be translated into a Turbo Pascal **while/do** or a **repeat/until**. Remember that a **repeat/until** loop *always executes at least once* because the loop condition is checked at the bottom of the loop; whereas a **while/do** loop may or may not execute because its condition is checked at the top. Therefore, you must look carefully at each constructed loop in BASIC to determine where the loop test is applied. For example, the BASIC code

```
100 S=S+1
200 Q=S/3.1415
300 PRINT Q;
400 IF S <100 THEN GOTO 100
```

is actually a **repeat/until** loop in disguise—it will always execute at least once. After line 100 has been executed, lines 200 through 400 will execute as well. If **S** is less than 100, the program will loop back to line 100. In Turbo Pascal, this code would be

```
repeat
   s:=s+1;
   q:=q/3.1415;
   Write(q);
until s=100;
```

In the following BASIC example, the loop test is performed at the start of the loop:

```
10 A=1
20 IF A>100 THEN GOTO 80
30 PRINT A
40 INPUT B
50 A=A+B
60 GOTO 20
80 PRINT "DONE"
```

This requires the use of the **while/do** loop in the Turbo Pascal equivalent:

```
a:=1;
while a<=100 do
begin
   WriteLn(a);
   ReadLn(b);
   a:=a+b;
end;
```

Avoid placing any initialization inside the loop itself by accident. In this example, the statement **a:=1** has to be outside the loop because it is a start-up condition and does not belong in the loop itself.

Converting the BASIC IF/THEN/ELSE

Most forms of BASIC have only the single-line **IF/THEN/ELSE** statement. This means that when a block of statements must be executed based on the outcome of an **IF**, the **GOTO** or the **GOSUB** must be used. You must recognize this situation because you will want to structure the code into a proper Turbo Pascal **if/then** or **if/then/else** statement when you translate it. As an example, consider this BASIC code fragment:

```
120 IF     T<500 THEN GOTO 500
130        Y=W
140        T=10
```

```
150        INPUT A$
  .
  .
  .
500 REM  RESUME DISK READS
```

To achieve an **IF** block in a BASIC program, the **IF** condition must be cast in the negative: the target of the **IF** must not be the condition that causes entry into the **IF** block, but rather the one that causes a jump around it. This is one of the worst problems in BASIC. Using **GOSUB** routines as the target of the **IF** or the **ELSE** does ease the problem slightly, but not entirely. If the BASIC code fragment were translated directly into Turbo Pascal it would look like this:

```
if t<500 then {do nothing}
else
begin
    y:=w;
    t:=10;
    ReadLn(a);
end;
{resume disk reads}
```

You can now see the problem: the target of the **if** is really an empty statement. The only way to resolve this is to recode the **if** condition so that if it is true, the block of code is entered. The code fragment then becomes

```
if t>=500 then
begin
    y:=w;
    t:=10;
    ReadLn(a);
end;
{resume disk reads}
```

Now the code, as written in Turbo Pascal, makes sense.

The differences between the way the BASIC **IF/THEN** is used and the way the Turbo Pascal **if/then** is used illustrate that the programming language often governs the approach to solving the problem. Most people find the positive form of the **if** more natural than the negative form.

Creating Turbo Pascal Subprograms From BASIC Programs

One reason that translating BASIC into Turbo Pascal is difficult is that BASIC does not support stand-alone subroutines with local variables. This means that a literal translation of a BASIC program into Turbo Pascal produces a very large main program with no subprograms. This negates many of the reasons that you may have wanted to translate the program in the first place: maintainability, structure, and ease of modification.

A better translation would create a Turbo Pascal program with a fairly small main program and many other subprograms, but to do this requires knowledge of the program and a keen eye for reading code. However, here are a few rules to guide you.

First, you should make all **GOSUB** routines into subprograms. Also, look for similar functions in which only the variables have changed, and collapse them into one subprogram with parameters. For example, this BASIC program has two subroutines—the first at line 100 and the second at line 200.

```
10  A=10
20  B=20
30  GOSUB 100
40  PRINT A,B
50  C=20
60  D=30
70  GOSUB 200
80  PRINT C,D
90  END
100 A=A*B
110 B=A/B
120 RETURN
200 C=C*D
210 D=C/D
220 RETURN
```

Both subroutines do exactly the same thing, except they operate on separate sets of variables. A proper translation of this program into Turbo Pascal has only one function, which uses parameters to avoid having two dedicated functions:

```
program x;
var
   a,b,c,d:real;

procedure f1(var x,y:integer):real;
begin
   x:=x*y;
   y:=x/y;
end;

begin
   a:=10;    b:=10;
   f1(a,b);
   WriteLn(a,' ',b);

   c:=20;  d:=30;
   f1(c,d);
   WriteLn(c,' ',d);
end.
```

This Turbo Pascal translation approximates the meaning of the code to the reader more closely than does the BASIC version, since BASIC implies that there are actually two separate functions involved.

The second rule is that you should make all repeated code into a function. In a BASIC program the same few lines of code may be repeated. A programmer occasionally does this to make the code slightly faster. Because Turbo Pascal is a compiled language, using functions instead of in-line code has very little negative effect on the speed of execution, and the increased clarity and structure outweigh any gain in speed.

Getting Rid of Global Variables

In BASIC, all variables are global: they are known throughout the entire program and may be modified anywhere in the program. In the translation process, try to convert as many of these global variables as possible into local ones, because it makes the program more resilient and bug-free. The more global variables there are, the more likely it is that side effects will occur.

It is sometimes difficult to know when to make a variable local to a subprogram. The easiest choices are the ones that control counters in short sections of code. For example, in this code

```
10 FOR X=1 TO 10
20    PRINT X
30 NEXT
```

X is clearly used only to control the FOR/NEXT loop and can therefore be made into a local variable within a subprogram.

Another type of variable that is a candidate for becoming local is a temporary variable. A temporary variable holds an intermediate result in a calculation. Temporary variables are often spread out in a program, and they can be hard to recognize. For example, the variable C12 shown here holds a temporary result in the calculation:

```
10 INPUT A,B
20 GOSUB 100
30 PRINT C12
40 END
100 C12=A*B
110 C12=C12/0.142
120 RETURN
```

The same code in Turbo Pascal, with C12 as a local variable, would be

```
program x;
var
   a,b:real;
```

```
function f2(x,y:real):real;
var
    C12:real;
begin
    C12:=a*b;
    C12:=C12/0.142;
    f2:=C12;
end;

begin
    ReadLn(a,b);
    WriteLn(f2(a,b));
end.
```

Remember, it is always best to have as few global variables as possible, so it is important to find good candidates for local variables.

Final Thoughts on Translating

Although translating programs can be the most tedious of all programming tasks, it is also one of the most common. A good approach is first to understand the way the program you are translating works. Once you know how it operates, the program will be easier to recode; you will know whether your new version is working correctly. Also, when you know the program you are translating, the job becomes more interesting because it is not just a simple symbol-substitution process.

The next chapter discusses a specialized case of translation: you will translate a Pascal program written on one compiler into a program that will compile and run with Turbo Pascal. Although this case may sound easy, it is often the hardest translation task of all.

ELEVEN

Efficiency, Porting, And Debugging

The ability to write programs that make efficient use of system resources, are transportable to other computers, and are error-free is the mark of a professional programmer. This ability transforms computer science into the "art of computer science," because so few formal techniques are available to ensure success. This chapter presents some of the methods by which efficiency, portability, and program debugging may be achieved.

Efficiency

When used to describe a computer program, the term *efficiency* refers to the use of system resources, the speed of execution, or both. System resources include RAM, disk space, printer paper, and basically anything that can be allocated and used up. Whether or not a program is efficient is sometimes a subjective judgment—it depends on the situation. Consider a program that uses 47K of RAM to execute, 2 megabytes of disk space, and takes an average run time of 7 minutes. If this is a sort program running on an Apple II, then the program is probably not very efficient. However, if it is a weather-forecasting program running on a Cray computer, then the program is probably very efficient.

Another point to consider when you're striving for efficiency is that optimizing one aspect of a program often degrades another. For example, making a program execute faster often means making it bigger if you use in-line code instead of function calls to increase speed. Also, making more efficient use of disk space by compacting data invariably makes disk access slower. These and other types of efficiency trade-offs can be very frustrating—especially to the nonprogramming end-user who cannot see why one thing

255

should affect the other.

In light of these problems, you may wonder how efficiency can be discussed at all. Actually, there are some programming practices that are always efficient—or at least are more efficient than others. There are also a few techniques that make programs *both* faster and smaller.

Avoiding Code Duplication

Even the best programmer sometimes writes *redundant code*. Redundant code does not refer to code that could be changed into a subroutine; even very inexperienced programmers understand this. Rather, it refers to the unnecessary duplication of similar statements within a routine. To get a better idea what redundant code is, examine this code fragment:

```
Read(a,y);
if a<10 then WriteLn('Invalid input');
if Length(y)=0 then WriteLn('Invalid input');
```

In this case, the statement **WriteLn('Invalid input');** occurs twice. However, this is unnecessary, because it could be written as

```
Read(a,y);
if (a<10) or (Length(y)=0) then WriteLn('Invalid input');
```

Here the object code is not only shorter, but it actually executes faster as well—only one **if/then** statement is executed, instead of two.

This example probably would not occur in an actual program, because the redundant statements were close together, making it quite easy to see. However, because duplicated statements are often separated by several lines of code, redundant code occurs in most computer programs.

Redundancy sometimes happens because of the method selected to code a routine. For example, here are two ways to code a function that searches an array of strings for a specific word:

```
type
   str80 = string[80];
   StrArray = array [1..100] of str80;

function StrSearch1(str:StrArray, word:str80):boolean;
{Correct, non-redundant method}
var
   t:integer;
begin
   StrSearch1=FALSE;
   for t:=1 to 100 do
      if str[t]=word then StrSearch1=TRUE;
end;
```

```
Function StrSeach2(str:StrArray,word:str80):boolean;
{Incorrect, redundant method}
var
   t:integer;
begin
  t:=1;
  StrSearch:=FALSE;
  if str[]=word  then StrSearch2=TRUE
  else
  begin
     t:=2;
     while(t<=100) do
     begin
        if str[t]=word then StrSearch2=TRUE;
        t:t+1;
     end;
  end;
end;
```

The second method not only duplicates the **if/then** comparison statements, but it also has two assignment statements (**t:=1** and **t:=2**) that are essentially duplications. The first version runs faster and requires much less memory. memory.

In short, redundant code can be caused either by sloppiness in coding or by poor judgment in choosing the way to implement a routine. Either way, it is something to avoid.

Use of Procedures and Functions

Always remember that the use of procedures and functions with local variables forms the basis of structured programming. Procedures and functions are the building blocks of Turbo Pascal programs, and they are Turbo Pascal's strongest assets. Do not let anything that is discussed in this section be construed otherwise. Now that you have been warned, you should know a few aspects of Turbo Pascal functions and their effects on the size and speed of your code.

First, Turbo Pascal is a *stack-oriented language:* all local variables and parameters to functions use the stack for temporary storage. When a function is called, the return address of the calling routine is placed on the stack as well. This allows the subroutine to return to the location from which it was called. When a function returns, this address—as well as all local variables and parameters—must be removed from the stack. The process of pushing this information onto the stack is generally referred to as the *calling sequence,* and the process of popping the information off of the stack is called the *returning sequence.* These sequences take time—sometimes quite a bit of time if several parameters are passed and temporary variables are used.

To understand how a function call can slow down your program, look at the
two code examples shown here:

```
Version 1                        Version 2

for x:=1 to 100 do               for x:=1 to 100
        t=compute(x);                    t:=Abs(Sin(q)/100/3.1416);


function compute(q:integer):real;
var
    t:real;
begin
    computer:=Abs(Sin(q)/100/3.1416);
end;
```

Although each loop performs the same function, Version 2 is much faster
because the overhead of the calling and returning sequences has been elimi-
nated by using in-line code. To understand just how much time is taken up,
study the following pseudo-assembly code, which shows in theory the calling
and returning sequences for the function **compute**:

```
; calling sequence
move A, x   ; put value of x into accumulator
push A
call compute   ; the call instruction places
               ; the return address on the stack


; returning sequence
; the return value of the function must be placed
; into a register - we will use B
move B, stack-1   ; get value in temporary t
return   ; return to the calling routine
; calling routine then does the following
pop A    ; clear parameter use in the call
```

Using the **compute** function inside the loop causes the calling and returning sequence to be executed 100 times. If you really want to write fast code,
then using **compute** inside a loop is not a good idea.

By now you may think that you should write a program that has just a few
large routines so that it will run quickly. In the majority of cases, however,
the slight time differential will not be meaningful, and the loss of structure
will be acute. But there is another problem. Replacing subprograms that are
used by several routines with in-line code will make your program very
large, because the same code will be duplicated several times. Keep in mind
that subroutines were invented primarily as a way to make efficient use of
memory. A rule of thumb is that making a program faster means making it

bigger, while making it smaller means making it slower. It only makes sense to use in-line code instead of a function call when speed is of absolute priority. Otherwise, the liberal use of procedures and functions is definitely recommended.

The case Statement Versus if/then/else Ladders

The following code fragments are functionally equivalent. However, one is more efficient than the other. Can you tell which one?

```
case ch of            if ch='a' then f1(ch)
   'a': f1(ch);        else if ch='b' then f2(ch)
   'b': f2(ch);        else if ch='c' then f3(ch)
   'c': f3(ch);        else if ch='d' then f4(ch);
   'd': f4(ch);
end;
```

The code fragment on the left is much more efficient than the one on the right, because in general, the **case** statement generates tighter, faster object code than a series of **if/then/else** statements.

The **if/then/else** arrangement, as shown in this example, is referred to as an **if/then/else** ladder because program execution seems to step its way down the sequence. The **if/then/else** ladder is important because it allows you to perform multibranch decisions on a variety of data types that cannot be used in a **case** statement. However, if you are using scalars—integers, characters, reals, and enumerations—you should use the **case** statement instead.

Porting Programs

It is common for a program written on one machine to be transported to another computer with a different processor, operating system, or both. This process is called *porting* and can be either very easy or extremely difficult, depending on how the program was originally written. A program is *portable* if it can be easily ported. A program is not easily portable if it contains numerous *machine dependencies*—code fragments that work only with one specific operating system or processor. Turbo Pascal has been designed to allow the porting of code between all of its versions, but it still requires care, attention to detail, and often the sacrifice of maximum efficiency because of variations in the operating systems.

Porting code originally written by using a different Pascal compiler to Turbo Pascal can present problems, because a different set of enhancements may have been used. The reverse situation is also true: if any of the Turbo Pascal enhancements were used, code that was written in Turbo Pascal must be modified if it is to be compiled and run on a different compiler.

This section examines a few specific problem areas and offers some solutions. You will also see how to write Pascal programs so that they are portable.

Using const

Perhaps the simplest way to make programs portable is to make *every* system- or processor-dependent "magic number" into a **const** declaration. These "magic numbers" include random-access record sizes for disk accesses, special screen and keyboard commands, memory allocation information, and anything else that has even the slightest chance of changing when the program is ported. If you make the magic numbers into **const** declarations, these definitions not only make the magic numbers obvious to the person doing the porting, but they also simplify editing; their values have to be changed only once instead of throughout the program.

For example, here are two declarations of an array and two procedures that access it. In the first version, the array dimensions are hard-coded, and in the second they are placed into **const** declarations.

```
{first version}
var
   count:array[1..100] of integer;

procedure f1;
var
   t:integer;
begin
   for t:=1 to 100 do count[t]:=t;
end;


{second version}
const
   MAX = 100;
var
   count:array[1..MAX] of integer;

procedure f2;
var
   t:integer;
begin
   for t:=1 to MAX do count[t]:=t;
end;
```

The second version is clearly better if you want to port this program to a machine that allows, for example, larger array sizes. In this case, only **MAX** would have to change, and all references to **MAX** would be automatically corrected. This version not only is easier to change, but it also avoids a great deal of editing errors. Remember that there will probably be many references to **MAX** in a real program, so the gain in portability is often quite substantial.

Operating-System Dependencies

Virtually all commercial programs have code in them that is specific to the operating system. For example, a spreadsheet program might make use of the IBM PC's video memory to allow fast switching between screens, or a graphics package may use special graphics commands that are only applicable to that operating system. Some operating-system dependencies are necessary for fast, commercially viable programs. However, there is no reason to hard-code any more dependencies than are necessary.

When you must use system calls to access the operating system, it is best to do them all through one master procedure so that you only have to change it to accommodate a new operating system and can leave the rest of the code intact. For example, if system calls were needed to clear the screen and the end-of-line, and to locate the cursor at an X,Y coordinate, then you would create a master procedure like **OpSysCall**, as shown here:

```
procedure OpSysCall(op,x,y:integer);
{Interface to operating system}
begin
    case op of
        1: ClearScreen;
        2: ClearEOL;
        3: GotoXY(x,y);
end;
```

Although these calls are standard in all versions of Turbo Pascal, if you ever have to port to another Pascal compiler (for example, a mainframe environment), you will find this interface technique to be valuable. Only the code that forms the actual functions would have to be changed, leaving a common interface intact.

Turbo Pascal's Extensions

If you are porting from another Pascal to Turbo Pascal, Turbo Pascal's extensions and enhancements can make the job easier and even improve the efficiency of your program. For example, the **string** extension makes working with strings much easier.

However, if you are transporting code from Turbo Pascal to another Pascal, then you almost certainly must remove all of the extensions and enhancements from your program. The worst task will be changing all **string** types into arrays of characters. But this is only the first step—you will also lose all routines that handle strings, such as **Copy**, **Concat**, and **Pos**. If your program uses such procedures, then you must create them yourself in the new version.

Generally, if you know that you are going to port a program to another Pascal before you write it, then you should avoid using Turbo Pascal's extensions and enhancements.

Debugging

To paraphrase Thomas Edison, programming is 10% inspiration and 90% debugging. Good programmers are good debuggers. Although you probably have good debugging skills, you should watch for certain types of bugs that can occur easily while you are using Turbo Pascal.

Pointer Problems

A common error in Turbo Pascal programs is the misuse of pointers. Pointer problems fall into two general categories: misunderstanding of indirection and the pointer operators, and the accidental use of invalid pointers. To solve the first type of problem, you must understand pointers in the Pascal language; to solve the second, you must always verify the validity of a pointer before you use it.

The following program illustrates a typical pointer error that Turbo Pascal programmers make:

```
program WRONG; {This program is in error}

type
   pntr = ^object;

   object = record
      x: char;
      y: integer;
      name:string[80];
   end;

var
   p:pntr;

begin
   p^.name:='tom';
   p^.x:='g';
   p^.y:=100;
end.
```

This program will probably crash (it could take the operating system with it) because the pointer **p** hasn't been assigned a value by using **New**. The pointer **p** contains an unknown, random number, which could be pointing anywhere in the memory of the computer. This is certainly not what you want. To correct this program, you must add the line

```
New(p);
```

before the first use of **p**.

"Wild" pointers are extremely difficult to track down. If you are making assignments to a pointer variable that does not contain a valid pointer address, your program may appear to function correctly some times but crash at other times. Statistically, the smaller your program, the more likely it will run correctly even with a stray pointer, because little memory is in use. As your program grows, failures become more common, but as you try to debug you will be thinking about recent additions or changes to your program, not about pointer errors. Hence, you will probably look in the wrong spot for the bug.

A second, more insidious problem can occur when you are using pointers: you can run out of memory during a call to **New** at run time. This causes a run-time error, and execution will stop. Fortunately, Turbo Pascal has the special built-in function **MemAvail** so that you can avoid this problem. **MemAvail** returns either the number of free bytes (8-bit systems) or paragraphs (16-bit systems) left on the heap. (A *paragraph* is 16 bytes.) Therefore, to make the program completely correct, check for available memory before you attempt to allocate it. To do this, you must know the number of bytes needed for each data type you are allocating. However, this number may change according to processors and operating systems, so you must consult the *Turbo Pascal Reference Manual* for the information concerning your system. To correct the previous program example for the IBM PC, you should add a check for 6 paragraphs, or 96 bytes. The actual amount needed by the record is only 84 — 81 for the string, 1 for the character, and 2 for the integer — but because the smallest allocation is a paragraph for 16-bit systems, you must round up. The correct program is shown here:

```
program RIGHT; {This program is OK}

type
   pntr = ^object;

   object = record
      x: char;
      y: integer;
      name:string[80];
   end;

var
   p:pntr;
```

```
begin
   if MaxAvail>=96 then
   begin  {there is memory available}
      New(p);
      p^.name:='tom';
      p^.x:='g';
      p^.y:=100;
   end;
end.
```

One indication of a pointer problem is that errors tend to be erratic. Your program may work correctly one time, and incorrectly another. Sometimes other variables will contain garbage for no reason. If these problems occur, check your pointers. As a matter of procedure, you should check all pointers when bugs begin to occur.

Although pointers can be troublesome, they are also one of the most powerful and useful aspects of the Pascal language, and they are worth whatever trouble they may cause you. Make the effort early on to learn to use them correctly.

Redefining Built-in Procedures And Functions

Although Turbo Pascal does not allow you to redefine the keywords that make up the language, it does allow you to redefine the words that reference its standard procedures and functions. Programmers sometimes think that it is a good idea to do this for various reasons; however, it can only lead to trouble. Here is an example of a direct problem caused by redefining a built-in procedure:

```
program WRONG;  {This program is incorrect}
var
   t:integer;

WriteLn(t:integer);
begin
   write(t,' ','bytes of memory available on the heap');
end;

begin
   {compute amount of free memory on the heap}
   WriteLn(MemAvail);
   WriteLn('All done');
end;
```

As shown in this example, the programmer redefined the standard procedure **WriteLn** but forgot that the message **All done** was supposed to be printed. Instead, the memory-available message would be displayed twice, because the redefinition of **WriteLn** replaced the built-in definition.

Although the problem in the preceding example is fairly easy to see, a worse redefinition problem occurs when a built-in procedure or function is redefined but is *not* used directly in the program at that time. At some later time, when the program is modified, the redefined function or procedure is referenced as if it were still the built-in function, as shown in this example:

```
Function MemAvail: boolean;
{See if room left in global array count}
var
   t:integer
begin
   MemAvail:=FALSE;
   for t:=1 to MAX do if count[t]=0 then MemAvail:=TRUE;
end;
```

The redefinition of **MemAvail** is fine as far as this example goes. The problem arises if the array **count** is changed later from a global variable to a dynamic variable that is allocated from the heap. In this case, if you tried to use **MemAvail** to see if sufficient memory were left on the heap, your program would fail.

The only way to avoid such problems is never to give a procedure or function you have written the same name as a built-in one. If you are not sure, append your initials to the start of the name, as in **HSMemAvail** instead of **MemAvail**.

Unexpected Syntax Errors

Occasionally you will see a syntax error that you cannot understand or even recognize as an error. One particularly unsettling error will occur when you try to compile this code:

```
program Errors;   {This program will not compile}

var
   s:string[80];

procedure F1(x:string[80]);
begin
   WriteLn(x);
end;

begin
   ReadLn(s);
   F1(s);
end.
```

If you try to compile this program, you will see the error message

```
Error 36: Type identifier expected
```

After pressing the ESC key, you will find that Turbo Pascal is pointing at the line

```
procedure F1(x:string[80]);
```
                 ↑

with the cursor at the position shown by the arrow. But the error message states that a type identifier is expected! Didn't you supply one with the **string[80]** statement? Is this a bug in Turbo Pascal? The answer is no. Turbo Pascal cannot use a **string** type in a procedure or function call. You must explicitly declare a user-defined type and use it instead. For this example, you first declare a type called **str80** with the following type statement:

```
type
   str80 = string[80];
```

You then use the newly created type **str80** as the type of the parameter to the function **F1**. The corrected program looks like this:

```
program CorrectedErrors;  {This program will compile}
type
   str80 = string[80];

var
   s:str80;

procedure F1(x:str80);
begin
   WriteLn(x);
end;

begin
   ReadLn(s);
   F1(s);
end.
```

Another confusing syntax error is generated by the following program:

```
program Error;  {This program will not compile}

procedure F2;
var
   t:integer;
begin
   for t:=1 to 10 do WriteLn('hi there');
end

begin
   F2;
end.
```

The error here is that the semicolon has been left off of the **end** in the procedure **F2**. However, Turbo Pascal will point to the error as being at the **begin**, which follows it. In this simple program, it is easy to catch the error. However, in certain situations, you may have to backtrack to find where a semicolon is missing.

if/then/if/else Errors

Even very experienced programmers occasionally fall prey to the **if/then/if/else** error. For example, are you *sure* what the following code does?

```
if count<100 then
   if count>50 then F1
else F2;
```

Don't be fooled by the improper formatting! The **else** is not associated with the first **if**, but rather with the second **if**. Remember, an **else** is always associated with the closest **if**. In this example, instead of executing **F2** when **count** is greater than 100, Turbo Pascal does nothing. Also, **F2** will execute only if **count** is less than 100, and then if it is less than 50. You will see this when the code is properly formatted:

```
if count<100 then
   if count>50 then F1
   else F2;
```

If you simply wanted to have **F2** execute when **count** is greater than 100, you would need to use a **begin/end** block, as shown here:

```
if count<100 then
begin
   if count>50 then F1;
end
else F2;
```

Forgetting the var Parameter
In Procedures and Functions

Sometimes, in the heat of programming, it is easy to forget that if a procedure or function changes its argument, then the argument must be specified as a **var** parameter. Forgetting this can cause bizarre results and hours of frustrating debugging time. For example, consider this incorrect program.

```
program Error;   {This program is incorrect}
var
   t:integer;
```

```
procedure F1(x:integer);
begin
   Write('Enter a value: ');
   ReadLn(x);
end;

begin
   F1(t);   {get a value for t}
   writeln('t has the value: ',t);
end;
```

This program does not work, because only the local variable **x** is assigned a value, and when **F1** returns, **t** is unmodified. To make this program work, you must declare **x** inside **F1** to be a **var** parameter. This makes certain that the calling variable **t** is modified. The corrected program is shown here:

```
program Fixed;   {This program is correct}
var
   t:integer;

procedure F1(var x:integer);
begin
   Write('Enter a value: ');
   ReadLn(x);
end;

begin
   F1(t);   {get a value for t}
   writeln('t has the value: ',t);
end;
```

Although this simple program was easy to correct, when this error occurs in large programs, it can be one of the most difficult bugs to find.

General Debugging Theory

Everyone has a different approach to programming and debugging. However, some techniques have proven to be better than others. In the case of debugging, incremental testing is considered to be the least costly and most time-effective method, even though it can appear to slow the development process.

Incremental testing is simply the process of always having working code. As soon as it is possible to run a piece of your program, you should do so, testing that section completely. As you add to your program, continue to test the new sections as well as the way they connect to the established operational code. In this way you can be sure that any possible bugs are concentrated into a small area of code.

Incremental testing theory is generally based on probability and areas. As you know, *area* is a squared dimension. Each time you add length, you double area. Therefore, as your program grows there is an n-squared area in which you must search for bugs. While debugging, you as a programmer want the smallest possible area to deal with. Through incremental testing you can subtract the area already tested from the total area, thereby reducing the region that may contain a bug.

Final Thoughts

Throughout this book, various algorithms and techniques have been discussed, some in considerable detail. Remember that computer science is both a theoretical and an empirical science. Although it is fairly easy to see why one algorithm is better than another, it is difficult to say what makes a successful program. When it comes to efficiency, portability and debugging, experimenting will sometimes yield information more easily than would theoretical musings.

Programming is both a science and an art. It is a science because you must know logic and understand how and why algorithms work; it is an art because you create the total entity that is a program. As a programmer, you really have one of the best jobs on earth—you walk the line between science and art, and get the best of both.

Index